FOOLKILLER

PSYCHO THERAPY

writer: **MAX BEMIS**

penciler: **DALIBOR TALAJIĆ**

inker: **JOSÉ MARZÁN, JR.**

colorist: **MIROSLAV MRVA**

letterer: **VC's TRAVIS LANHAM**

cover art: **DAVE JOHNSON**

assistant editor: **KATHLEEN WISNESKI**

editor: **DARREN SHAN**

consulting editor: **JORDAN D. WHITE**

FOOLKILLER: PSYCHO THERAPY. Contains material originally published in magazine form as FOOLKILLER #1-5. First printing 2017. ISBN# 978-1-302-90478-4. Published by MARVEL WORLDWIDE, INC., a subsidiary of MARVEL ENTERTAINMENT, LLC. OFFICE OF PUBLICATION: 135 West 50th Street, New York, NY 10020. Copyright © 2017 MARVEL. No similarity between any of the names, characters, persons, and/or institutions in this magazine with those of any living or dead person or institution is intended, and any such similarity which may exist is purely coincidental. Printed in the U.S.A. DAN BUCKLEY, President, Marvel Entertainment; JOE QUESADA, Chief Creative Officer; TOM BREVOORT, SVP of Publishing; DAVID BOGART, SVP of Business Affairs & Operations, Publishing & Partnership; C.B. CEBULSKI, VP of Brand Management & Development, Asia; DAVID GABRIEL, SVP of Sales & Marketing, Publishing; JEFF YOUNGQUIST, VP of Production & Special Projects; DAN CARR, Executive Director of Publishing Technology; ALEX MORALES, Director of Publishing Operations; SUSAN CRESPI, Production Manager; STAN LEE, Chairman Emeritus. For information regarding advertising in Marvel Comics or on Marvel.com, please contact Vit DeBellis, Integrated Sales Manager, at vdebellis@marvel.com. For Marvel subscription inquiries, please call 888-511-5480. Manufactured between 5/5/2017 and 6/6/2017 by QUADGRAPHICS WASECA, WASECA, MN, USA.

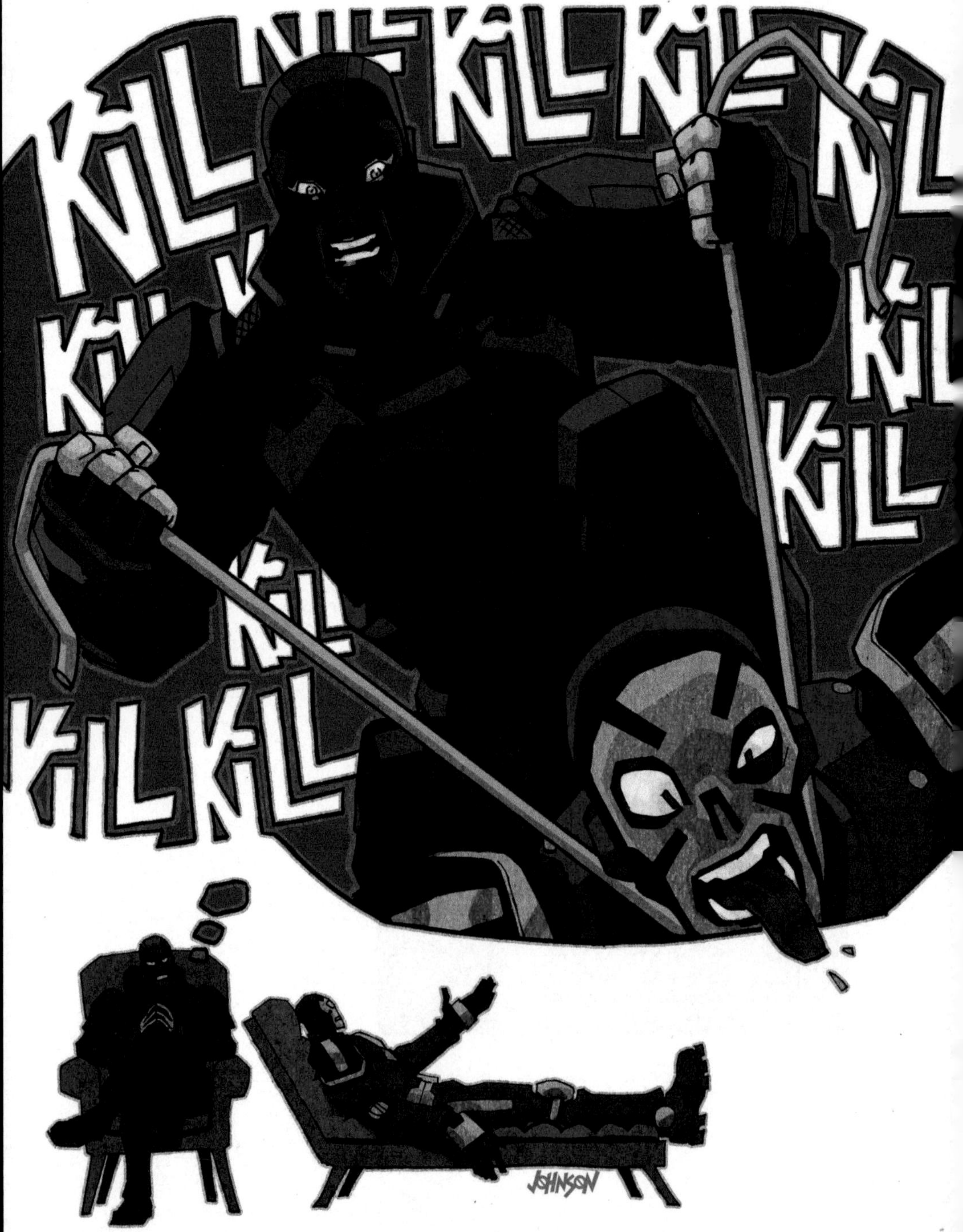
KILL
KILL
KILL
KILL
KILL
KILL KILL
JOHNSON

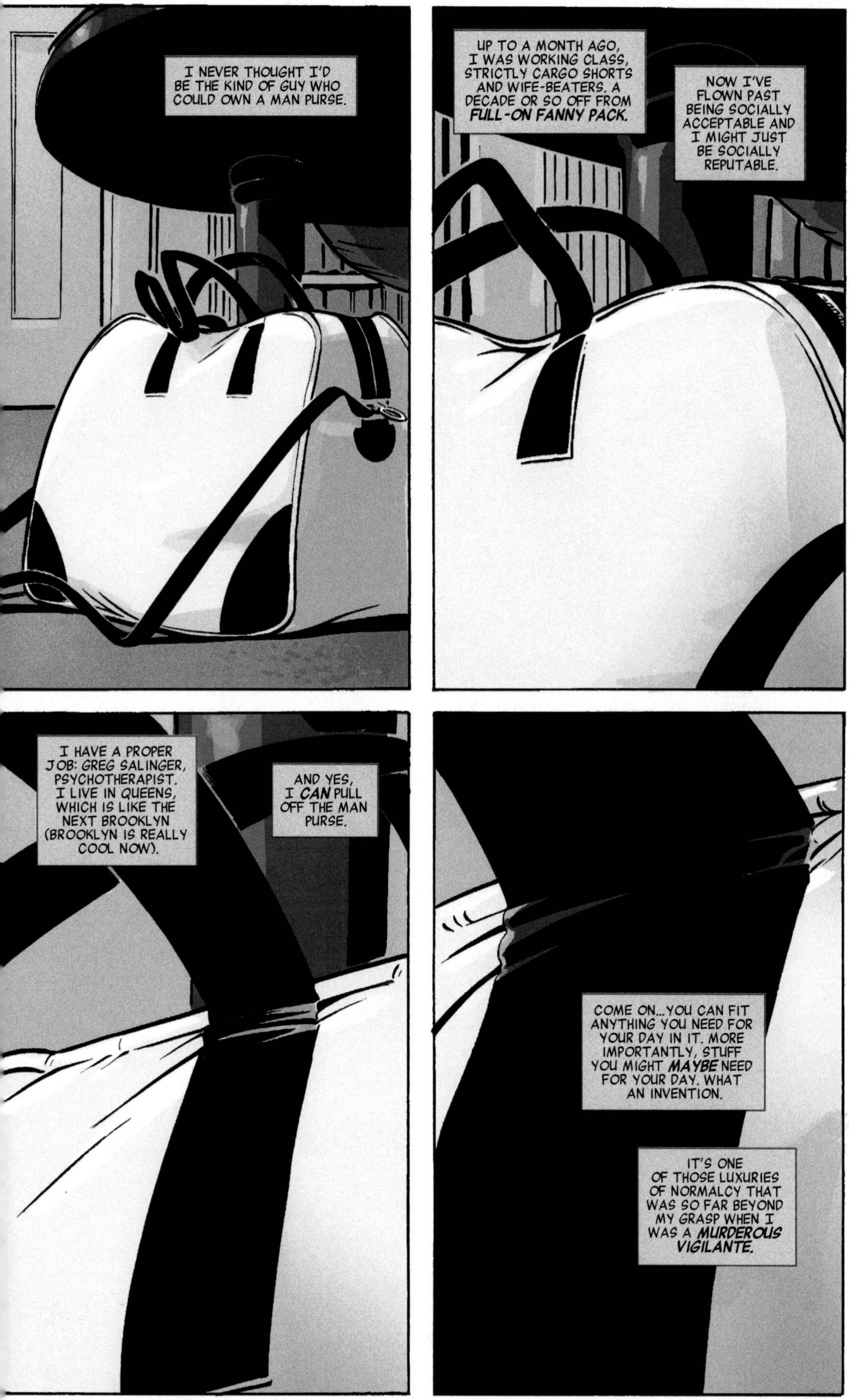
I NEVER THOUGHT I'D BE THE KIND OF GUY WHO COULD OWN A MAN PURSE.
UP TO A MONTH AGO, I WAS WORKING CLASS, STRICTLY CARGO SHORTS AND WIFE-BEATERS. A DECADE OR SO OFF FROM **FULL-ON FANNY PACK.**
NOW I'VE FLOWN PAST BEING SOCIALLY ACCEPTABLE AND I MIGHT JUST BE SOCIALLY REPUTABLE.
I HAVE A PROPER JOB: GREG SALINGER, PSYCHOTHERAPIST. I LIVE IN QUEENS, WHICH IS LIKE THE NEXT BROOKLYN (BROOKLYN IS REALLY COOL NOW).
AND YES, I ***CAN*** PULL OFF THE MAN PURSE.
COME ON...YOU CAN FIT ANYTHING YOU NEED FOR YOUR DAY IN IT. MORE IMPORTANTLY, STUFF YOU MIGHT ***MAYBE*** NEED FOR YOUR DAY. WHAT AN INVENTION.
IT'S ONE OF THOSE LUXURIES OF NORMALCY THAT WAS SO FAR BEYOND MY GRASP WHEN I WAS A ***MURDEROUS VIGILANTE.***

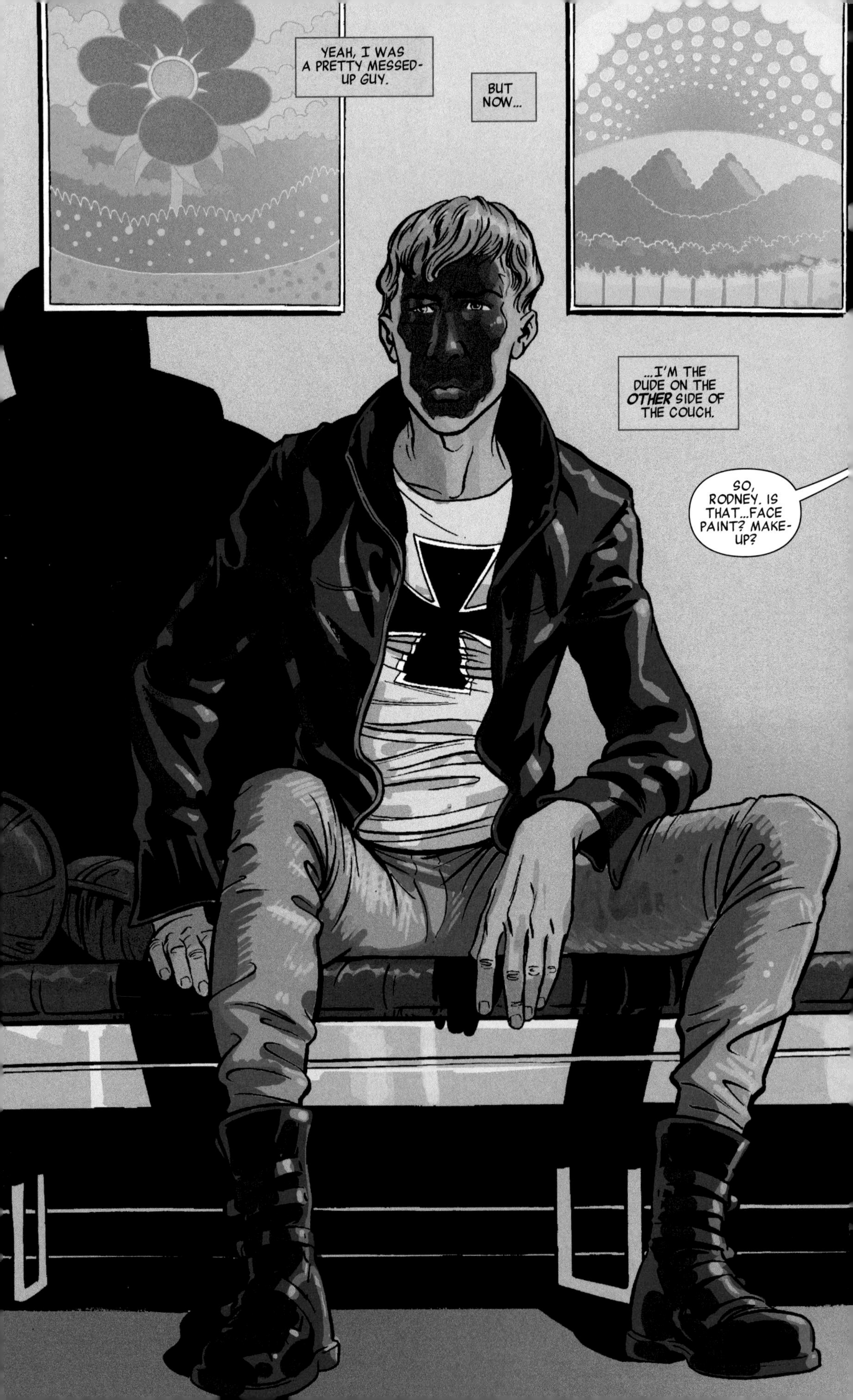
YEAH, I WAS A PRETTY MESSED-UP GUY.
BUT NOW...
...I'M THE DUDE ON THE OTHER SIDE OF THE COUCH.
SO, RODNEY. IS THAT...FACE PAINT? MAKE-UP?

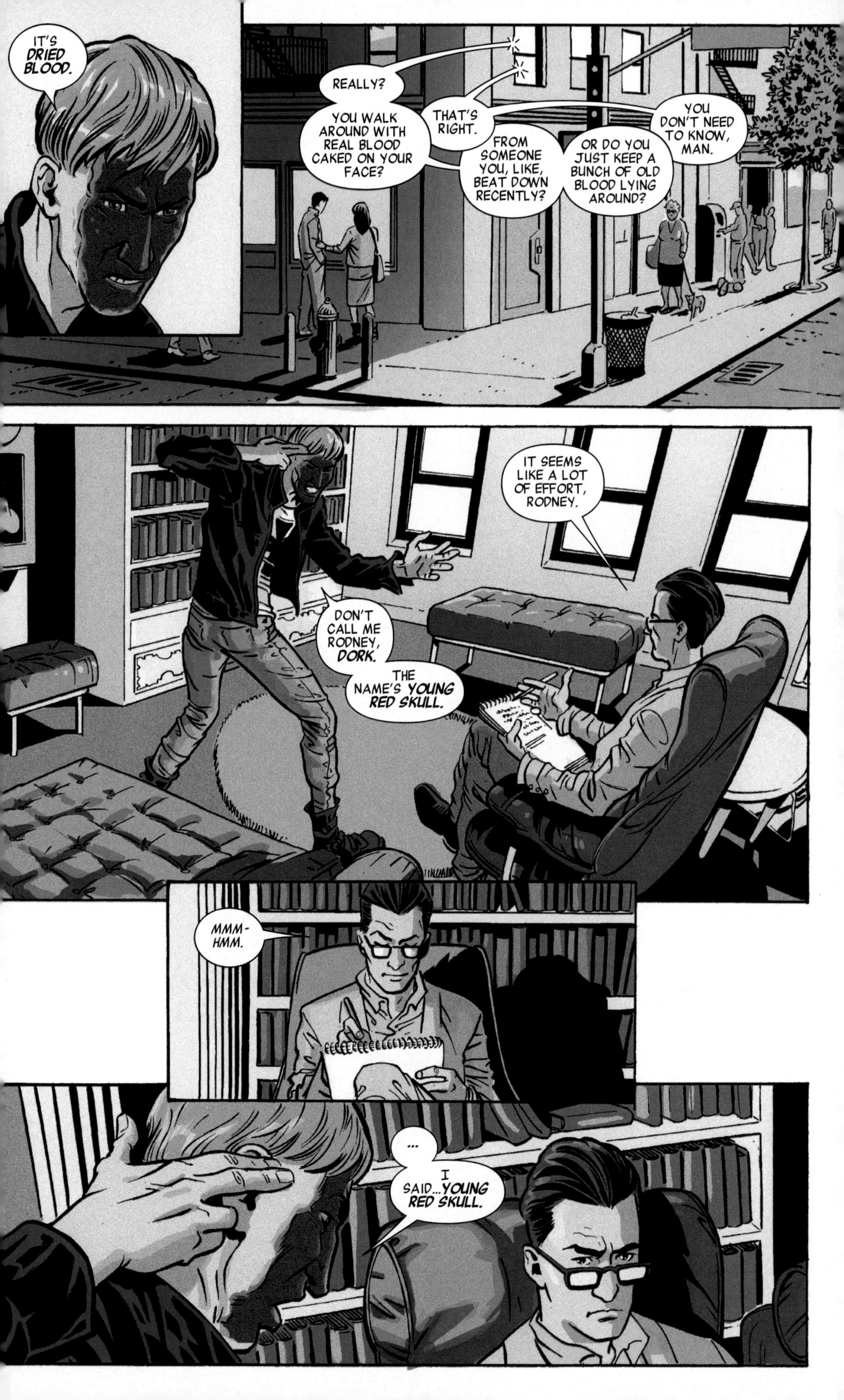
IT'S DRIED BLOOD.
REALLY?
YOU WALK AROUND WITH REAL BLOOD CAKED ON YOUR FACE?
THAT'S RIGHT.
FROM SOMEONE YOU, LIKE, BEAT DOWN RECENTLY?
OR DO YOU JUST KEEP A BUNCH OF OLD BLOOD LYING AROUND?
YOU DON'T NEED TO KNOW, MAN.
IT SEEMS LIKE A LOT OF EFFORT, RODNEY.
DON'T CALL ME RODNEY, DORK.
THE NAME'S YOUNG RED SKULL.
MMM-HMM.
...
I SAID...YOUNG RED SKULL.

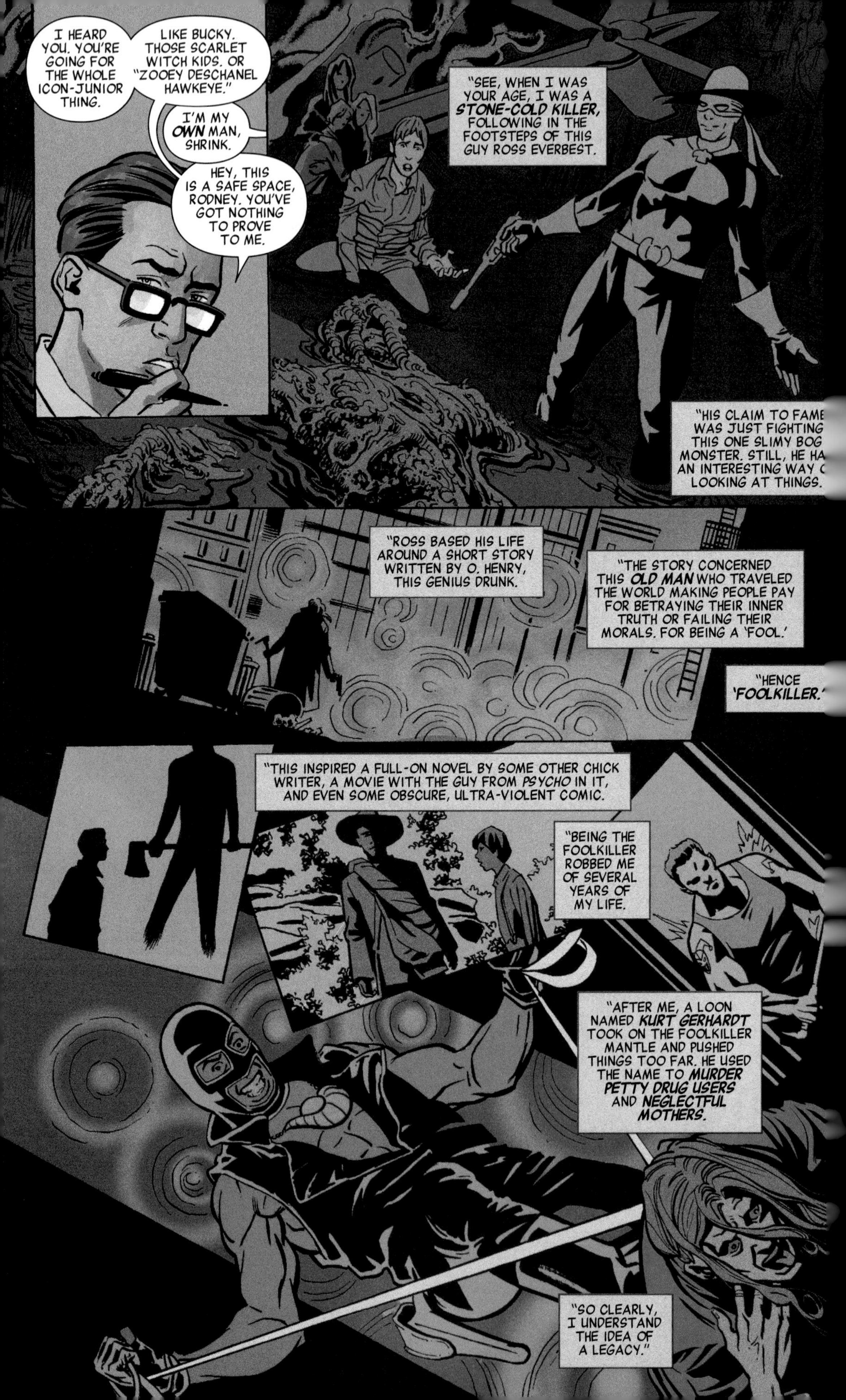
I HEARD YOU. YOU'RE GOING FOR THE WHOLE ICON-JUNIOR THING.
LIKE BUCKY. THOSE SCARLET WITCH KIDS. OR "ZOOEY DESCHANEL HAWKEYE."
I'M MY OWN MAN, SHRINK.
HEY, THIS IS A SAFE SPACE, RODNEY. YOU'VE GOT NOTHING TO PROVE TO ME.
"SEE, WHEN I WAS YOUR AGE, I WAS A STONE-COLD KILLER, FOLLOWING IN THE FOOTSTEPS OF THIS GUY ROSS EVERBEST.
"HIS CLAIM TO FAME WAS JUST FIGHTING THIS ONE SLIMY BOG MONSTER. STILL, HE HA AN INTERESTING WAY O LOOKING AT THINGS.
"ROSS BASED HIS LIFE AROUND A SHORT STORY WRITTEN BY O. HENRY, THIS GENIUS DRUNK.
"THE STORY CONCERNED THIS OLD MAN WHO TRAVELED THE WORLD MAKING PEOPLE PAY FOR BETRAYING THEIR INNER TRUTH OR FAILING THEIR MORALS. FOR BEING A 'FOOL.'
"HENCE 'FOOLKILLER.'
"THIS INSPIRED A FULL-ON NOVEL BY SOME OTHER CHICK WRITER, A MOVIE WITH THE GUY FROM PSYCHO IN IT, AND EVEN SOME OBSCURE, ULTRA-VIOLENT COMIC.
"BEING THE FOOLKILLER ROBBED ME OF SEVERAL YEARS OF MY LIFE.
"AFTER ME, A LOON NAMED KURT GERHARDT TOOK ON THE FOOLKILLER MANTLE AND PUSHED THINGS TOO FAR. HE USED THE NAME TO MURDER PETTY DRUG USERS AND NEGLECTFUL MOTHERS.
"SO CLEARLY, I UNDERSTAND THE IDEA OF A LEGACY."

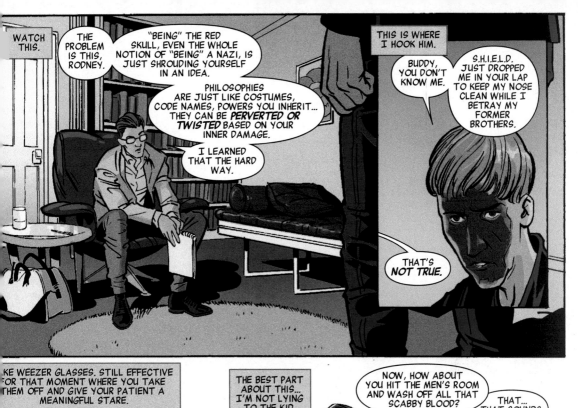

WATCH THIS.

THE PROBLEM IS THIS, RODNEY.

"BEING" THE RED SKULL, EVEN THE WHOLE NOTION OF "BEING" A NAZI, IS JUST SHROUDING YOURSELF IN AN IDEA.

PHILOSOPHIES ARE JUST LIKE COSTUMES, CODE NAMES, POWERS YOU INHERIT... THEY CAN BE *PERVERTED OR TWISTED* BASED ON YOUR INNER DAMAGE.

I LEARNED THAT THE HARD WAY.

THIS IS WHERE I HOOK HIM.

BUDDY, YOU DON'T KNOW ME.

S.H.I.E.L.D. JUST DROPPED ME IN YOUR LAP TO KEEP MY NOSE CLEAN WHILE I BETRAY MY FORMER BROTHERS.

THAT'S *NOT TRUE.*

...KE WEEZER GLASSES. STILL EFFECTIVE FOR THAT MOMENT WHERE YOU TAKE THEM OFF AND GIVE YOUR PATIENT A MEANINGFUL STARE.

I WAS JUST LIKE YOU BEFORE I FLIPPED MY SCRIPT.

NOW I'VE GOT A DEGREE IN PSYCHOLOGY. I HAVE A SICK APARTMENT, A LADY WHO LOVES ME AND A STEADY GIG THAT DOESN'T INVOLVE IMPALING ANYONE ON A STICK.

I KNOW YOU...BECAUSE I TOO WAS THE *VICTIM OF AN IDEA.*

THE BEST PART ABOUT THIS... I'M NOT LYING TO THE KID.

NOW, HOW ABOUT YOU HIT THE MEN'S ROOM AND WASH OFF ALL THAT SCABBY BLOOD?

THAT... THAT SOUNDS GOOD.

I MEAN SERIOUSLY, I CAN SMELL IT FROM HERE. LIKE *NICKELS AND BUTT SWEAT.*

OKAY.

THEN WHAT?

AND THAT FILLS ME WITH A NEWFOUND SENSE OF JOY.

THEN WE START TO TALK ABOUT YOUR DAD.

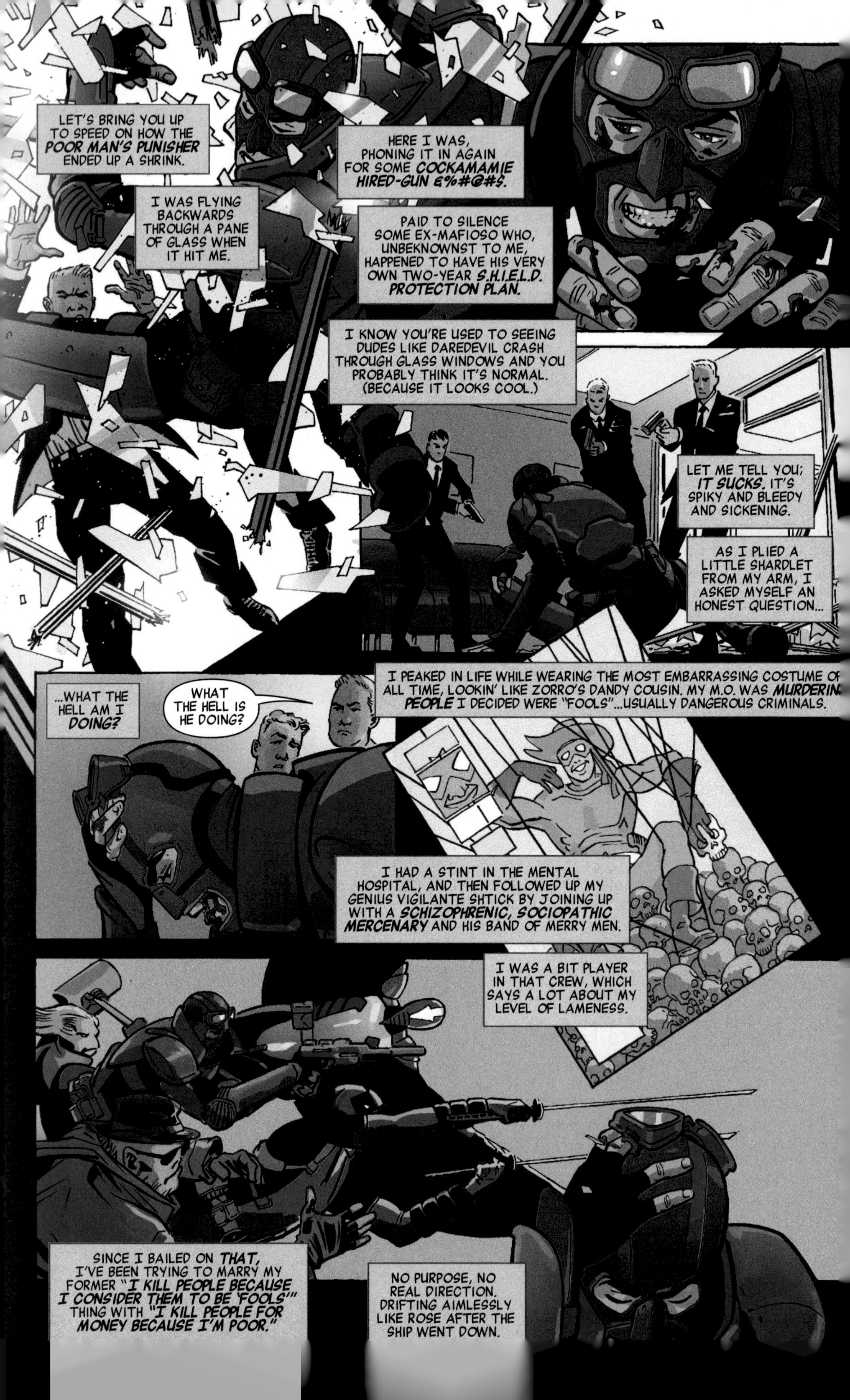
LET'S BRING YOU UP TO SPEED ON HOW THE POOR MAN'S PUNISHER ENDED UP A SHRINK.
I WAS FLYING BACKWARDS THROUGH A PANE OF GLASS WHEN IT HIT ME.
HERE I WAS, PHONING IT IN AGAIN FOR SOME COCKAMAMIE HIRED-GUN &%#@#$.
PAID TO SILENCE SOME EX-MAFIOSO WHO, UNBEKNOWNST TO ME, HAPPENED TO HAVE HIS VERY OWN TWO-YEAR S.H.I.E.L.D. PROTECTION PLAN.
I KNOW YOU'RE USED TO SEEING DUDES LIKE DAREDEVIL CRASH THROUGH GLASS WINDOWS AND YOU PROBABLY THINK IT'S NORMAL. (BECAUSE IT LOOKS COOL.)
LET ME TELL YOU; IT SUCKS. IT'S SPIKY AND BLEEDY AND SICKENING.
AS I PLIED A LITTLE SHARDLET FROM MY ARM, I ASKED MYSELF AN HONEST QUESTION...
...WHAT THE HELL AM I DOING?
WHAT THE HELL IS HE DOING?
I PEAKED IN LIFE WHILE WEARING THE MOST EMBARRASSING COSTUME OF ALL TIME, LOOKIN' LIKE ZORRO'S DANDY COUSIN. MY M.O. WAS MURDERING PEOPLE I DECIDED WERE "FOOLS"...USUALLY DANGEROUS CRIMINALS.
I HAD A STINT IN THE MENTAL HOSPITAL, AND THEN FOLLOWED UP MY GENIUS VIGILANTE SHTICK BY JOINING UP WITH A SCHIZOPHRENIC, SOCIOPATHIC MERCENARY AND HIS BAND OF MERRY MEN.
I WAS A BIT PLAYER IN THAT CREW, WHICH SAYS A LOT ABOUT MY LEVEL OF LAMENESS.
SINCE I BAILED ON THAT, I'VE BEEN TRYING TO MARRY MY FORMER "I KILL PEOPLE BECAUSE I CONSIDER THEM TO BE 'FOOLS'" THING WITH "I KILL PEOPLE FOR MONEY BECAUSE I'M POOR."
NO PURPOSE, NO REAL DIRECTION. DRIFTING AIMLESSLY LIKE ROSE AFTER THE SHIP WENT DOWN.

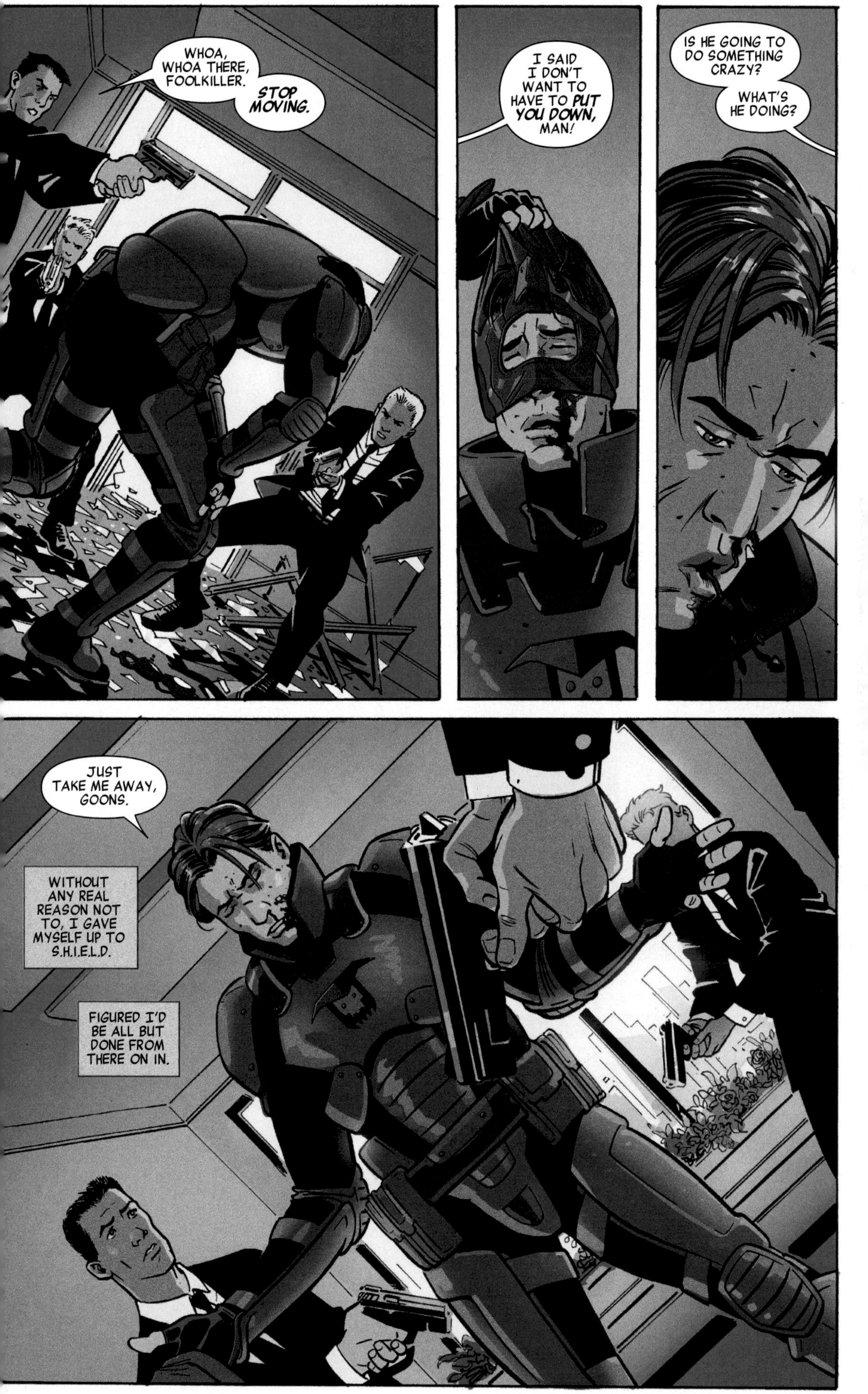

WHOA, WHOA THERE, FOOLKILLER.
STOP MOVING.
I SAID I DON'T WANT TO HAVE TO PUT YOU DOWN, MAN!
IS HE GOING TO DO SOMETHING CRAZY?
WHAT'S HE DOING?
JUST TAKE ME AWAY, GOONS.
WITHOUT ANY REAL REASON NOT TO, I GAVE MYSELF UP TO S.H.I.E.L.D.
FIGURED I'D BE ALL BUT DONE FROM THERE ON IN.

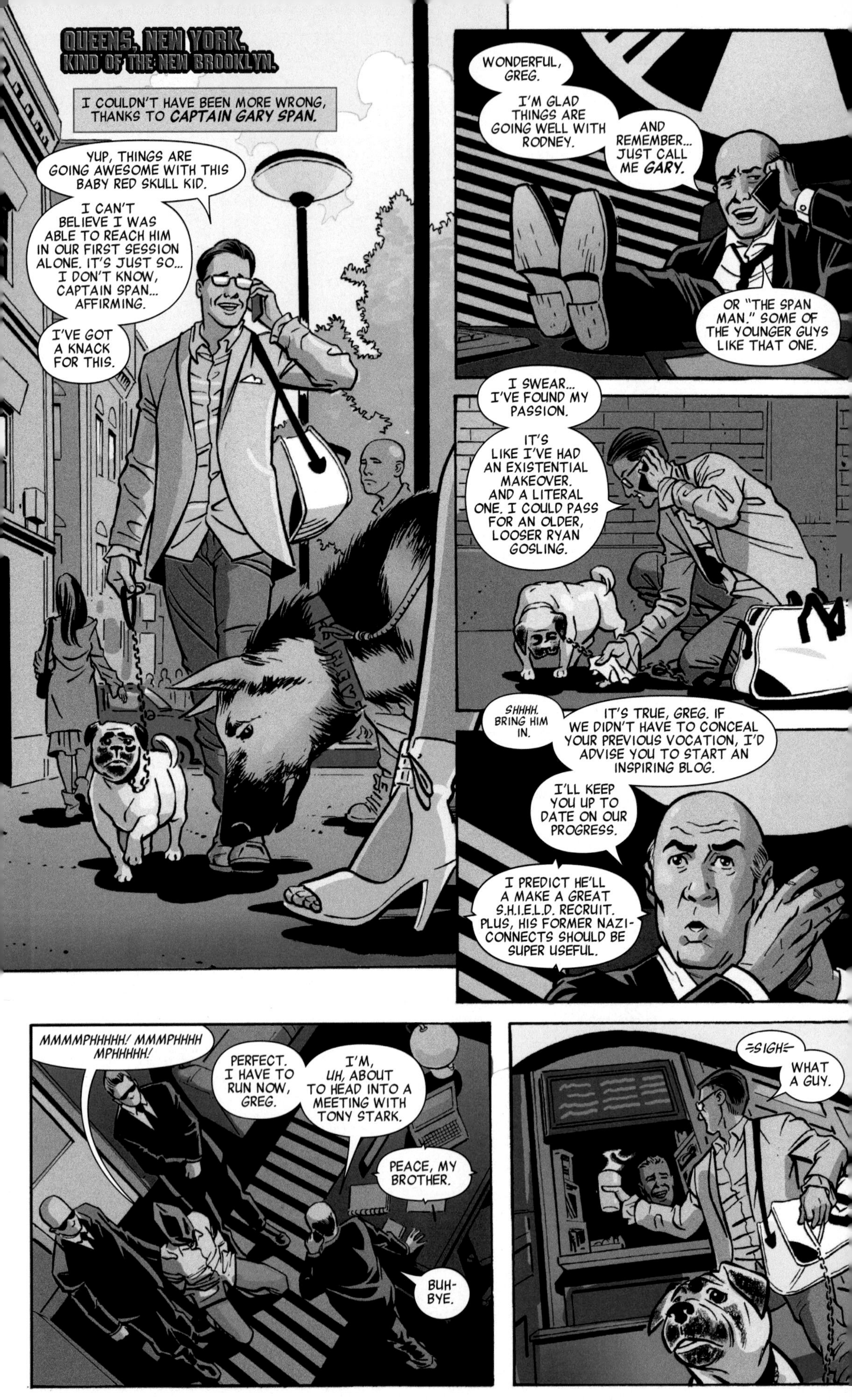
QUEENS, NEW YORK. KIND OF THE NEW BROOKLYN.
I COULDN'T HAVE BEEN MORE WRONG, THANKS TO CAPTAIN GARY SPAN.
YUP, THINGS ARE GOING AWESOME WITH THIS BABY RED SKULL KID.
I CAN'T BELIEVE I WAS ABLE TO REACH HIM IN OUR FIRST SESSION ALONE. IT'S JUST SO... I DON'T KNOW, CAPTAIN SPAN... AFFIRMING.
I'VE GOT A KNACK FOR THIS.
WONDERFUL, GREG.
I'M GLAD THINGS ARE GOING WELL WITH RODNEY.
AND REMEMBER... JUST CALL ME GARY.
OR "THE SPAN MAN." SOME OF THE YOUNGER GUYS LIKE THAT ONE.
I SWEAR... I'VE FOUND MY PASSION.
IT'S LIKE I'VE HAD AN EXISTENTIAL MAKEOVER. AND A LITERAL ONE. I COULD PASS FOR AN OLDER, LOOSER RYAN GOSLING.
SHHHH. BRING HIM IN.
IT'S TRUE, GREG. IF WE DIDN'T HAVE TO CONCEAL YOUR PREVIOUS VOCATION, I'D ADVISE YOU TO START AN INSPIRING BLOG.
I'LL KEEP YOU UP TO DATE ON OUR PROGRESS.
I PREDICT HE'LL A MAKE A GREAT S.H.I.E.L.D. RECRUIT. PLUS, HIS FORMER NAZI-CONNECTS SHOULD BE SUPER USEFUL.
MMMMPHHHHH! MMMPHHHH MPHHHHH!
PERFECT. I HAVE TO RUN NOW, GREG.
I'M, UH, ABOUT TO HEAD INTO A MEETING WITH TONY STARK.
PEACE, MY BROTHER.
BUH-BYE.
=SIGH=
WHAT A GUY.

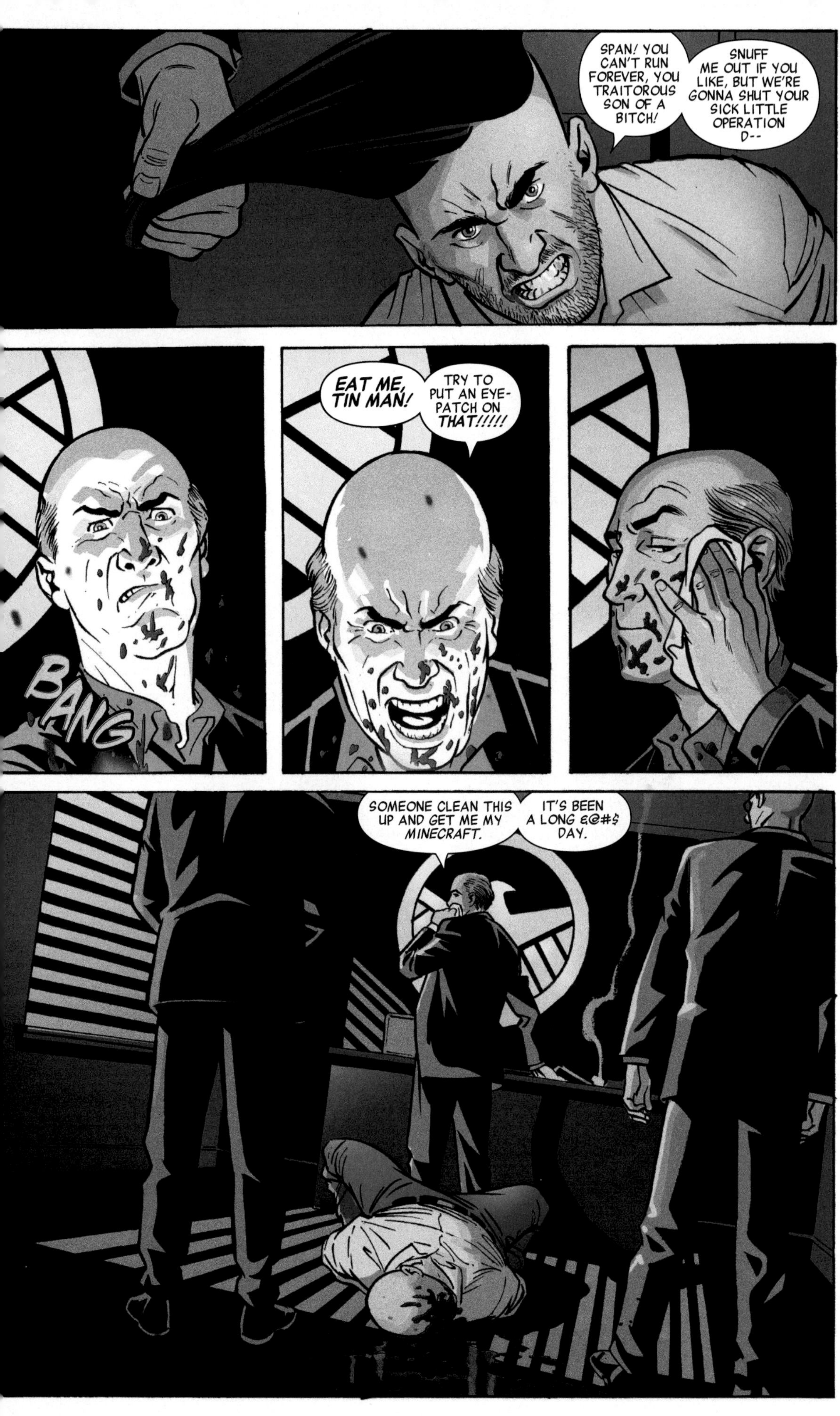
SPAN! YOU CAN'T RUN FOREVER, YOU TRAITOROUS SON OF A BITCH!
SNUFF ME OUT IF YOU LIKE, BUT WE'RE GONNA SHUT YOUR SICK LITTLE OPERATION D--
BANG
EAT ME, TIN MAN!
TRY TO PUT AN EYE-PATCH ON THAT!!!!!
SOMEONE CLEAN THIS UP AND GET ME MY MINECRAFT.
IT'S BEEN A LONG &@#$ DAY.

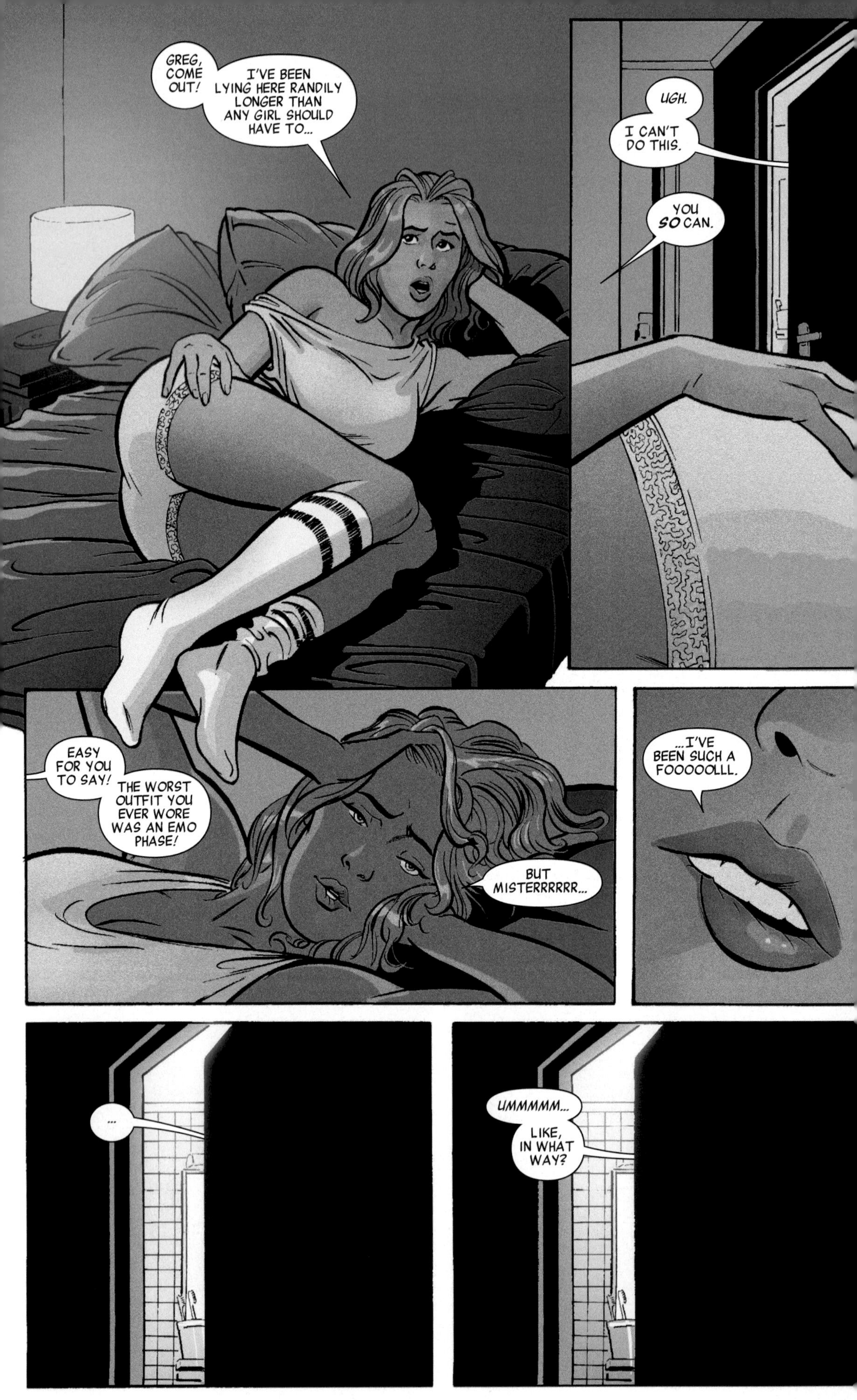
GREG, COME OUT!
I'VE BEEN LYING HERE RANDILY LONGER THAN ANY GIRL SHOULD HAVE TO...
UGH.
I CAN'T DO THIS.
YOU SO CAN.
EASY FOR YOU TO SAY!
THE WORST OUTFIT YOU EVER WORE WAS AN EMO PHASE!
BUT MISTERRRRRR...
...I'VE BEEN SUCH A FOOOOOLLL.
...
UMMMMM...
LIKE, IN WHAT WAY?

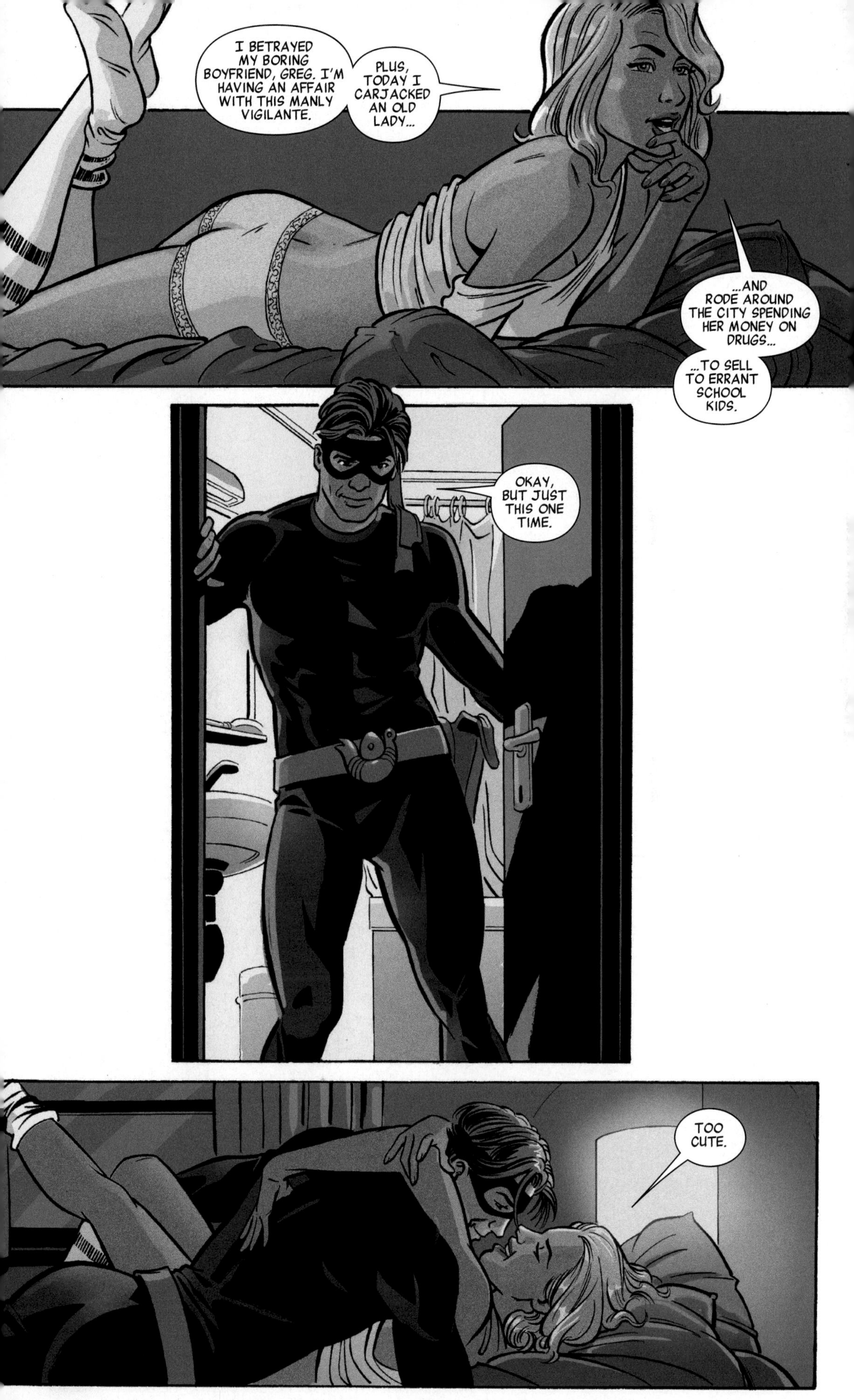
I BETRAYED MY BORING BOYFRIEND, GREG. I'M HAVING AN AFFAIR WITH THIS MANLY VIGILANTE.
PLUS, TODAY I CARJACKED AN OLD LADY...
...AND RODE AROUND THE CITY SPENDING HER MONEY ON DRUGS...
...TO SELL TO ERRANT SCHOOL KIDS.
OKAY, BUT JUST THIS ONE TIME.
TOO CUTE.

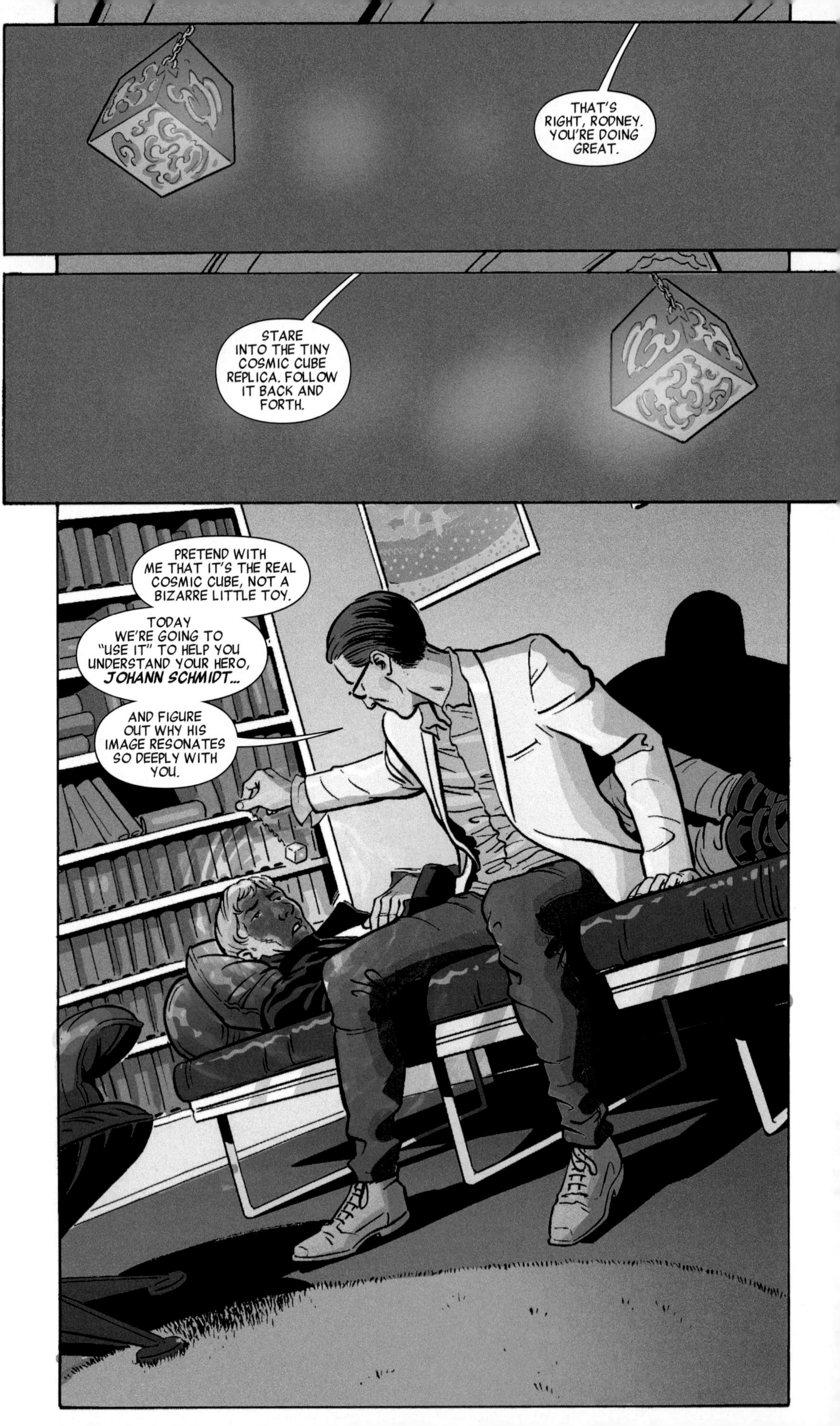
THAT'S RIGHT, RODNEY. YOU'RE DOING GREAT.
STARE INTO THE TINY COSMIC CUBE REPLICA. FOLLOW IT BACK AND FORTH.
PRETEND WITH ME THAT IT'S THE REAL COSMIC CUBE, NOT A BIZARRE LITTLE TOY.
TODAY WE'RE GOING TO "USE IT" TO HELP YOU UNDERSTAND YOUR HERO, JOHANN SCHMIDT...
AND FIGURE OUT WHY HIS IMAGE RESONATES SO DEEPLY WITH YOU.

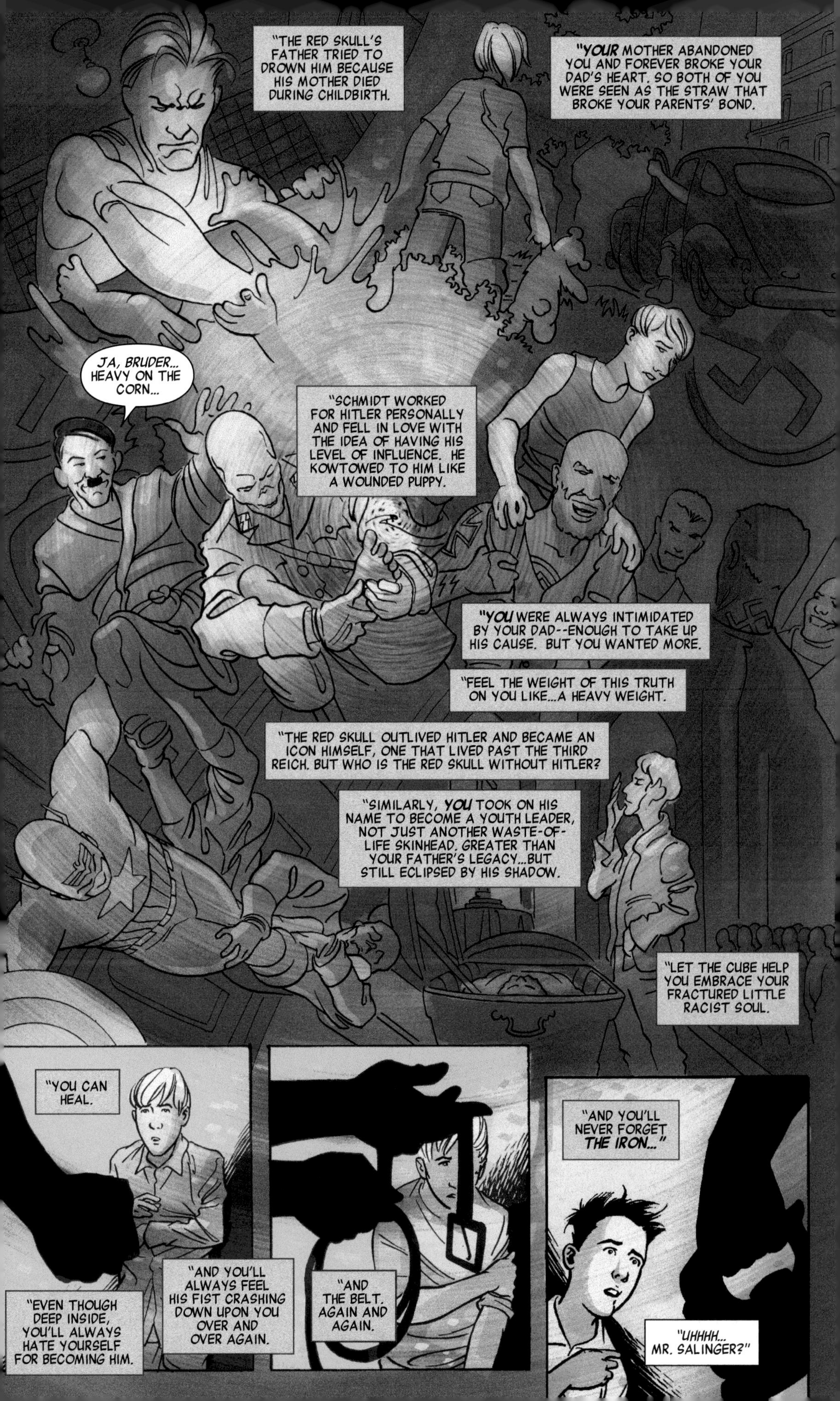

"THE RED SKULL'S FATHER TRIED TO DROWN HIM BECAUSE HIS MOTHER DIED DURING CHILDBIRTH.
"YOUR MOTHER ABANDONED YOU AND FOREVER BROKE YOUR DAD'S HEART. SO BOTH OF YOU WERE SEEN AS THE STRAW THAT BROKE YOUR PARENTS' BOND.
JA, BRUDER... HEAVY ON THE CORN...
"SCHMIDT WORKED FOR HITLER PERSONALLY AND FELL IN LOVE WITH THE IDEA OF HAVING HIS LEVEL OF INFLUENCE. HE KOWTOWED TO HIM LIKE A WOUNDED PUPPY.
"YOU WERE ALWAYS INTIMIDATED BY YOUR DAD--ENOUGH TO TAKE UP HIS CAUSE. BUT YOU WANTED MORE.
"FEEL THE WEIGHT OF THIS TRUTH ON YOU LIKE...A HEAVY WEIGHT.
"THE RED SKULL OUTLIVED HITLER AND BECAME AN ICON HIMSELF, ONE THAT LIVED PAST THE THIRD REICH. BUT WHO IS THE RED SKULL WITHOUT HITLER?
"SIMILARLY, YOU TOOK ON HIS NAME TO BECOME A YOUTH LEADER, NOT JUST ANOTHER WASTE-OF-LIFE SKINHEAD. GREATER THAN YOUR FATHER'S LEGACY...BUT STILL ECLIPSED BY HIS SHADOW.
"LET THE CUBE HELP YOU EMBRACE YOUR FRACTURED LITTLE RACIST SOUL.
"YOU CAN HEAL.
"EVEN THOUGH DEEP INSIDE, YOU'LL ALWAYS HATE YOURSELF FOR BECOMING HIM.
"AND YOU'LL ALWAYS FEEL HIS FIST CRASHING DOWN UPON YOU OVER AND OVER AGAIN.
"AND THE BELT. AGAIN AND AGAIN.
"AND YOU'LL NEVER FORGET THE IRON..."
"UHHHH... MR. SALINGER?"

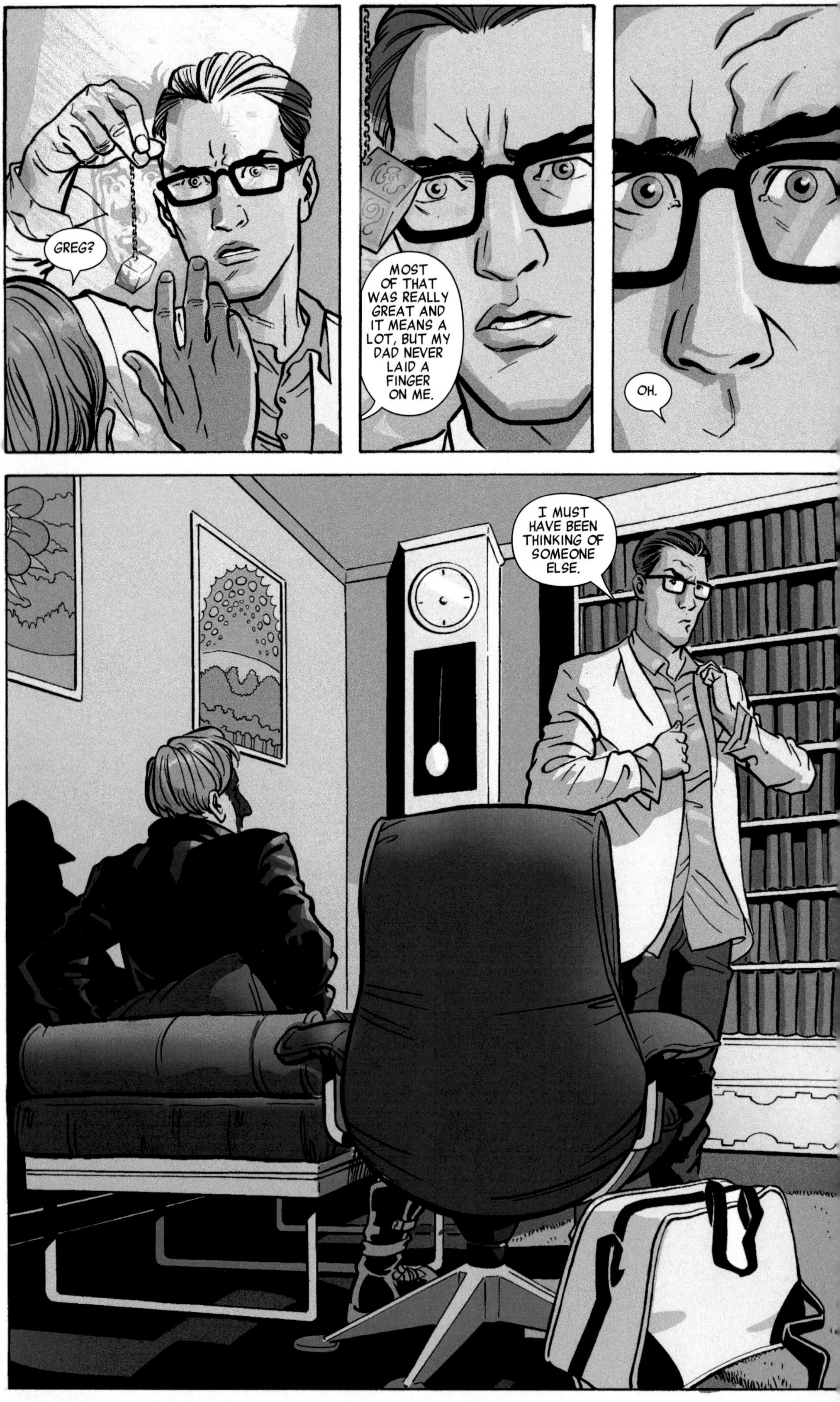
GREG?
MOST OF THAT WAS REALLY GREAT AND IT MEANS A LOT, BUT MY DAD NEVER LAID A FINGER ON ME.
OH.
I MUST HAVE BEEN THINKING OF SOMEONE ELSE.

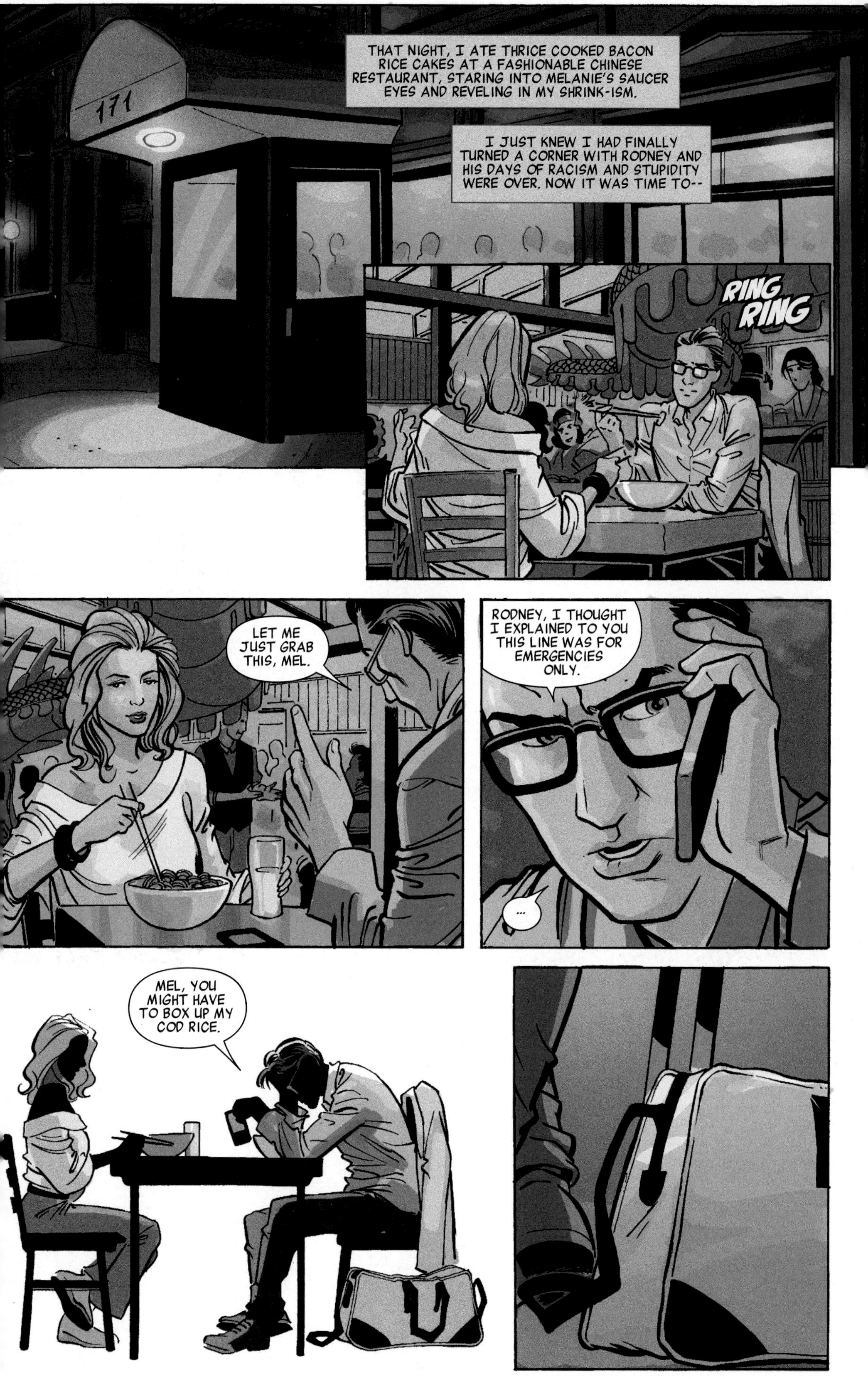
171
THAT NIGHT, I ATE THRICE COOKED BACON RICE CAKES AT A FASHIONABLE CHINESE RESTAURANT, STARING INTO MELANIE'S SAUCER EYES AND REVELING IN MY SHRINK-ISM.
I JUST KNEW I HAD FINALLY TURNED A CORNER WITH RODNEY AND HIS DAYS OF RACISM AND STUPIDITY WERE OVER. NOW IT WAS TIME TO--
RING RING
LET ME JUST GRAB THIS, MEL.
RODNEY, I THOUGHT I EXPLAINED TO YOU THIS LINE WAS FOR EMERGENCIES ONLY.
...
MEL, YOU MIGHT HAVE TO BOX UP MY COD RICE.

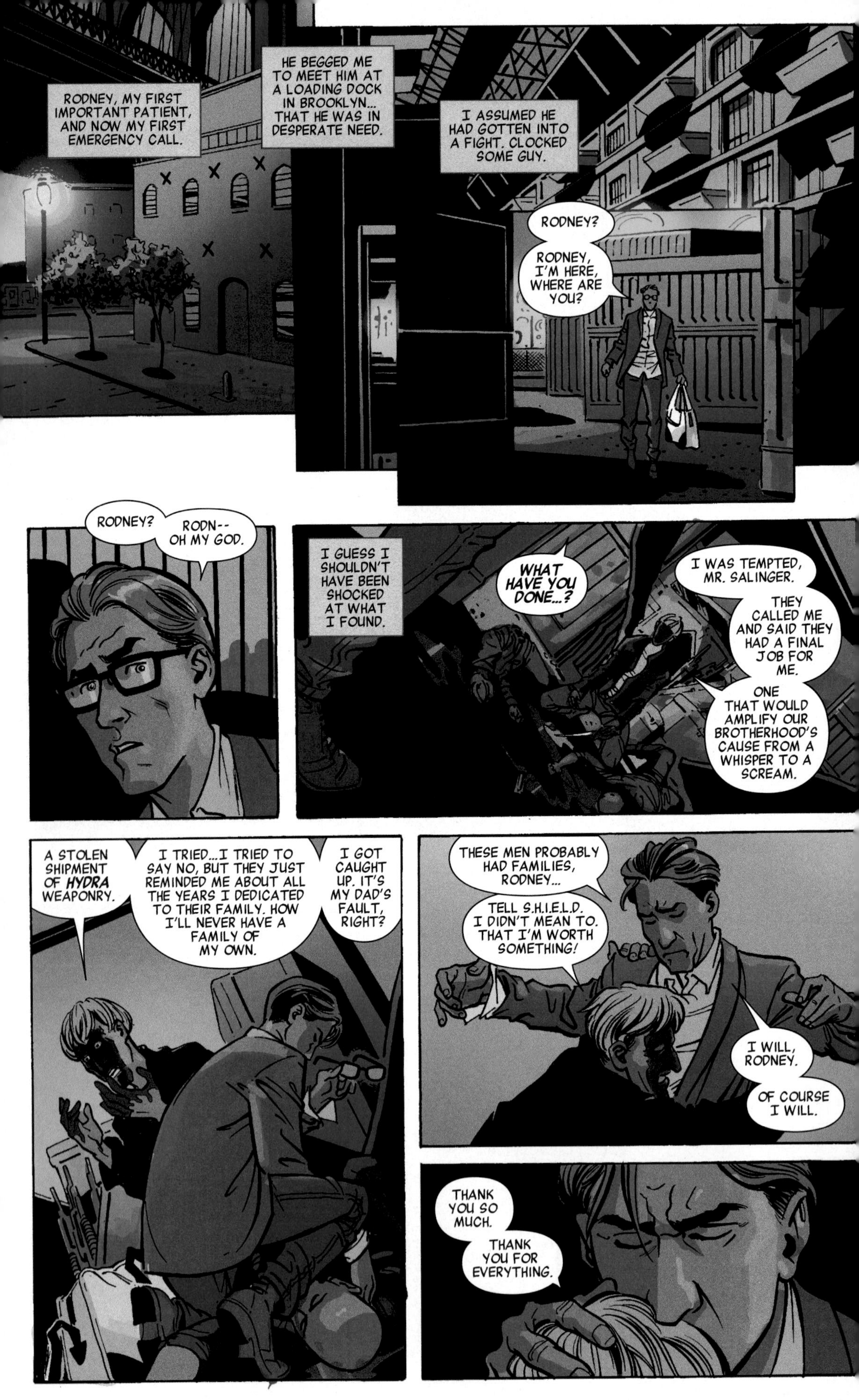

RODNEY, MY FIRST IMPORTANT PATIENT, AND NOW MY FIRST EMERGENCY CALL.
HE BEGGED ME TO MEET HIM AT A LOADING DOCK IN BROOKLYN... THAT HE WAS IN DESPERATE NEED.
I ASSUMED HE HAD GOTTEN INTO A FIGHT. CLOCKED SOME GUY.
RODNEY?
RODNEY, I'M HERE, WHERE ARE YOU?
RODNEY?
RODN-- OH MY GOD.
I GUESS I SHOULDN'T HAVE BEEN SHOCKED AT WHAT I FOUND.
WHAT HAVE YOU DONE...?
I WAS TEMPTED, MR. SALINGER.
THEY CALLED ME AND SAID THEY HAD A FINAL JOB FOR ME.
ONE THAT WOULD AMPLIFY OUR BROTHERHOOD'S CAUSE FROM A WHISPER TO A SCREAM.
A STOLEN SHIPMENT OF HYDRA WEAPONRY.
I TRIED...I TRIED TO SAY NO, BUT THEY JUST REMINDED ME ABOUT ALL THE YEARS I DEDICATED TO THEIR FAMILY. HOW I'LL NEVER HAVE A FAMILY OF MY OWN.
I GOT CAUGHT UP. IT'S MY DAD'S FAULT, RIGHT?
THESE MEN PROBABLY HAD FAMILIES, RODNEY...
TELL S.H.I.E.L.D. I DIDN'T MEAN TO. THAT I'M WORTH SOMETHING!
I WILL, RODNEY.
OF COURSE I WILL.
THANK YOU SO MUCH.
THANK YOU FOR EVERYTHING.

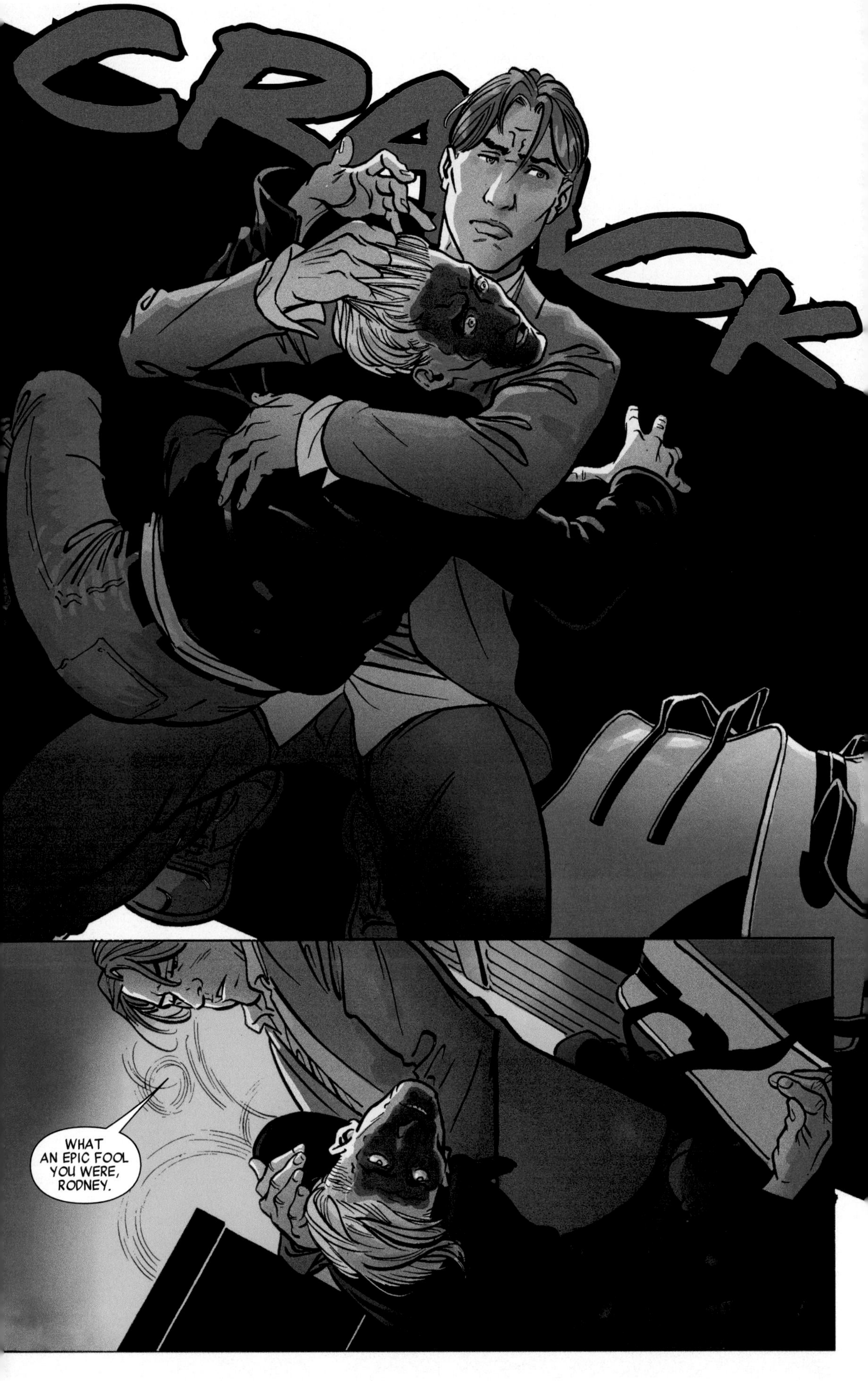
CRACK
WHAT AN EPIC FOOL YOU WERE, RODNEY.

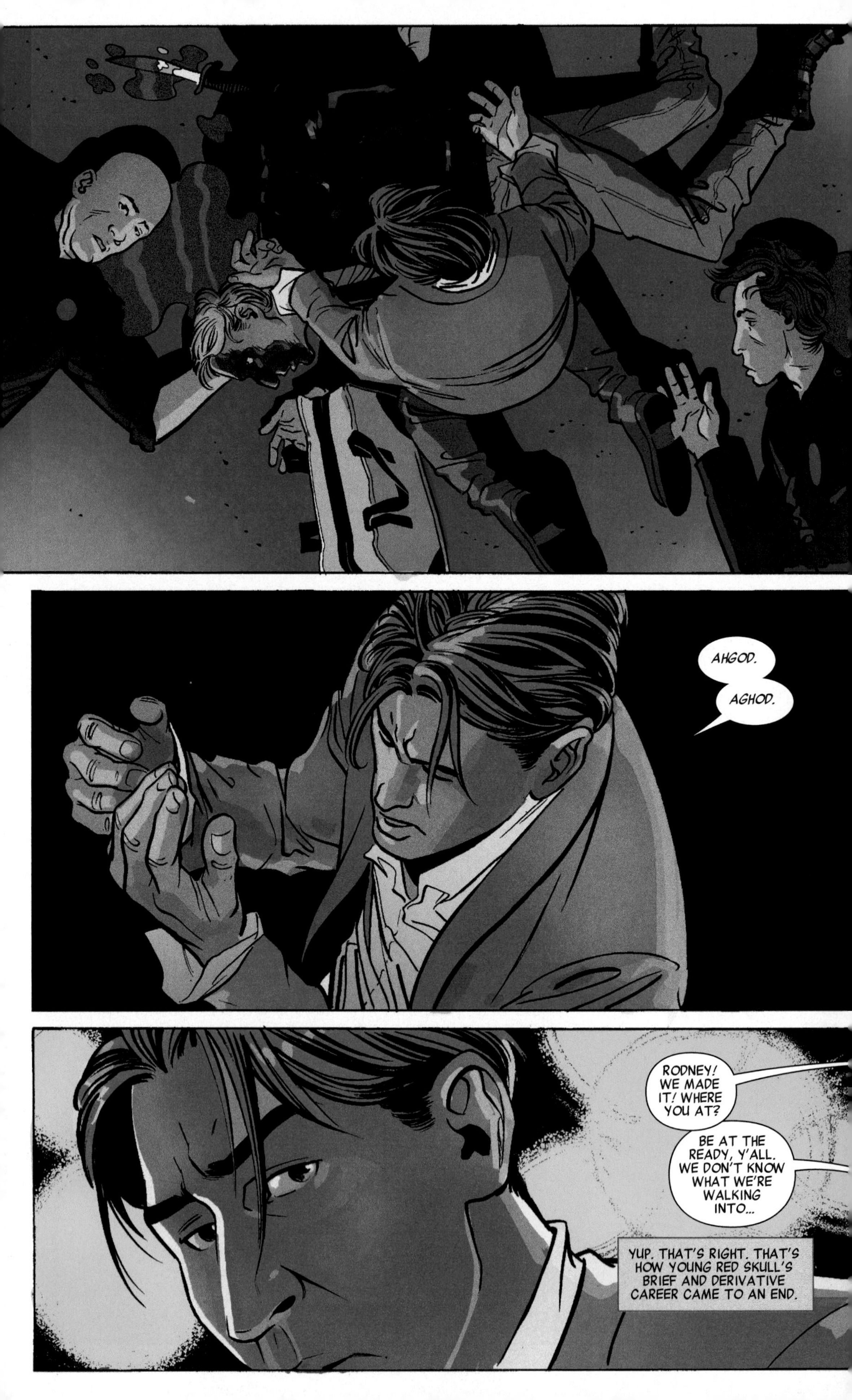
AHGOD.
AGHOD.
RODNEY! WE MADE IT! WHERE YOU AT?
BE AT THE READY, Y'ALL. WE DON'T KNOW WHAT WE'RE WALKING INTO...
YUP. THAT'S RIGHT. THAT'S HOW YOUNG RED SKULL'S BRIEF AND DERIVATIVE CAREER CAME TO AN END.

ADMITTEDLY, RODNEY WAS PRETTY MESSED UP... BUT DEEP INSIDE HIS HEART, HE WAS A GOOD GUY.

NOW DEEP INSIDE HIS HEART HE'S A DEAD GUY...

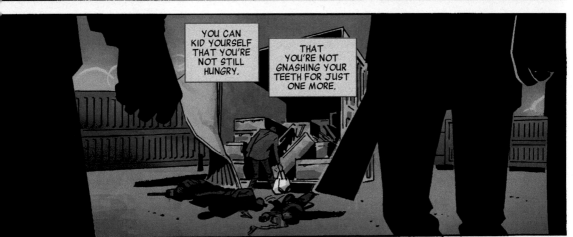

...AND AT MY HANDS. EVER BEEN ON A DIET AND THEN BREAK THE SEAL WITH A TWINKIE?

YOU CAN KID YOURSELF THAT YOU'RE NOT STILL HUNGRY.

THAT YOU'RE NOT GNASHING YOUR TEETH FOR JUST ONE MORE.

BUT AS A THERAPIST, I'M A SCOURGE OF DENIAL.

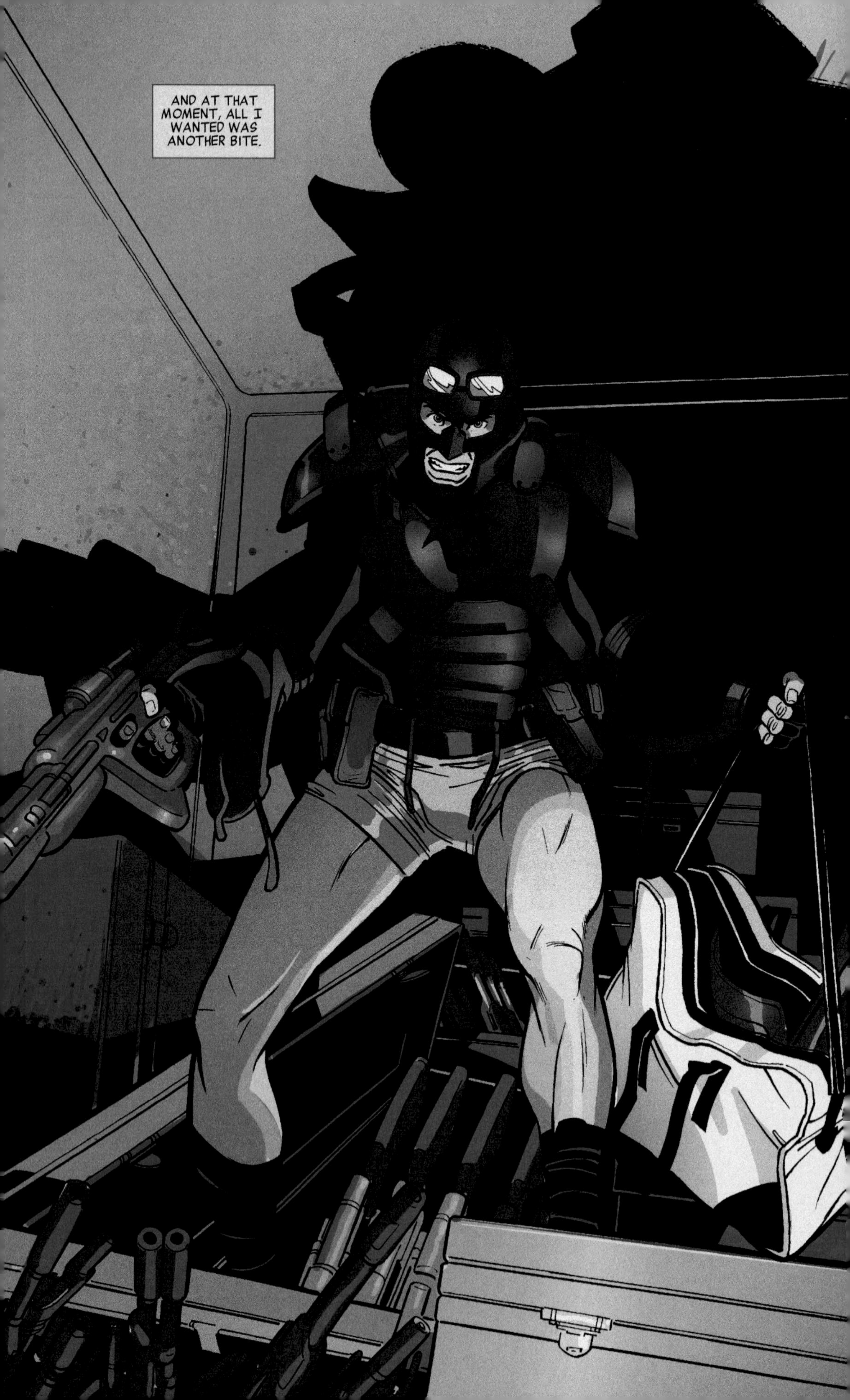
AND AT THAT MOMENT, ALL I WANTED WAS ANOTHER BITE.

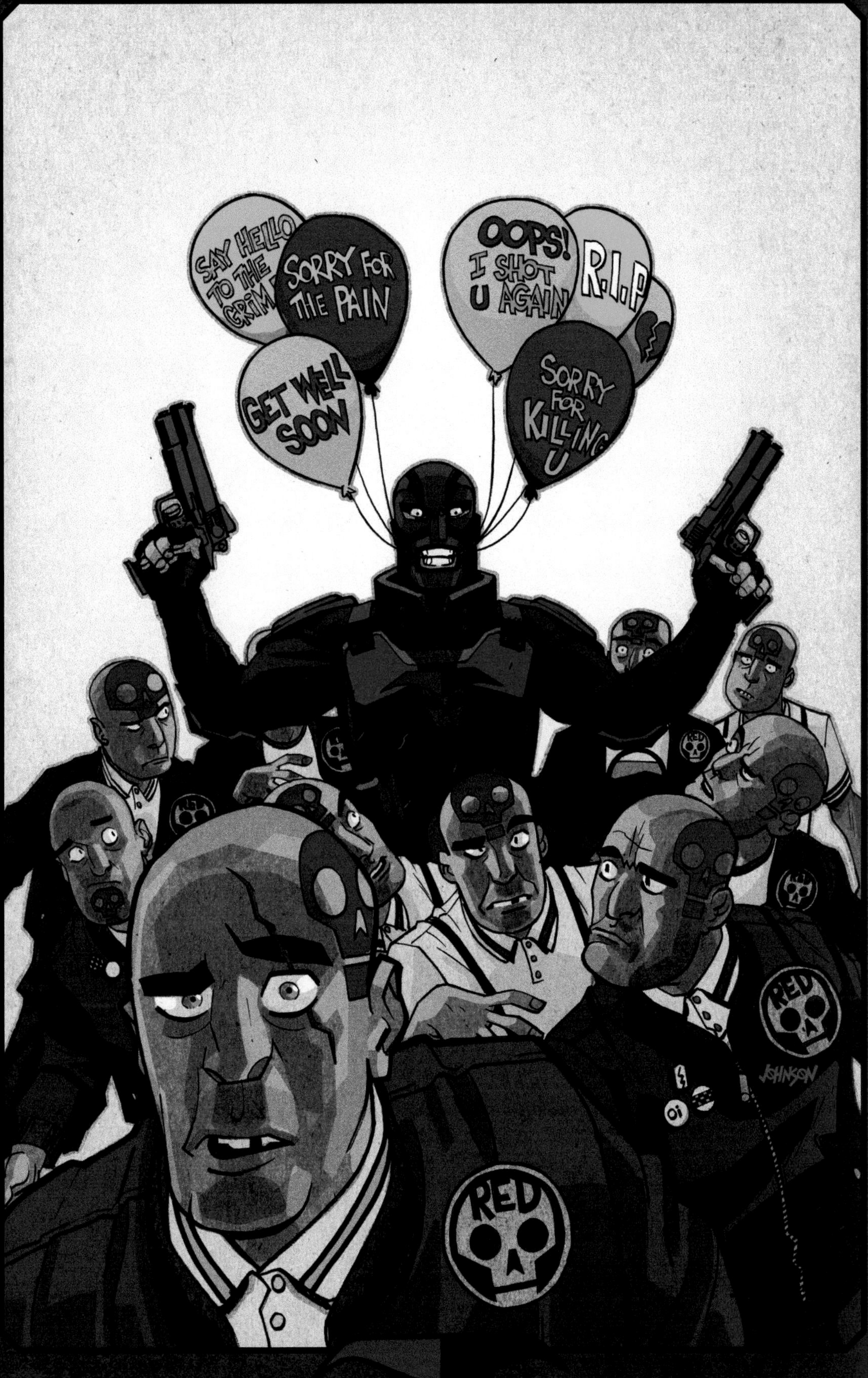
SAY HELLO TO THE GRIM
SORRY FOR THE PAIN
OOPS! I SHOT U AGAIN
R.I.P
GET WELL SOON
SORRY FOR KILLING U
RED
RED
Oi
JOHNSON

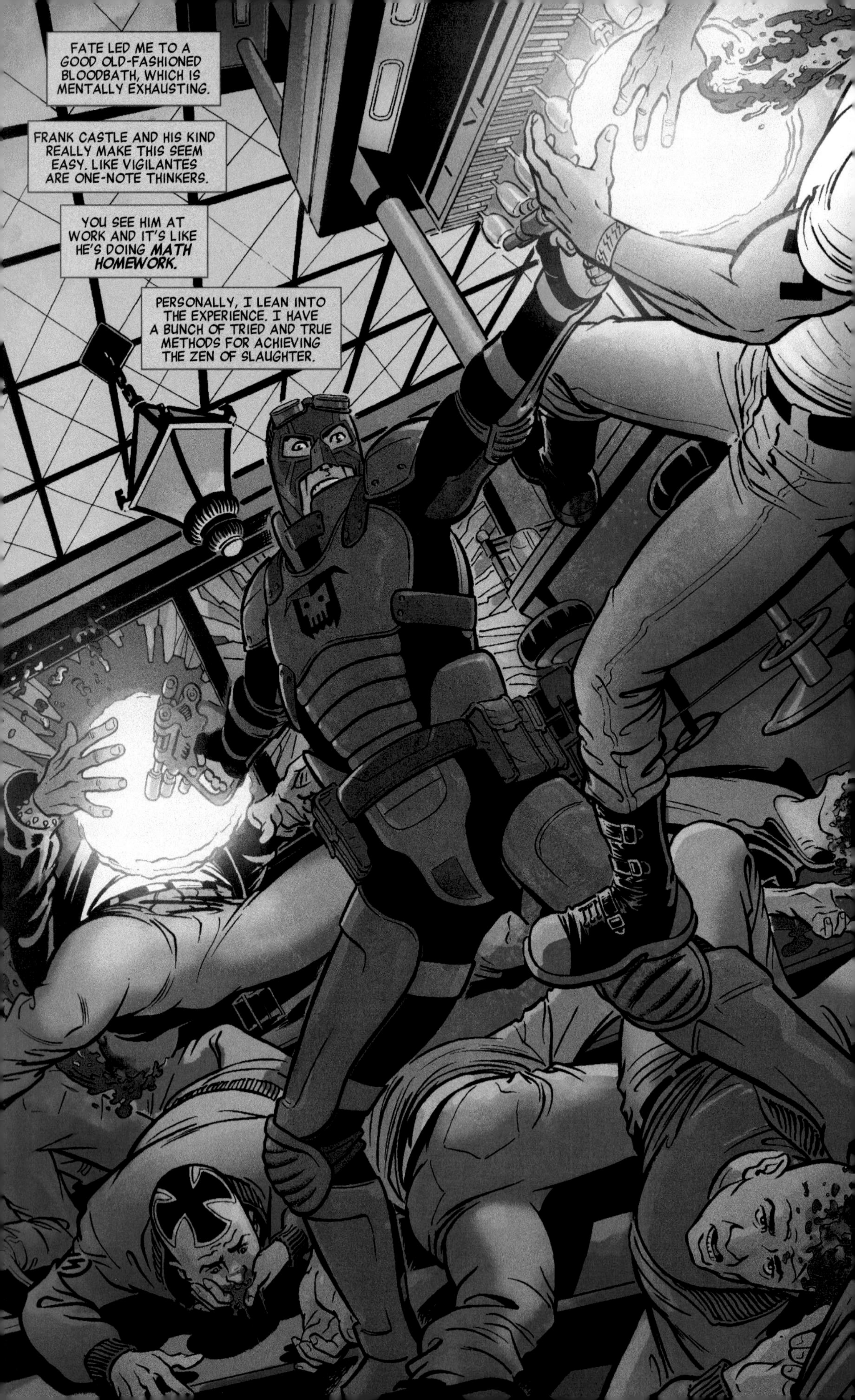
FATE LED ME TO A GOOD OLD-FASHIONED BLOODBATH, WHICH IS MENTALLY EXHAUSTING.
FRANK CASTLE AND HIS KIND REALLY MAKE THIS SEEM EASY. LIKE VIGILANTES ARE ONE-NOTE THINKERS.
YOU SEE HIM AT WORK AND IT'S LIKE HE'S DOING *MATH HOMEWORK.*
PERSONALLY, I LEAN INTO THE EXPERIENCE. I HAVE A BUNCH OF TRIED AND TRUE METHODS FOR ACHIEVING THE ZEN OF SLAUGHTER.

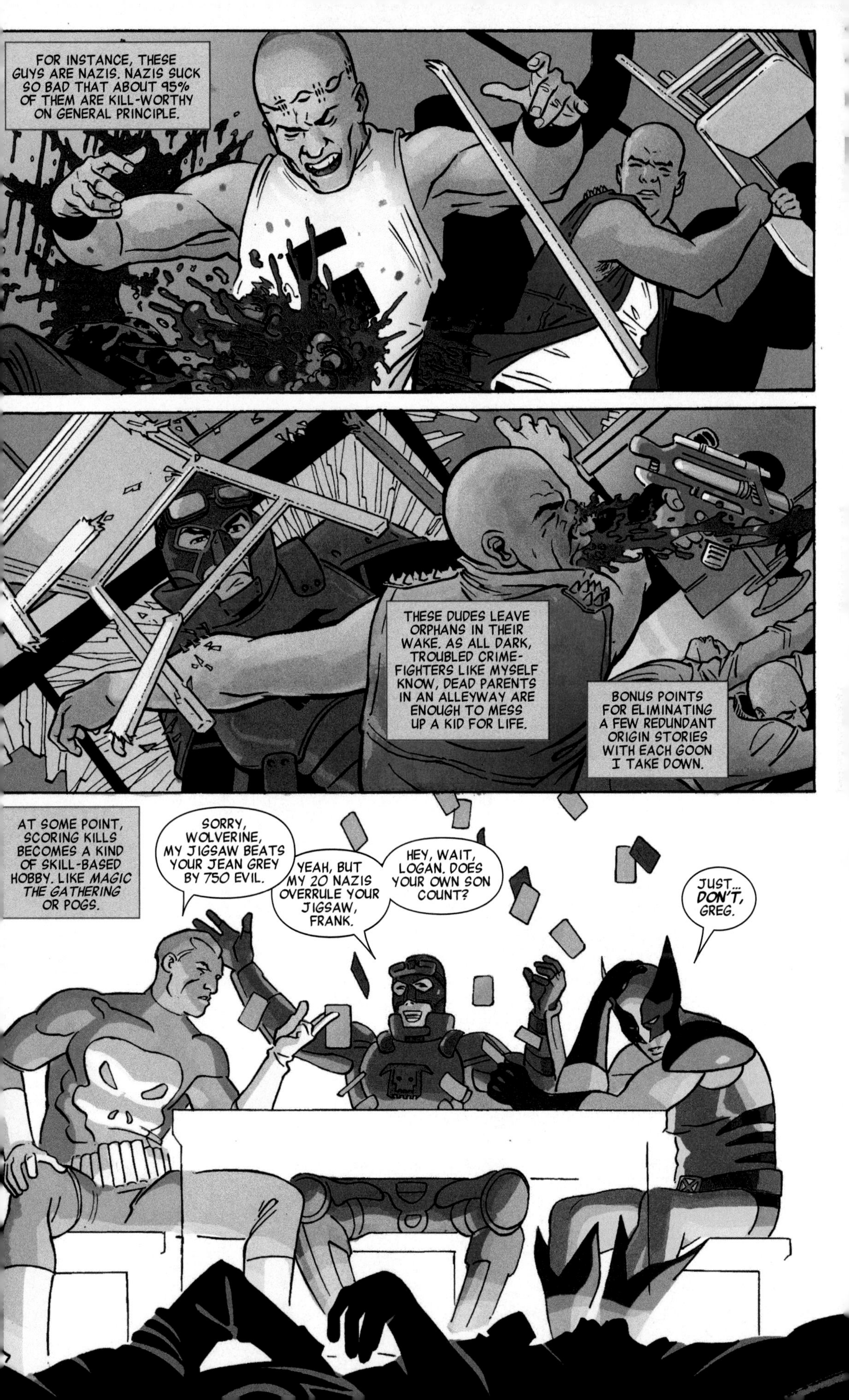
FOR INSTANCE, THESE GUYS ARE NAZIS. NAZIS SUCK SO BAD THAT ABOUT 95% OF THEM ARE KILL-WORTHY ON GENERAL PRINCIPLE.
THESE DUDES LEAVE ORPHANS IN THEIR WAKE. AS ALL DARK, TROUBLED CRIME-FIGHTERS LIKE MYSELF KNOW, DEAD PARENTS IN AN ALLEYWAY ARE ENOUGH TO MESS UP A KID FOR LIFE.
BONUS POINTS FOR ELIMINATING A FEW REDUNDANT ORIGIN STORIES WITH EACH GOON I TAKE DOWN.
AT SOME POINT, SCORING KILLS BECOMES A KIND OF SKILL-BASED HOBBY. LIKE *MAGIC THE GATHERING* OR POGS.
SORRY, WOLVERINE, MY JIGSAW BEATS YOUR JEAN GREY BY 750 EVIL.
YEAH, BUT MY 20 NAZIS OVERRULE YOUR JIGSAW, FRANK.
HEY, WAIT, LOGAN. DOES YOUR OWN SON COUNT?
JUST... **DON'T,** GREG.

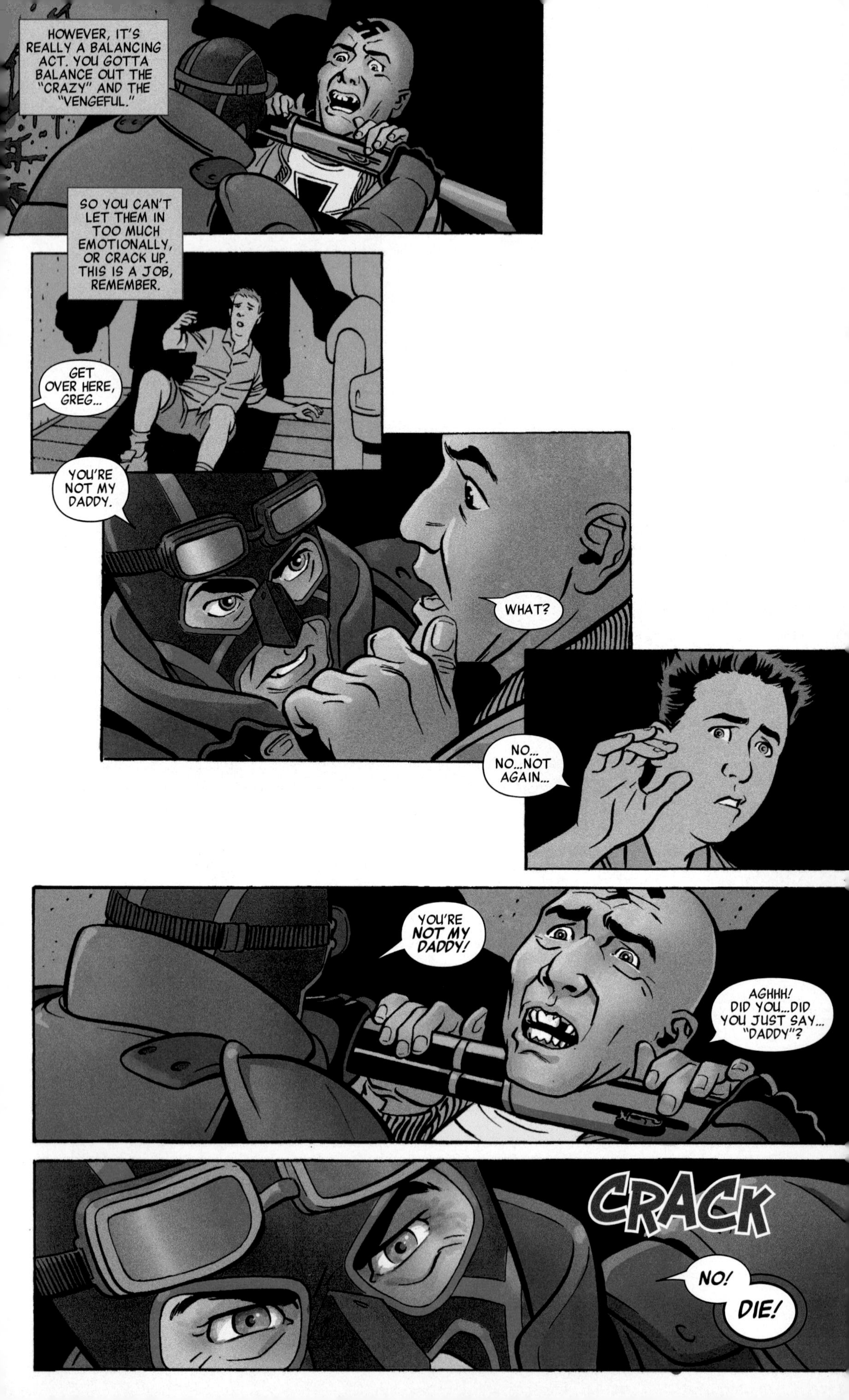
HOWEVER, IT'S REALLY A BALANCING ACT. YOU GOTTA BALANCE OUT THE "CRAZY" AND THE "VENGEFUL."
SO YOU CAN'T LET THEM IN TOO MUCH EMOTIONALLY, OR CRACK UP. THIS IS A JOB, REMEMBER.
GET OVER HERE, GREG...
YOU'RE NOT MY DADDY.
WHAT?
NO... NO...NOT AGAIN...
YOU'RE NOT MY DADDY!
AGHHH! DID YOU...DID YOU JUST SAY... "DADDY"?
CRACK
NO!
DIE!

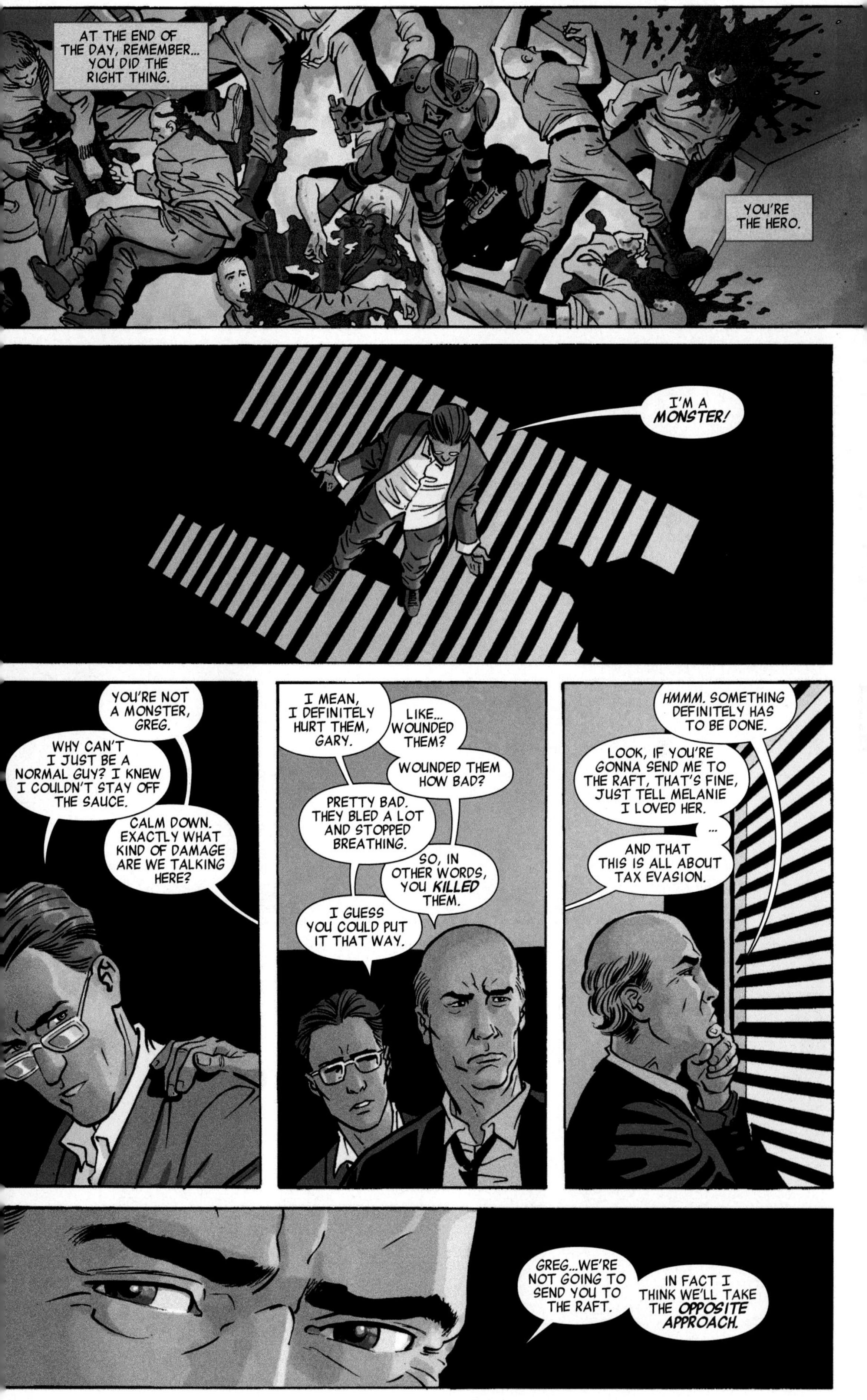

AT THE END OF THE DAY, REMEMBER... YOU DID THE RIGHT THING.
YOU'RE THE HERO.
I'M A MONSTER!
YOU'RE NOT A MONSTER, GREG.
WHY CAN'T I JUST BE A NORMAL GUY? I KNEW I COULDN'T STAY OFF THE SAUCE.
CALM DOWN. EXACTLY WHAT KIND OF DAMAGE ARE WE TALKING HERE?
I MEAN, I DEFINITELY HURT THEM, GARY.
LIKE... WOUNDED THEM?
WOUNDED THEM HOW BAD?
PRETTY BAD. THEY BLED A LOT AND STOPPED BREATHING.
SO, IN OTHER WORDS, YOU KILLED THEM.
I GUESS YOU COULD PUT IT THAT WAY.
HMMM. SOMETHING DEFINITELY HAS TO BE DONE.
LOOK, IF YOU'RE GONNA SEND ME TO THE RAFT, THAT'S FINE, JUST TELL MELANIE I LOVED HER.
...
AND THAT THIS IS ALL ABOUT TAX EVASION.
GREG...WE'RE NOT GOING TO SEND YOU TO THE RAFT.
IN FACT I THINK WE'LL TAKE THE OPPOSITE APPROACH.

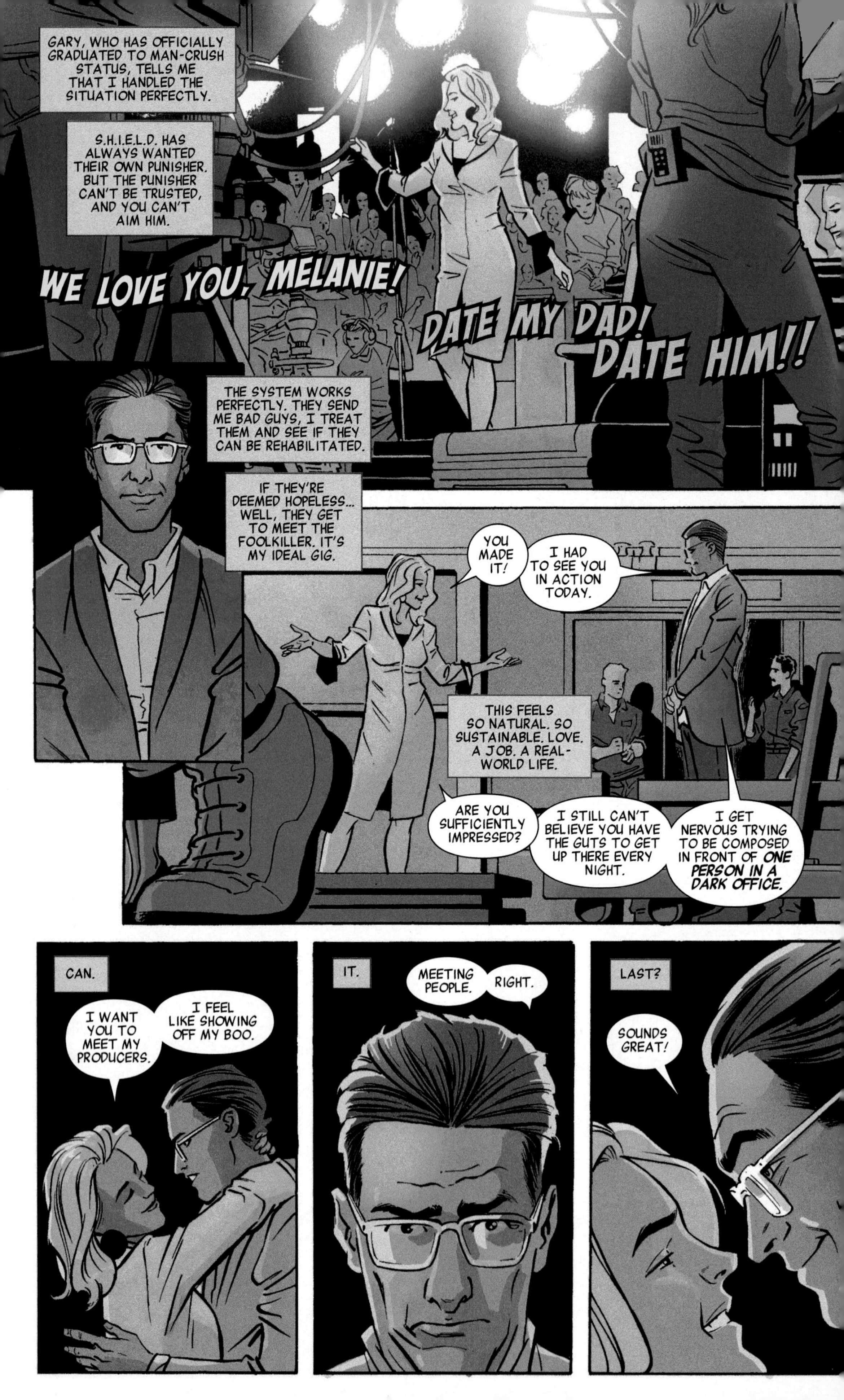
GARY, WHO HAS OFFICIALLY GRADUATED TO MAN-CRUSH STATUS, TELLS ME THAT I HANDLED THE SITUATION PERFECTLY.
S.H.I.E.L.D. HAS ALWAYS WANTED THEIR OWN PUNISHER. BUT THE PUNISHER CAN'T BE TRUSTED, AND YOU CAN'T AIM HIM.
WE LOVE YOU, MELANIE!
DATE MY DAD! DATE HIM!!
THE SYSTEM WORKS PERFECTLY. THEY SEND ME BAD GUYS, I TREAT THEM AND SEE IF THEY CAN BE REHABILITATED.
IF THEY'RE DEEMED HOPELESS... WELL, THEY GET TO MEET THE FOOLKILLER. IT'S MY IDEAL GIG.
YOU MADE IT!
I HAD TO SEE YOU IN ACTION TODAY.
THIS FEELS SO NATURAL. SO SUSTAINABLE. LOVE. A JOB. A REAL-WORLD LIFE.
ARE YOU SUFFICIENTLY IMPRESSED?
I STILL CAN'T BELIEVE YOU HAVE THE GUTS TO GET UP THERE EVERY NIGHT.
I GET NERVOUS TRYING TO BE COMPOSED IN FRONT OF ONE PERSON IN A DARK OFFICE.
CAN.
I WANT YOU TO MEET MY PRODUCERS.
I FEEL LIKE SHOWING OFF MY BOO.
IT.
MEETING PEOPLE.
RIGHT.
LAST?
SOUNDS GREAT!

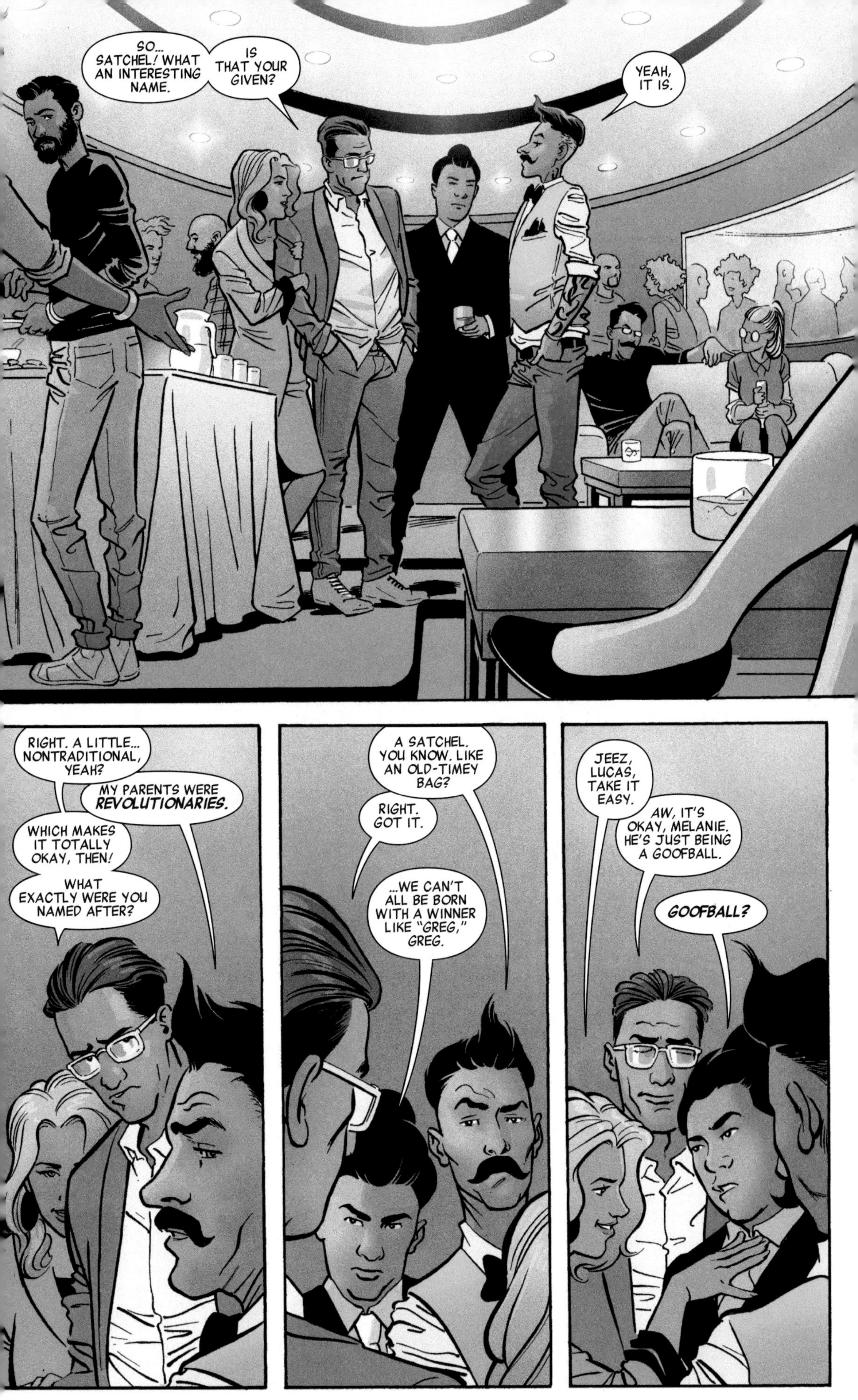
SO... SATCHEL! WHAT AN INTERESTING NAME.
IS THAT YOUR GIVEN?
YEAH, IT IS.
RIGHT. A LITTLE... NONTRADITIONAL, YEAH?
MY PARENTS WERE REVOLUTIONARIES.
WHICH MAKES IT TOTALLY OKAY, THEN!
WHAT EXACTLY WERE YOU NAMED AFTER?
A SATCHEL. YOU KNOW. LIKE AN OLD-TIMEY BAG?
RIGHT. GOT IT.
...WE CAN'T ALL BE BORN WITH A WINNER LIKE "GREG," GREG.
JEEZ, LUCAS, TAKE IT EASY.
AW, IT'S OKAY, MELANIE. HE'S JUST BEING A GOOFBALL.
GOOFBALL?

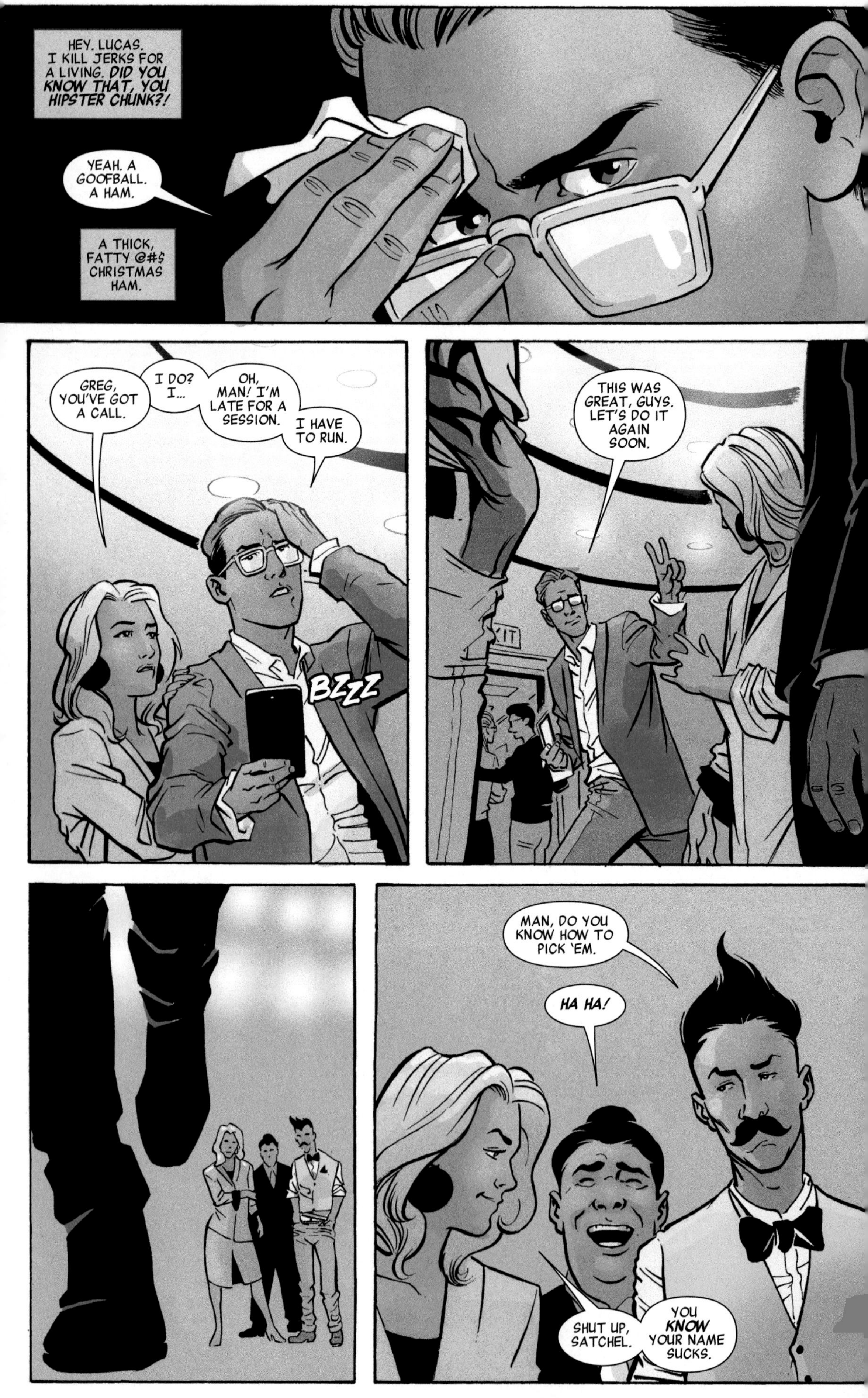

HEY. LUCAS. I KILL JERKS FOR A LIVING. DID YOU KNOW THAT, YOU HIPSTER CHUNK?!
YEAH. A GOOFBALL. A HAM.
A THICK, FATTY @#$ CHRISTMAS HAM.
GREG, YOU'VE GOT A CALL.
I DO? I...
OH, MAN! I'M LATE FOR A SESSION.
I HAVE TO RUN.
BZZZ
THIS WAS GREAT, GUYS. LET'S DO IT AGAIN SOON.
MAN, DO YOU KNOW HOW TO PICK 'EM.
HA HA!
SHUT UP, SATCHEL.
YOU KNOW YOUR NAME SUCKS.

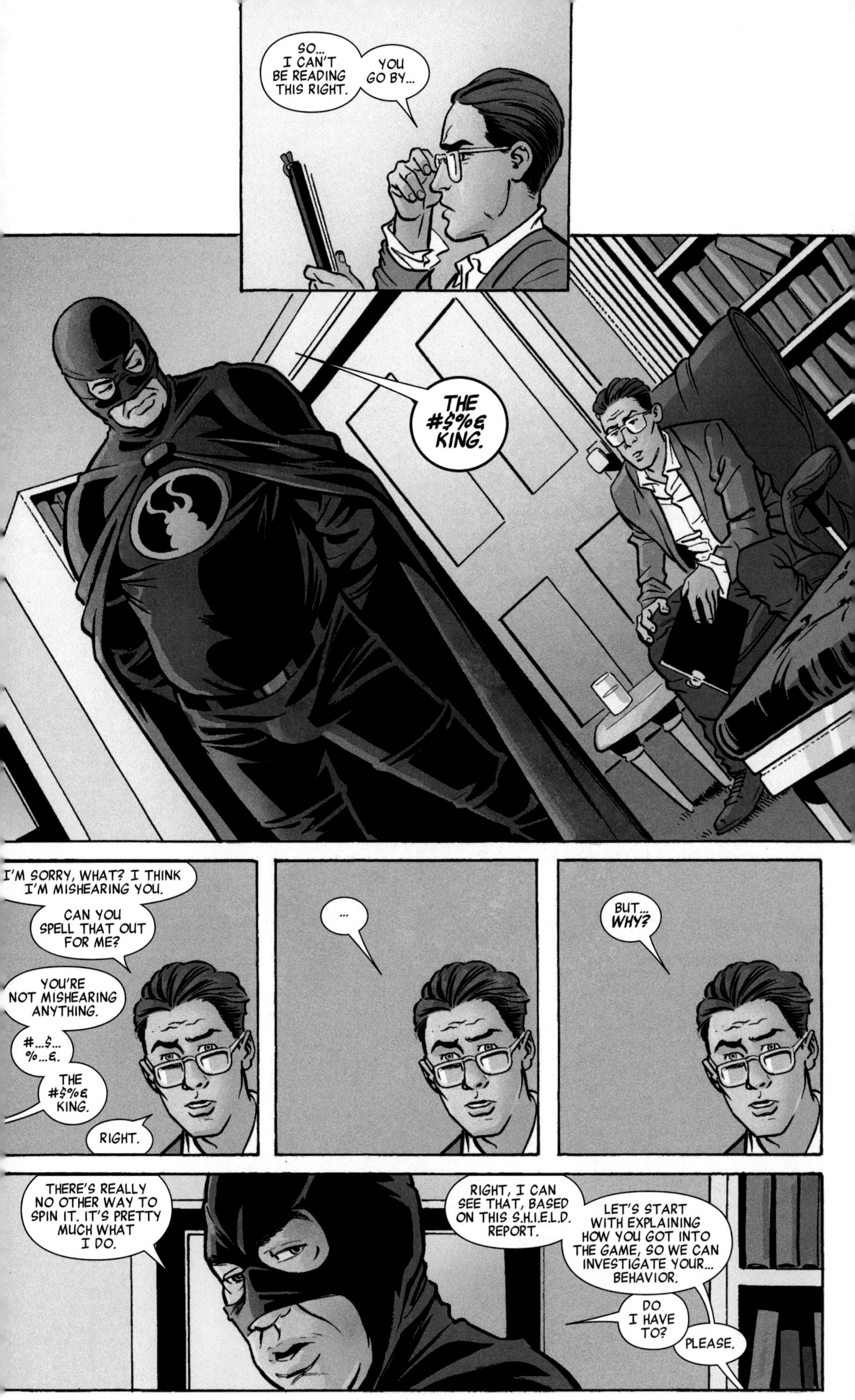
SO... I CAN'T BE READING THIS RIGHT.
YOU GO BY...
THE #$%€ KING.
I'M SORRY, WHAT? I THINK I'M MISHEARING YOU.
CAN YOU SPELL THAT OUT FOR ME?
YOU'RE NOT MISHEARING ANYTHING.
#...$... %...€.
THE #$%€ KING.
RIGHT.
...
BUT... WHY?
THERE'S REALLY NO OTHER WAY TO SPIN IT. IT'S PRETTY MUCH WHAT I DO.
RIGHT, I CAN SEE THAT, BASED ON THIS S.H.I.E.L.D. REPORT.
LET'S START WITH EXPLAINING HOW YOU GOT INTO THE GAME, SO WE CAN INVESTIGATE YOUR... BEHAVIOR.
DO I HAVE TO?
PLEASE.

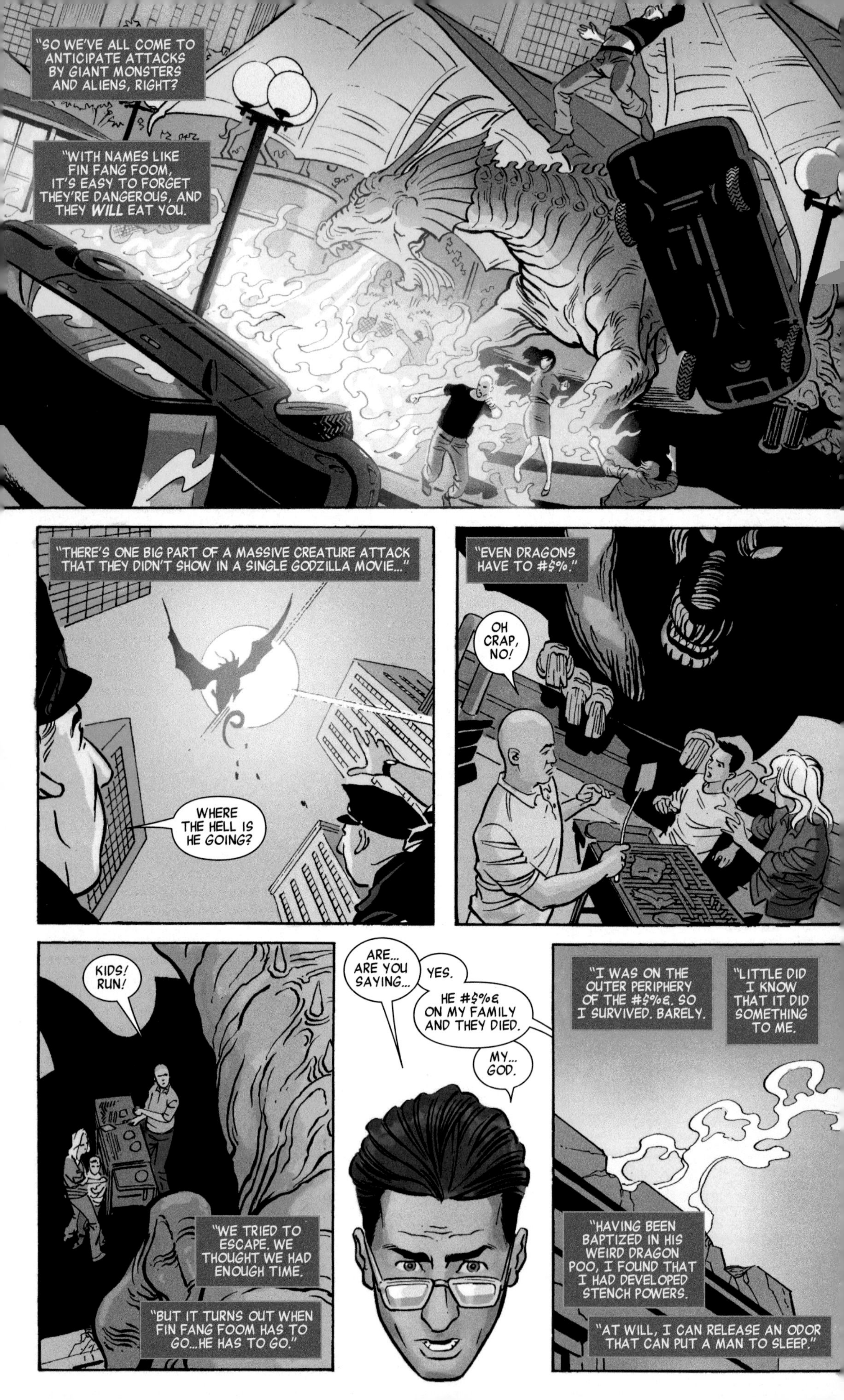
"SO WE'VE ALL COME TO ANTICIPATE ATTACKS BY GIANT MONSTERS AND ALIENS, RIGHT?
"WITH NAMES LIKE FIN FANG FOOM, IT'S EASY TO FORGET THEY'RE DANGEROUS, AND THEY WILL EAT YOU.
"THERE'S ONE BIG PART OF A MASSIVE CREATURE ATTACK THAT THEY DIDN'T SHOW IN A SINGLE GODZILLA MOVIE..."
WHERE THE HELL IS HE GOING?
"EVEN DRAGONS HAVE TO #$%."
OH CRAP, NO!
KIDS! RUN!
"WE TRIED TO ESCAPE. WE THOUGHT WE HAD ENOUGH TIME.
"BUT IT TURNS OUT WHEN FIN FANG FOOM HAS TO GO...HE HAS TO GO."
ARE... ARE YOU SAYING...
YES.
HE #$%€ ON MY FAMILY AND THEY DIED.
MY... GOD.
"I WAS ON THE OUTER PERIPHERY OF THE #$%€. SO I SURVIVED. BARELY.
"LITTLE DID I KNOW THAT IT DID SOMETHING TO ME.
"HAVING BEEN BAPTIZED IN HIS WEIRD DRAGON POO, I FOUND THAT I HAD DEVELOPED STENCH POWERS.
"AT WILL, I CAN RELEASE AN ODOR THAT CAN PUT A MAN TO SLEEP."

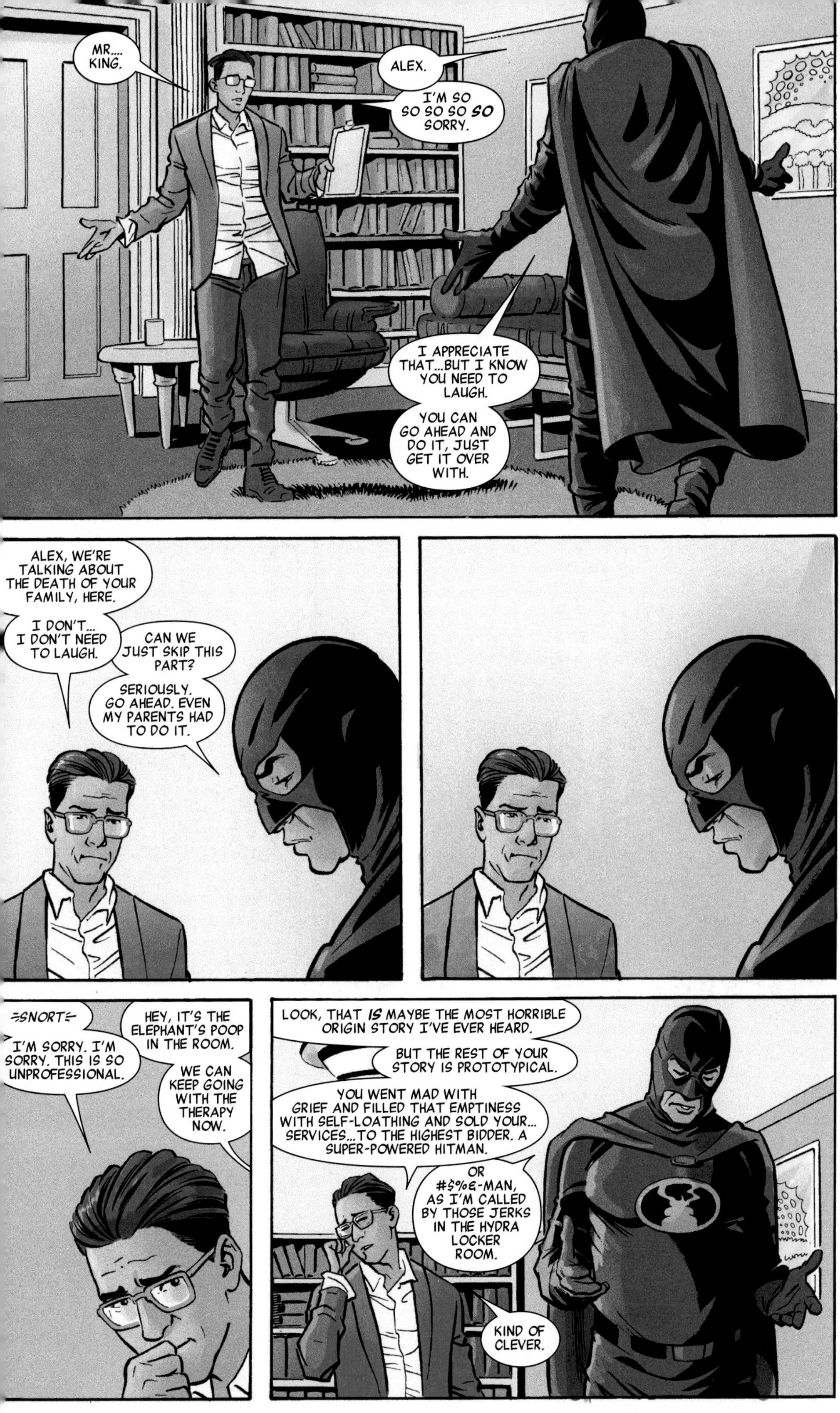
MR.... KING.
ALEX.
I'M SO SO SO SO SO SORRY.
I APPRECIATE THAT...BUT I KNOW YOU NEED TO LAUGH.
YOU CAN GO AHEAD AND DO IT, JUST GET IT OVER WITH.
ALEX, WE'RE TALKING ABOUT THE DEATH OF YOUR FAMILY, HERE.
I DON'T... I DON'T NEED TO LAUGH.
CAN WE JUST SKIP THIS PART?
SERIOUSLY. GO AHEAD. EVEN MY PARENTS HAD TO DO IT.
=SNORT=
I'M SORRY. I'M SORRY. THIS IS SO UNPROFESSIONAL.
HEY, IT'S THE ELEPHANT'S POOP IN THE ROOM.
WE CAN KEEP GOING WITH THE THERAPY NOW.
LOOK, THAT IS MAYBE THE MOST HORRIBLE ORIGIN STORY I'VE EVER HEARD.
BUT THE REST OF YOUR STORY IS PROTOTYPICAL.
YOU WENT MAD WITH GRIEF AND FILLED THAT EMPTINESS WITH SELF-LOATHING AND SOLD YOUR... SERVICES...TO THE HIGHEST BIDDER. A SUPER-POWERED HITMAN.
OR #$%&-MAN, AS I'M CALLED BY THOSE JERKS IN THE HYDRA LOCKER ROOM.
KIND OF CLEVER.

WHAT MATTERS IS IF YOU'RE GOING TO LET WHAT'S HAPPENED TO YOU...AND WHAT COMES OUT OF YOU...DEFINE YOU.

ALEX, YOU HAVE TO LET THIS GO.

YOU HAVE TO LET THEM GO.

I WANT TO! I WANT TO LIVE A NORMAL LIFE!

EVERY WAKING HOUR IS PAIN AND MALICE AND ANGER.

AND I SMELL, MAN! I SMELL REAL BAD!

YOU DO.

MR. SALINGER...IT'S NOT GOING TO HAPPEN.

I HAVE NO REASON TO LIVE, AND NO REASON TO HOPE.

I APPRECIATE S.H.I.E.L.D. GIVING ME THIS CHANCE, BUT THE TRUTH?

THE WORLD HAS TO PAY FOR WHAT IT'S DONE TO ME.

I'LL BE BACK TO FLINGING THE FIRST CHANCE I GET. NO MATTER WHO GETS IN MY WAY.

YOU SURE ABOUT THAT?

YEAH... I'M SURE.

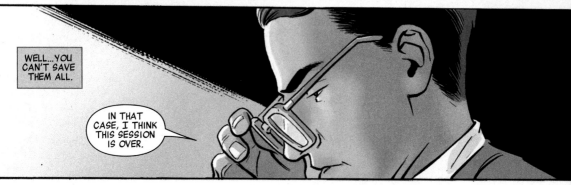

WELL...YOU CAN'T SAVE THEM ALL.

IN THAT CASE, I THINK THIS SESSION IS OVER.

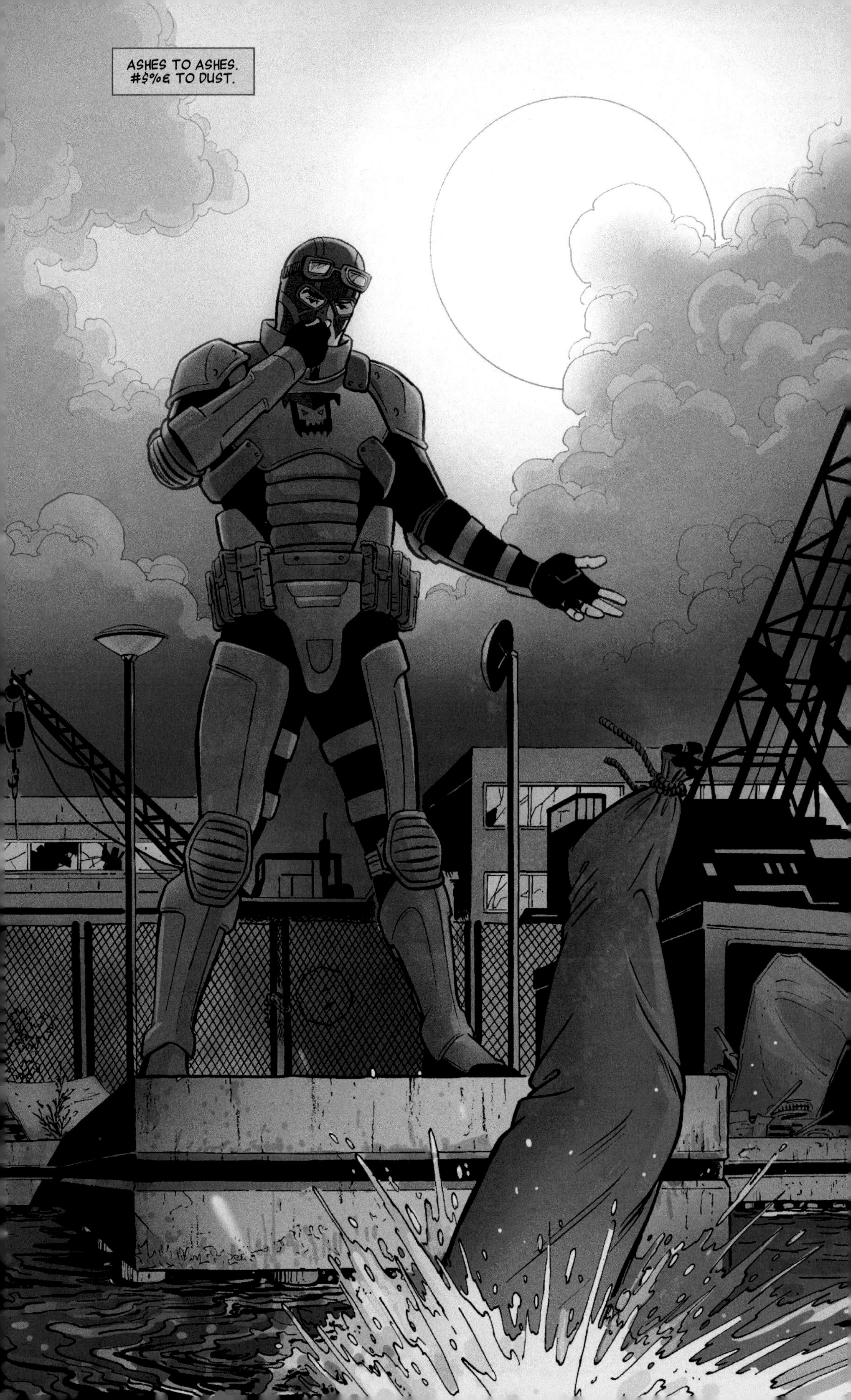
ASHES TO ASHES.
#$%& TO DUST.

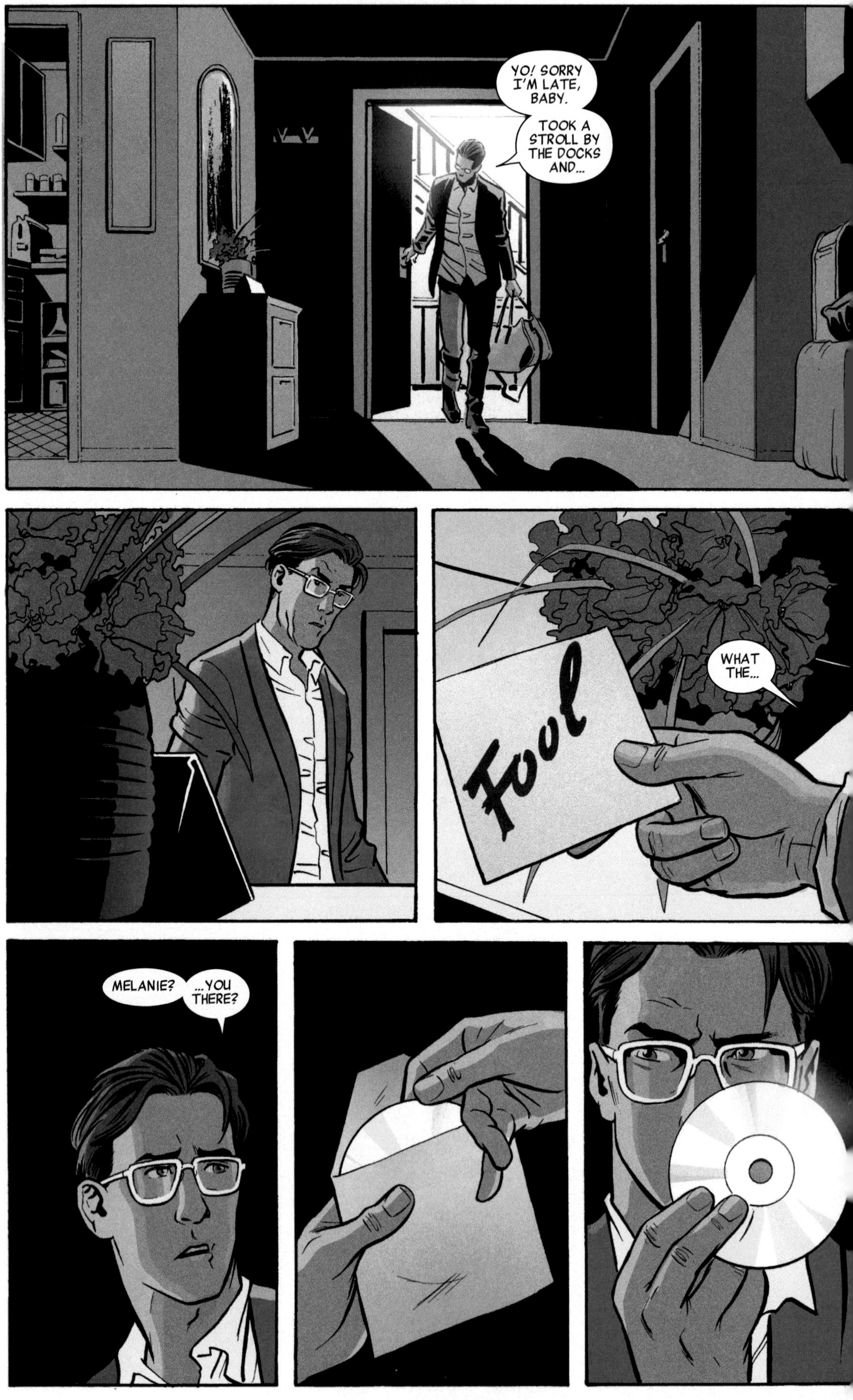
YO! SORRY I'M LATE, BABY.
TOOK A STROLL BY THE DOCKS AND...
Fool
WHAT THE...
MELANIE?
...YOU THERE?

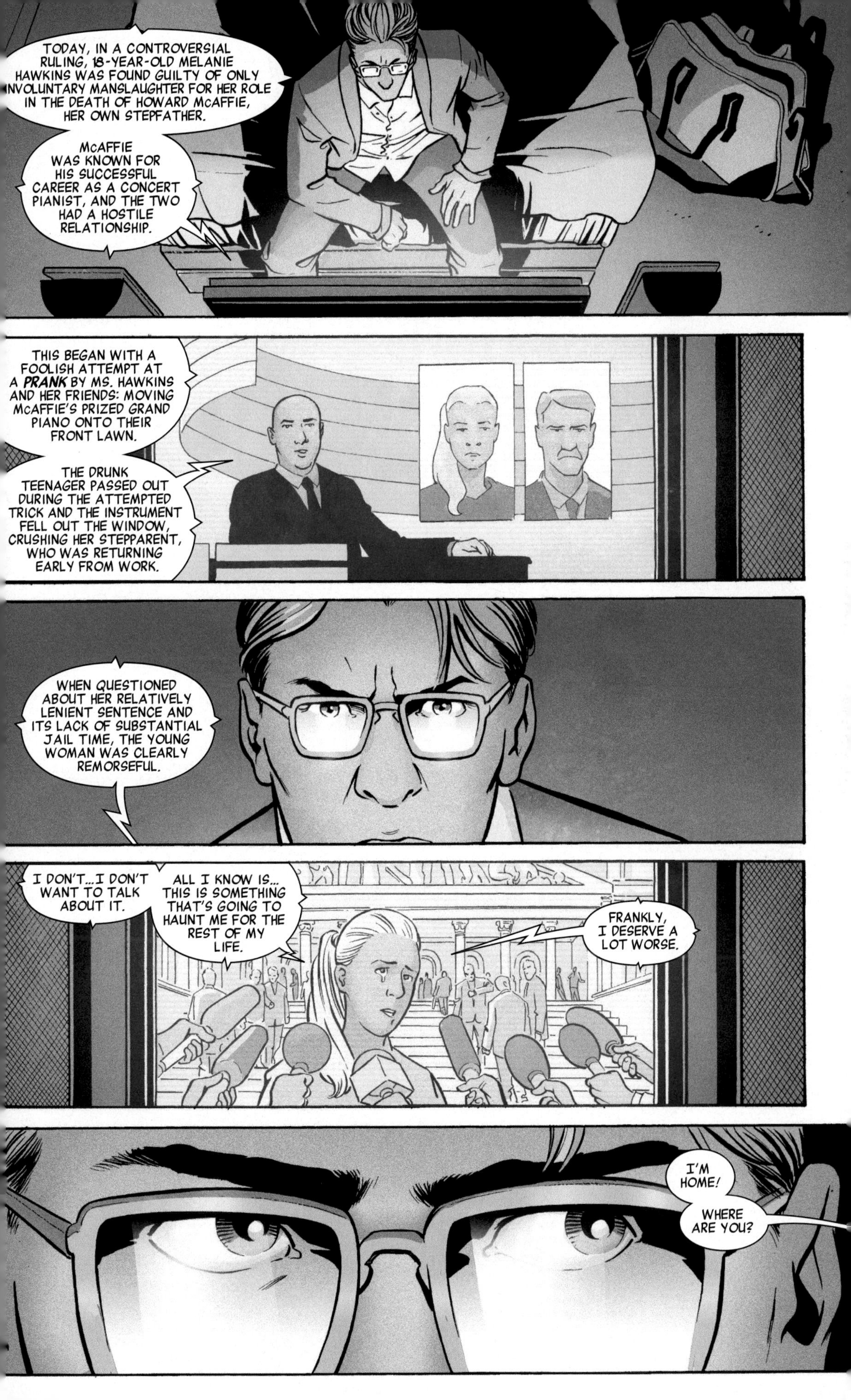
TODAY, IN A CONTROVERSIAL RULING, 18-YEAR-OLD MELANIE HAWKINS WAS FOUND GUILTY OF ONLY INVOLUNTARY MANSLAUGHTER FOR HER ROLE IN THE DEATH OF HOWARD McAFFIE, HER OWN STEPFATHER.
McAFFIE WAS KNOWN FOR HIS SUCCESSFUL CAREER AS A CONCERT PIANIST, AND THE TWO HAD A HOSTILE RELATIONSHIP.
THIS BEGAN WITH A FOOLISH ATTEMPT AT A PRANK BY MS. HAWKINS AND HER FRIENDS: MOVING McAFFIE'S PRIZED GRAND PIANO ONTO THEIR FRONT LAWN.
THE DRUNK TEENAGER PASSED OUT DURING THE ATTEMPTED TRICK AND THE INSTRUMENT FELL OUT THE WINDOW, CRUSHING HER STEPPARENT, WHO WAS RETURNING EARLY FROM WORK.
WHEN QUESTIONED ABOUT HER RELATIVELY LENIENT SENTENCE AND ITS LACK OF SUBSTANTIAL JAIL TIME, THE YOUNG WOMAN WAS CLEARLY REMORSEFUL.
I DON'T...I DON'T WANT TO TALK ABOUT IT.
ALL I KNOW IS... THIS IS SOMETHING THAT'S GOING TO HAUNT ME FOR THE REST OF MY LIFE.
FRANKLY, I DESERVE A LOT WORSE.
I'M HOME!
WHERE ARE YOU?

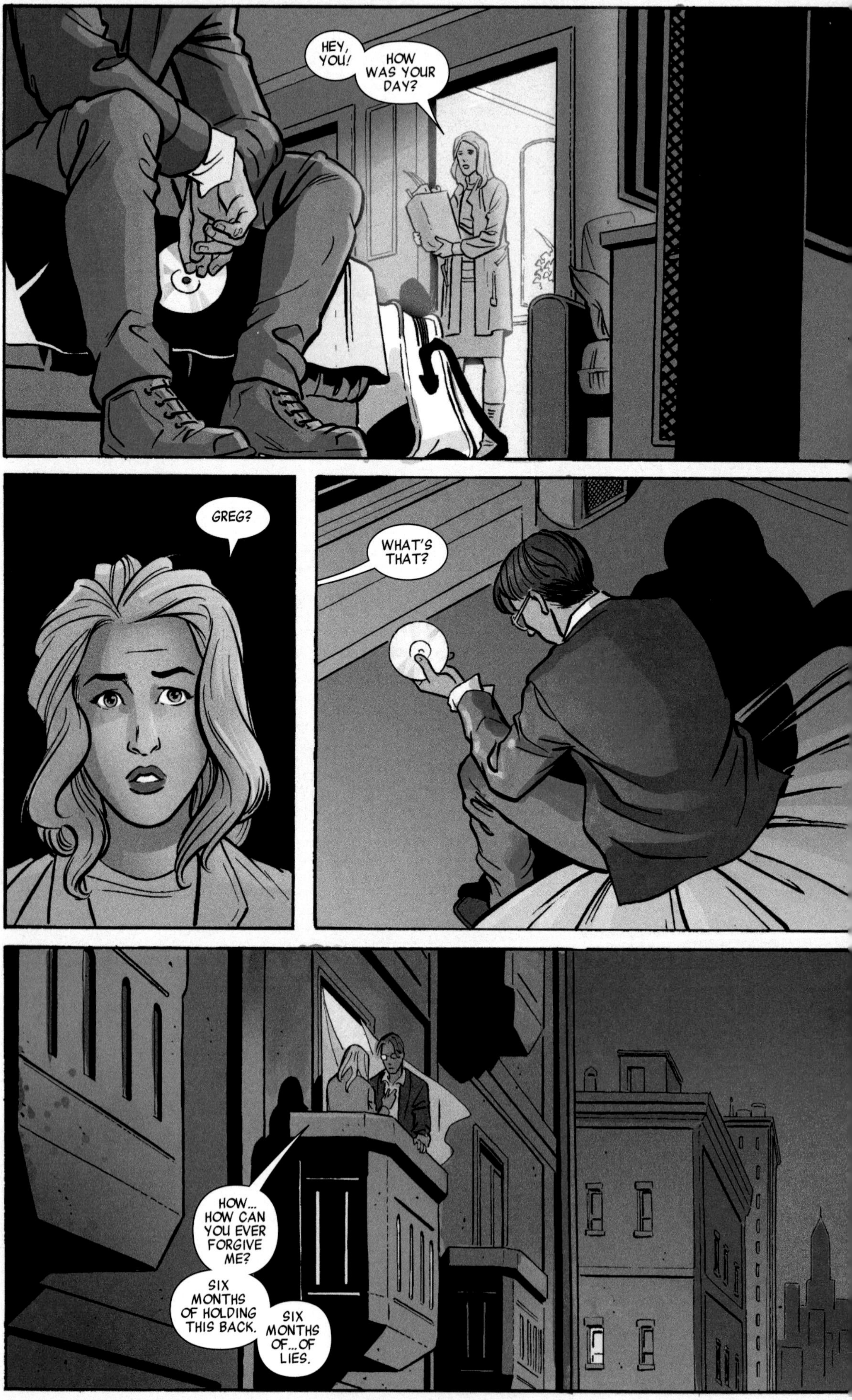
HEY, YOU!
HOW WAS YOUR DAY?
GREG?
WHAT'S THAT?
HOW... HOW CAN YOU EVER FORGIVE ME?
SIX MONTHS OF HOLDING THIS BACK.
SIX MONTHS OF... OF LIES.

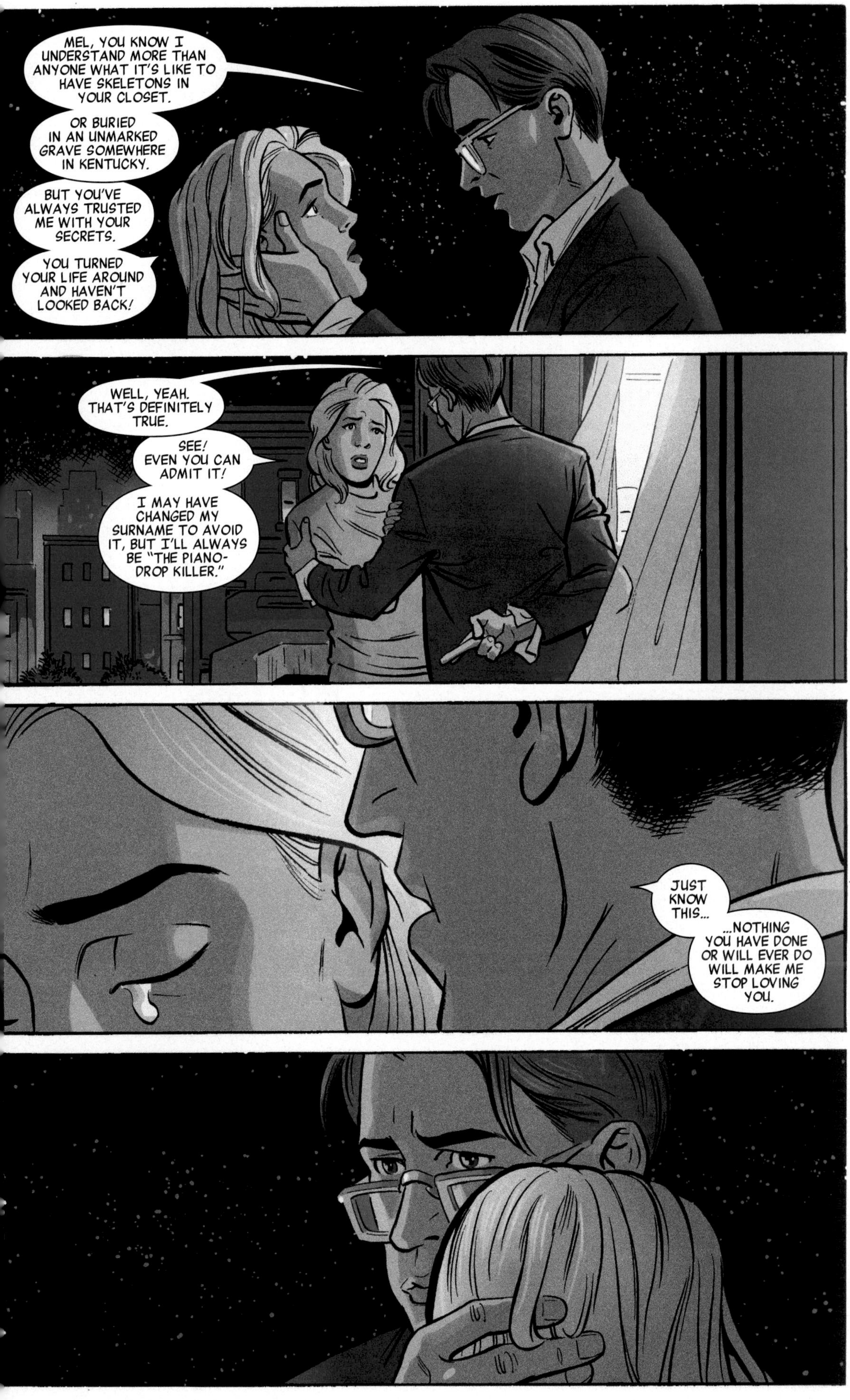
MEL, YOU KNOW I UNDERSTAND MORE THAN ANYONE WHAT IT'S LIKE TO HAVE SKELETONS IN YOUR CLOSET.
OR BURIED IN AN UNMARKED GRAVE SOMEWHERE IN KENTUCKY.
BUT YOU'VE ALWAYS TRUSTED ME WITH YOUR SECRETS.
YOU TURNED YOUR LIFE AROUND AND HAVEN'T LOOKED BACK!
WELL, YEAH. THAT'S DEFINITELY TRUE.
SEE! EVEN YOU CAN ADMIT IT!
I MAY HAVE CHANGED MY SURNAME TO AVOID IT, BUT I'LL ALWAYS BE "THE PIANO-DROP KILLER."
JUST KNOW THIS...
...NOTHING YOU HAVE DONE OR WILL EVER DO WILL MAKE ME STOP LOVING YOU.

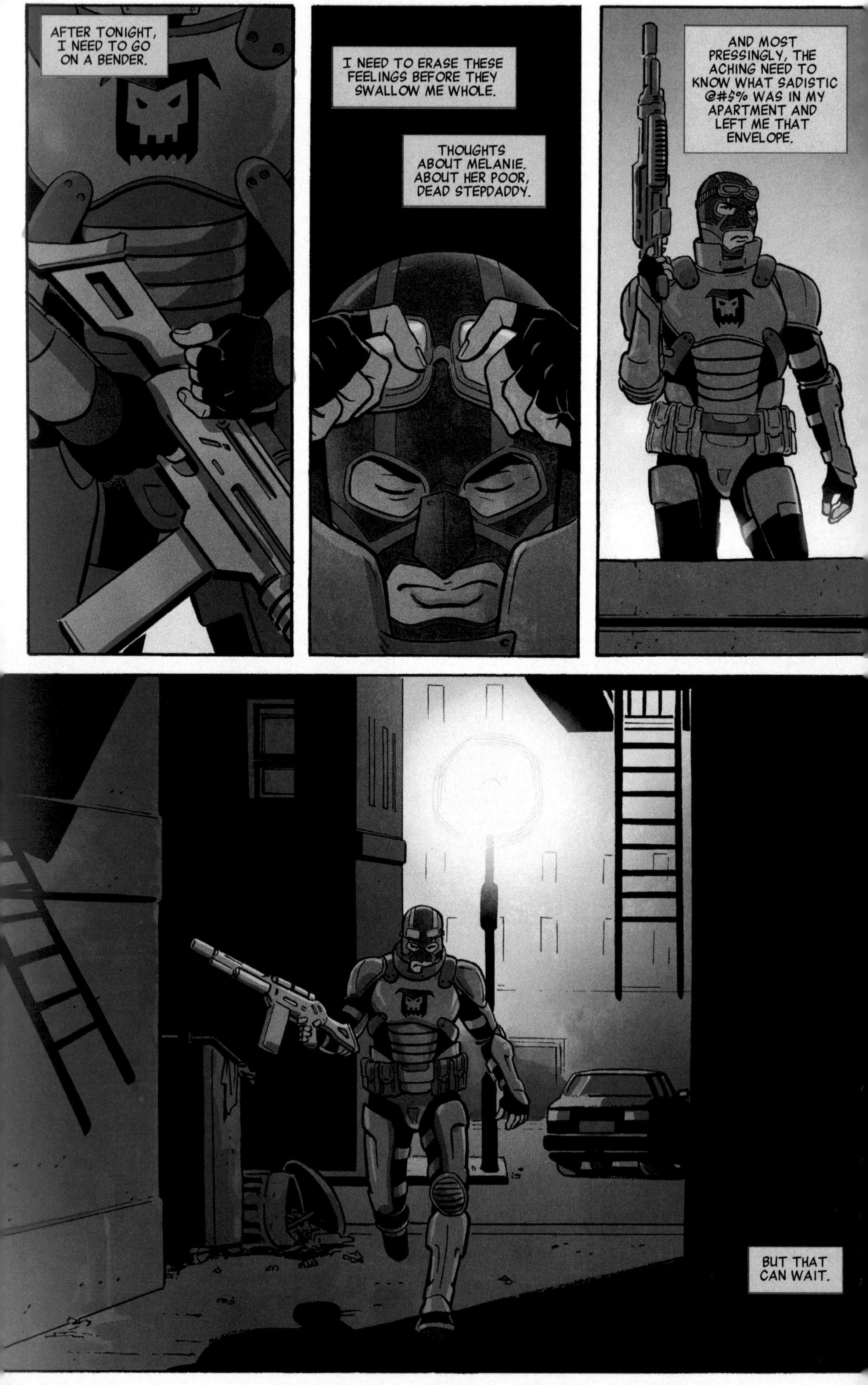
AFTER TONIGHT, I NEED TO GO ON A BENDER.
I NEED TO ERASE THESE FEELINGS BEFORE THEY SWALLOW ME WHOLE.
THOUGHTS ABOUT MELANIE. ABOUT HER POOR, DEAD STEPDADDY.
AND MOST PRESSINGLY, THE ACHING NEED TO KNOW WHAT SADISTIC @#$% WAS IN MY APARTMENT AND LEFT ME THAT ENVELOPE.
BUT THAT CAN WAIT.

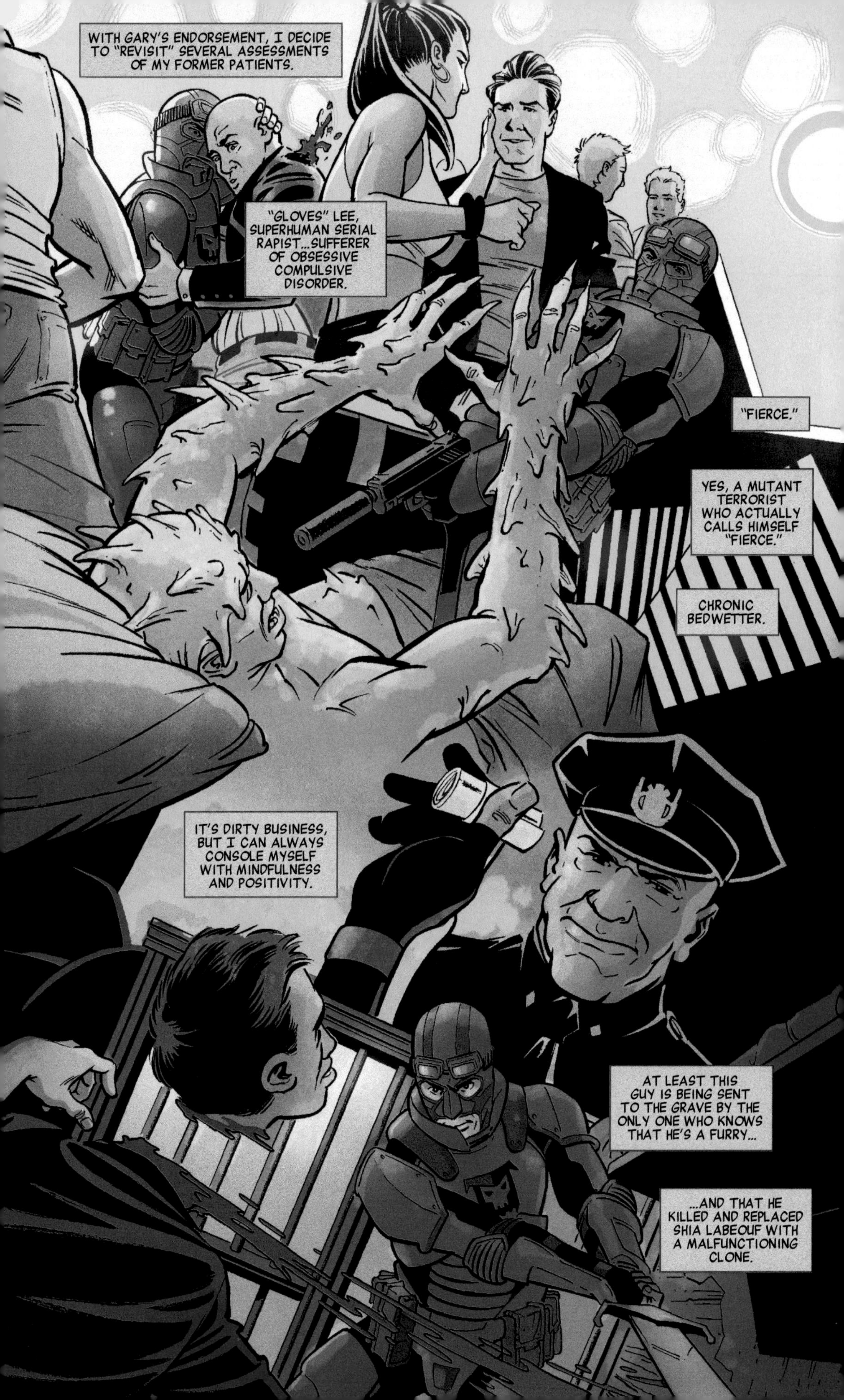
WITH GARY'S ENDORSEMENT, I DECIDE TO "REVISIT" SEVERAL ASSESSMENTS OF MY FORMER PATIENTS.
"GLOVES" LEE, SUPERHUMAN SERIAL RAPIST...SUFFERER OF OBSESSIVE COMPULSIVE DISORDER.
"FIERCE."
YES, A MUTANT TERRORIST WHO ACTUALLY CALLS HIMSELF "FIERCE."
CHRONIC BEDWETTER.
IT'S DIRTY BUSINESS, BUT I CAN ALWAYS CONSOLE MYSELF WITH MINDFULNESS AND POSITIVITY.
AT LEAST THIS GUY IS BEING SENT TO THE GRAVE BY THE ONLY ONE WHO KNOWS THAT HE'S A FURRY...
...AND THAT HE KILLED AND REPLACED SHIA LABEOUF WITH A MALFUNCTIONING CLONE.

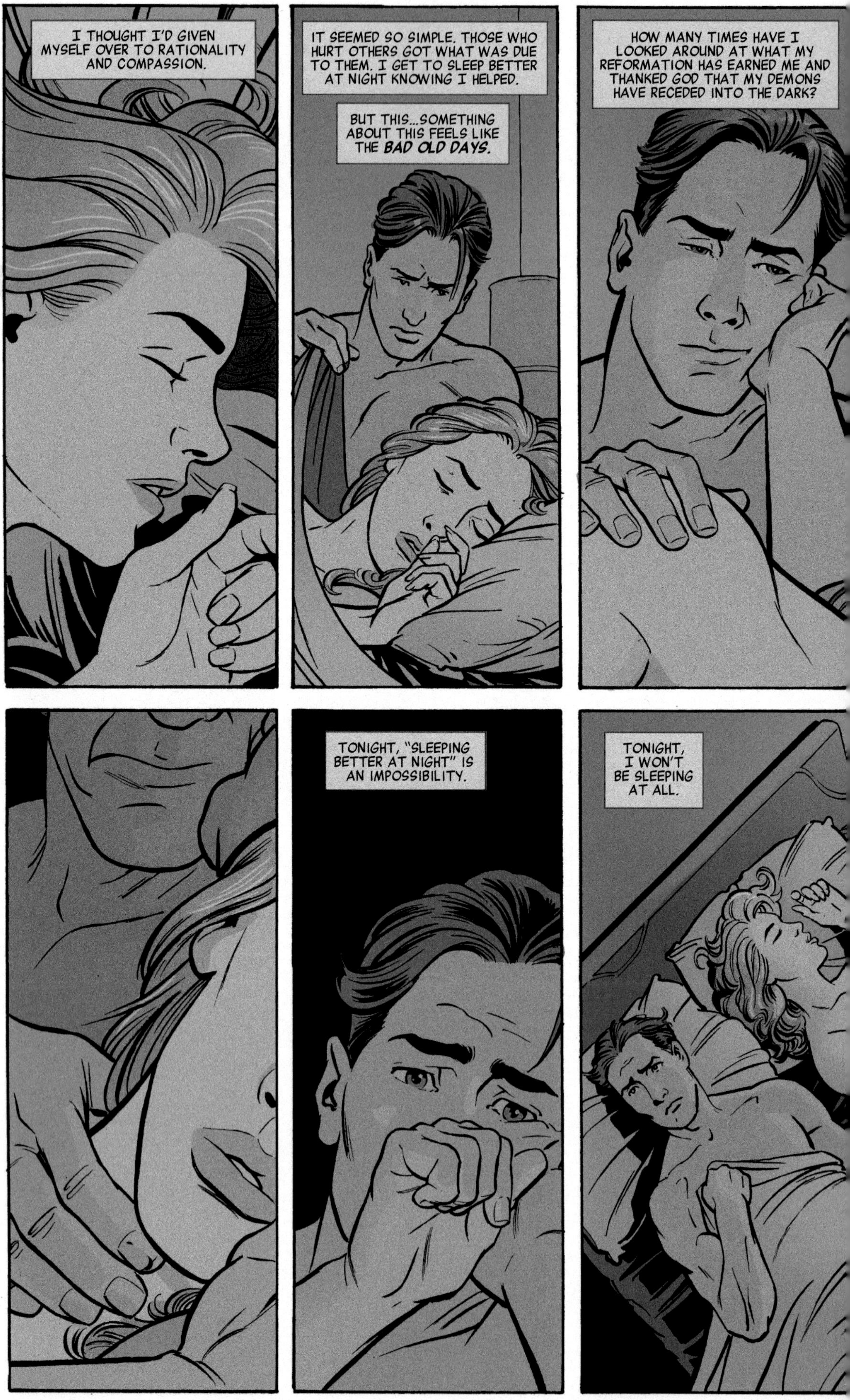
I THOUGHT I'D GIVEN MYSELF OVER TO RATIONALITY AND COMPASSION.
IT SEEMED SO SIMPLE. THOSE WHO HURT OTHERS GOT WHAT WAS DUE TO THEM. I GET TO SLEEP BETTER AT NIGHT KNOWING I HELPED.
BUT THIS...SOMETHING ABOUT THIS FEELS LIKE THE *BAD OLD DAYS.*
HOW MANY TIMES HAVE I LOOKED AROUND AT WHAT MY REFORMATION HAS EARNED ME AND THANKED GOD THAT MY DEMONS HAVE RECEDED INTO THE DARK?
TONIGHT, "SLEEPING BETTER AT NIGHT" IS AN IMPOSSIBILITY.
TONIGHT, I WON'T BE SLEEPING AT ALL.

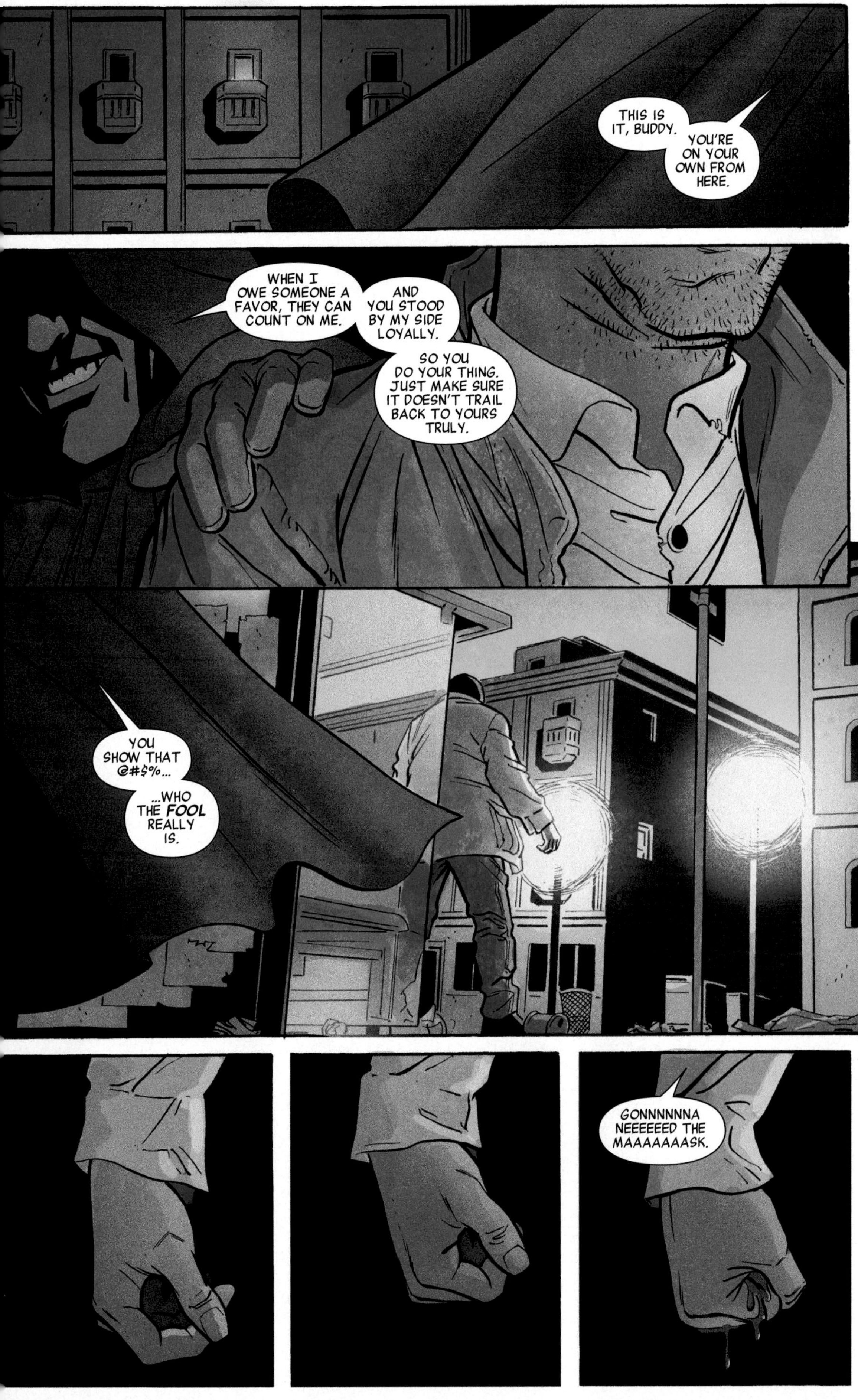
THIS IS IT, BUDDY.
YOU'RE ON YOUR OWN FROM HERE.
WHEN I OWE SOMEONE A FAVOR, THEY CAN COUNT ON ME.
AND YOU STOOD BY MY SIDE LOYALLY.
SO YOU DO YOUR THING. JUST MAKE SURE IT DOESN'T TRAIL BACK TO YOURS TRULY.
YOU SHOW THAT @#$%...
...WHO THE FOOL REALLY IS.
GONNNNNNA NEEEEEED THE MAAAAAAASK.

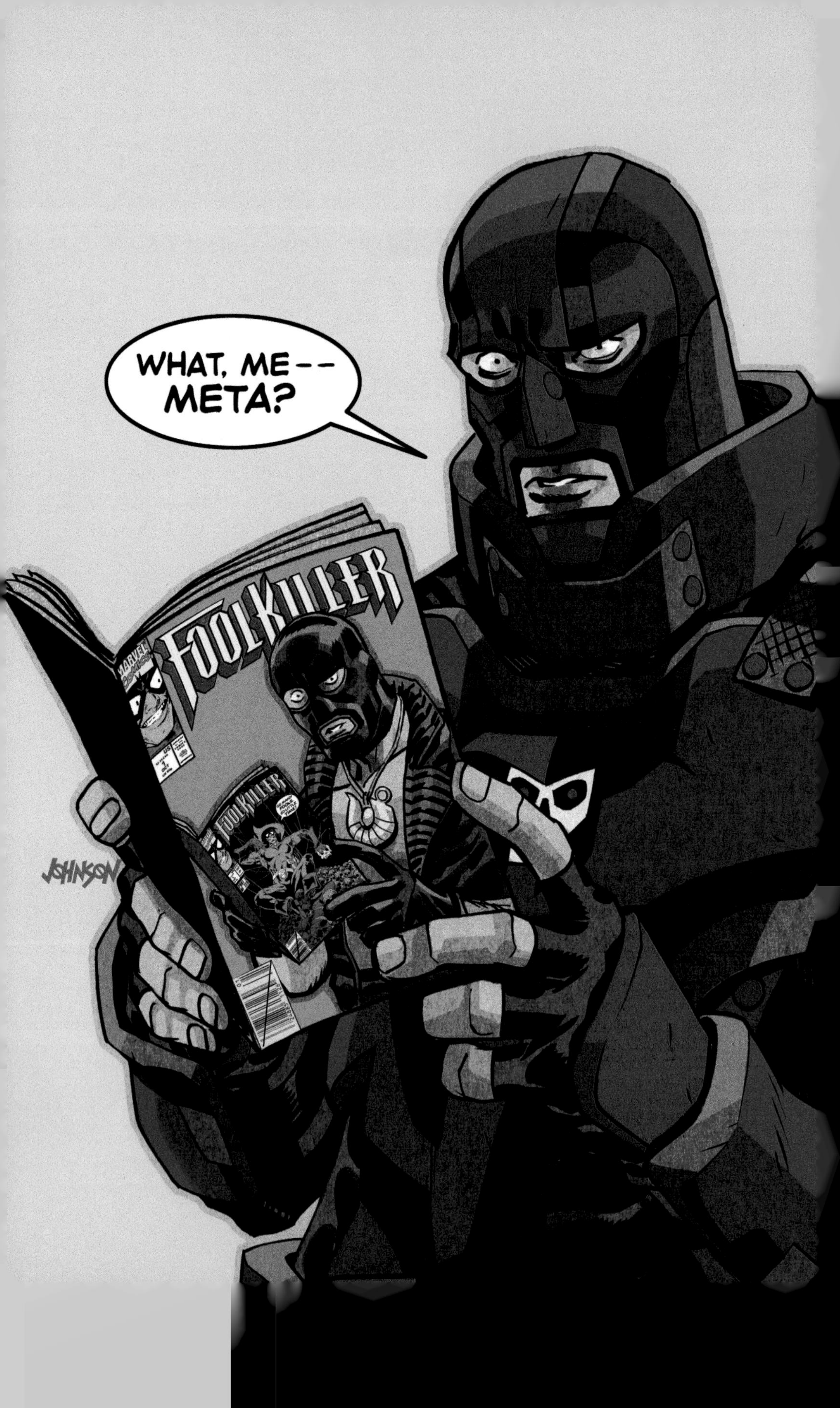
WHAT, ME--
META?
FOOLKILLER
JOHNSON

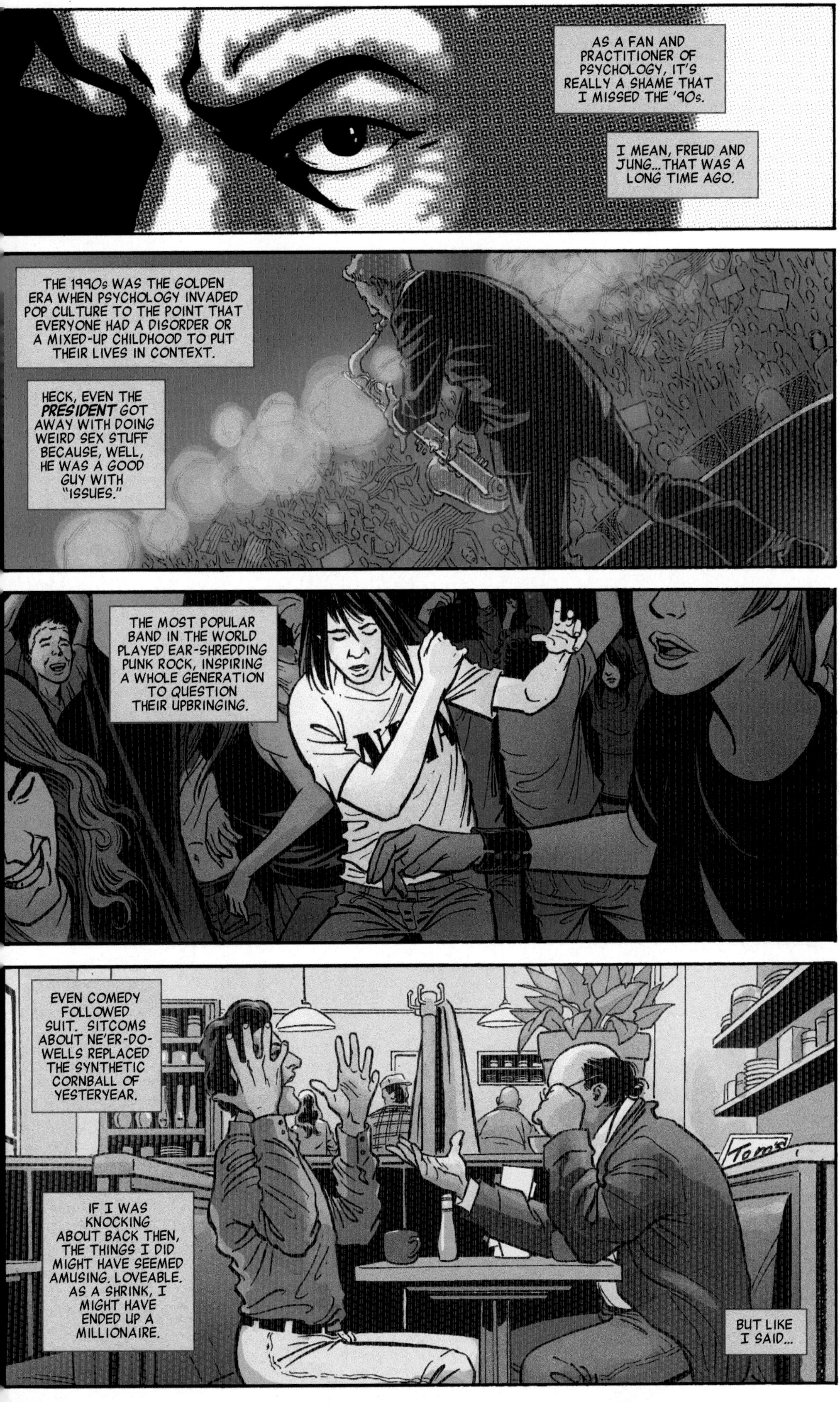
AS A FAN AND PRACTITIONER OF PSYCHOLOGY, IT'S REALLY A SHAME THAT I MISSED THE '90s.
I MEAN, FREUD AND JUNG... THAT WAS A LONG TIME AGO.
THE 1990s WAS THE GOLDEN ERA WHEN PSYCHOLOGY INVADED POP CULTURE TO THE POINT THAT EVERYONE HAD A DISORDER OR A MIXED-UP CHILDHOOD TO PUT THEIR LIVES IN CONTEXT.
HECK, EVEN THE *PRESIDENT* GOT AWAY WITH DOING WEIRD SEX STUFF BECAUSE, WELL, HE WAS A GOOD GUY WITH "ISSUES."
THE MOST POPULAR BAND IN THE WORLD PLAYED EAR-SHREDDING PUNK ROCK, INSPIRING A WHOLE GENERATION TO QUESTION THEIR UPBRINGING.
EVEN COMEDY FOLLOWED SUIT. SITCOMS ABOUT NE'ER-DO-WELLS REPLACED THE SYNTHETIC CORNBALL OF YESTERYEAR.
IF I WAS KNOCKING ABOUT BACK THEN, THE THINGS I DID MIGHT HAVE SEEMED AMUSING. LOVEABLE. AS A SHRINK, I MIGHT HAVE ENDED UP A MILLIONAIRE.
BUT LIKE I SAID...

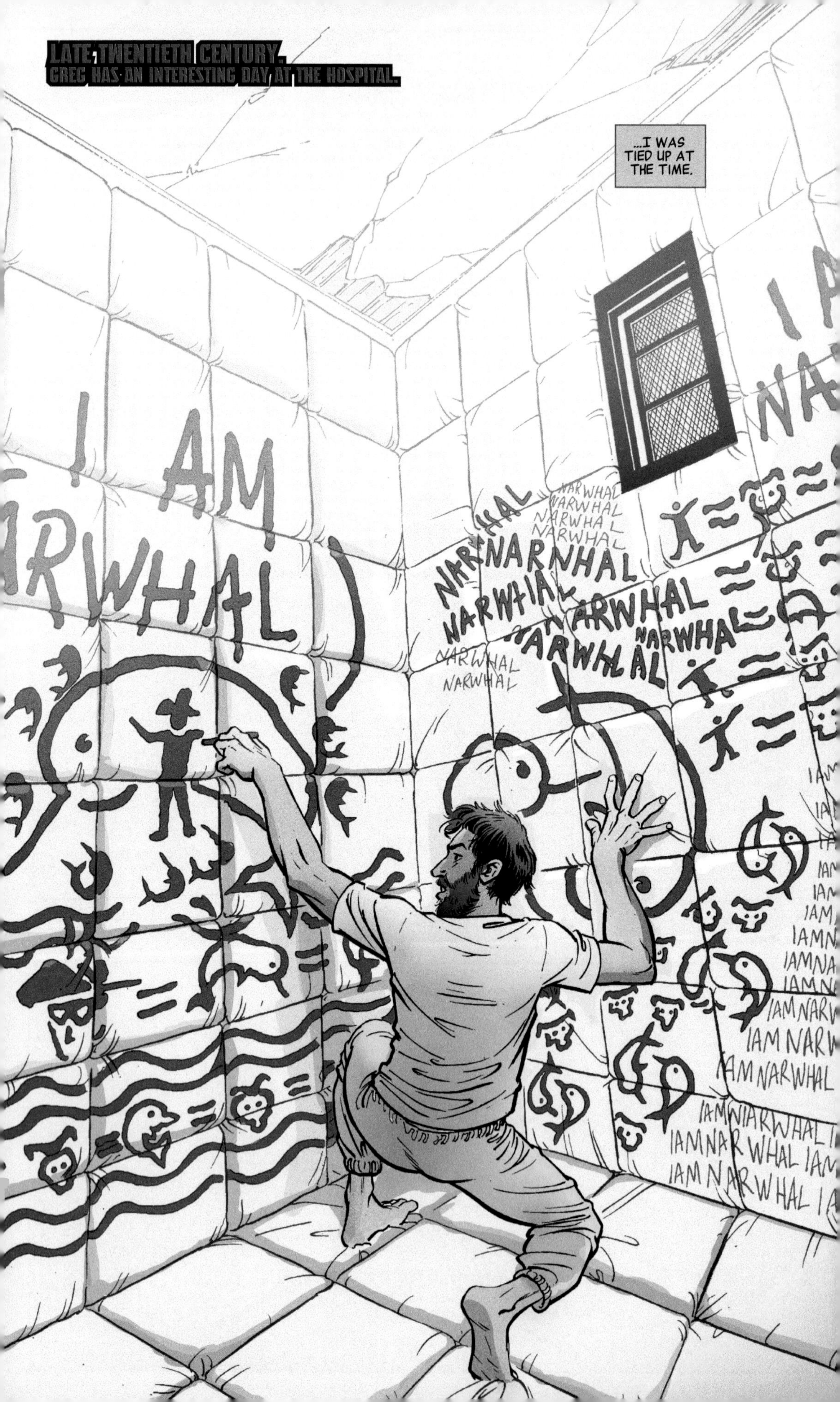
LATE TWENTIETH CENTURY.
GREG HAS AN INTERESTING DAY AT THE HOSPITAL.
...I WAS TIED UP AT THE TIME.
I AM NARWHAL

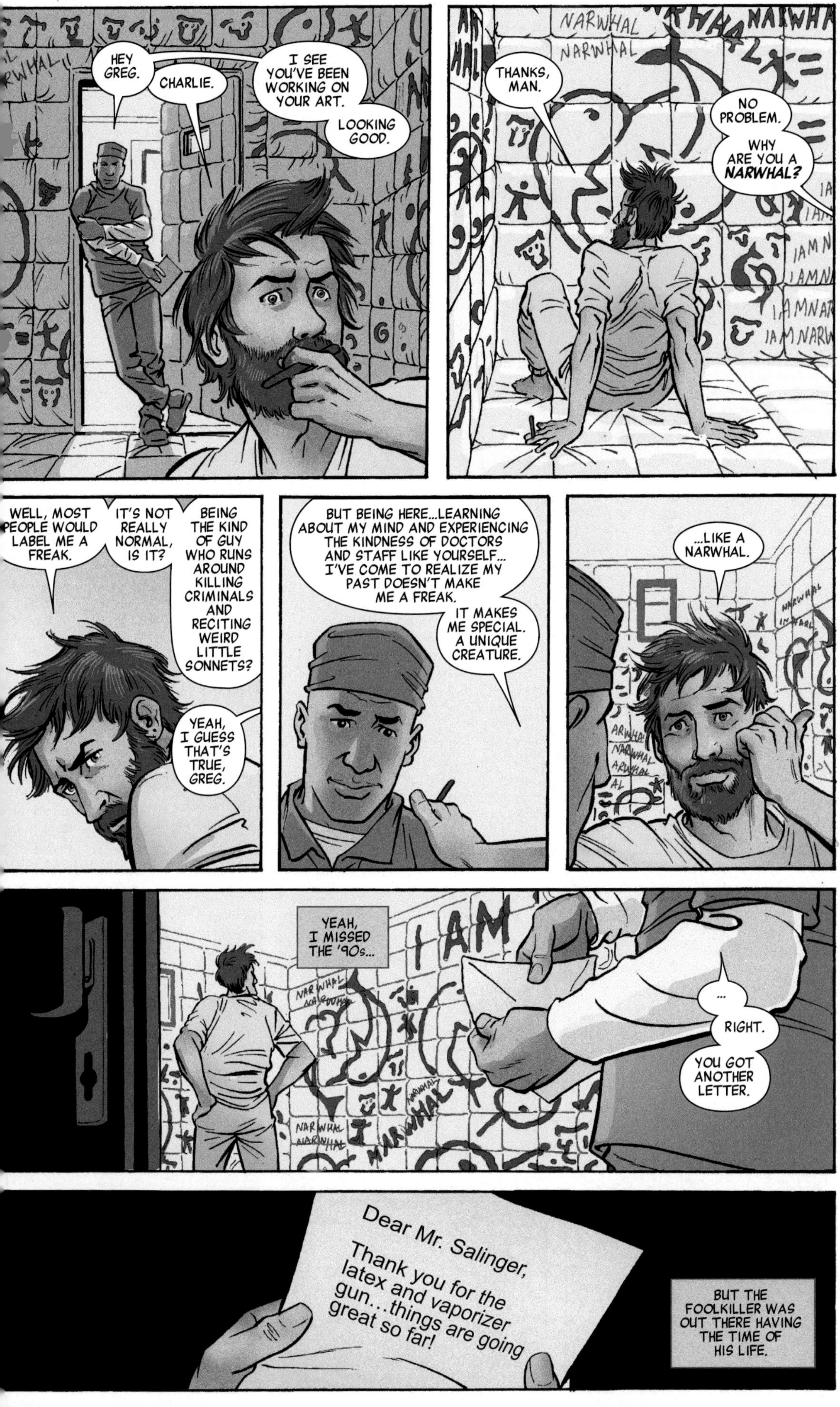
HEY GREG.
CHARLIE.
I SEE YOU'VE BEEN WORKING ON YOUR ART.
LOOKING GOOD.
THANKS, MAN.
NO PROBLEM.
WHY ARE YOU A **NARWHAL?**
WELL, MOST PEOPLE WOULD LABEL ME A FREAK.
IT'S NOT REALLY NORMAL, IS IT?
BEING THE KIND OF GUY WHO RUNS AROUND KILLING CRIMINALS AND RECITING WEIRD LITTLE SONNETS?
YEAH, I GUESS THAT'S TRUE, GREG.
BUT BEING HERE...LEARNING ABOUT MY MIND AND EXPERIENCING THE KINDNESS OF DOCTORS AND STAFF LIKE YOURSELF... I'VE COME TO REALIZE MY PAST DOESN'T MAKE ME A FREAK.
IT MAKES ME SPECIAL. A UNIQUE CREATURE.
...LIKE A NARWHAL.
YEAH, I MISSED THE '90s...
...
RIGHT.
YOU GOT ANOTHER LETTER.
I AM
NARWHAL
Dear Mr. Salinger,
Thank you for the latex and vaporizer gun…things are going great so far!
BUT THE FOOLKILLER WAS OUT THERE HAVING THE TIME OF HIS LIFE.

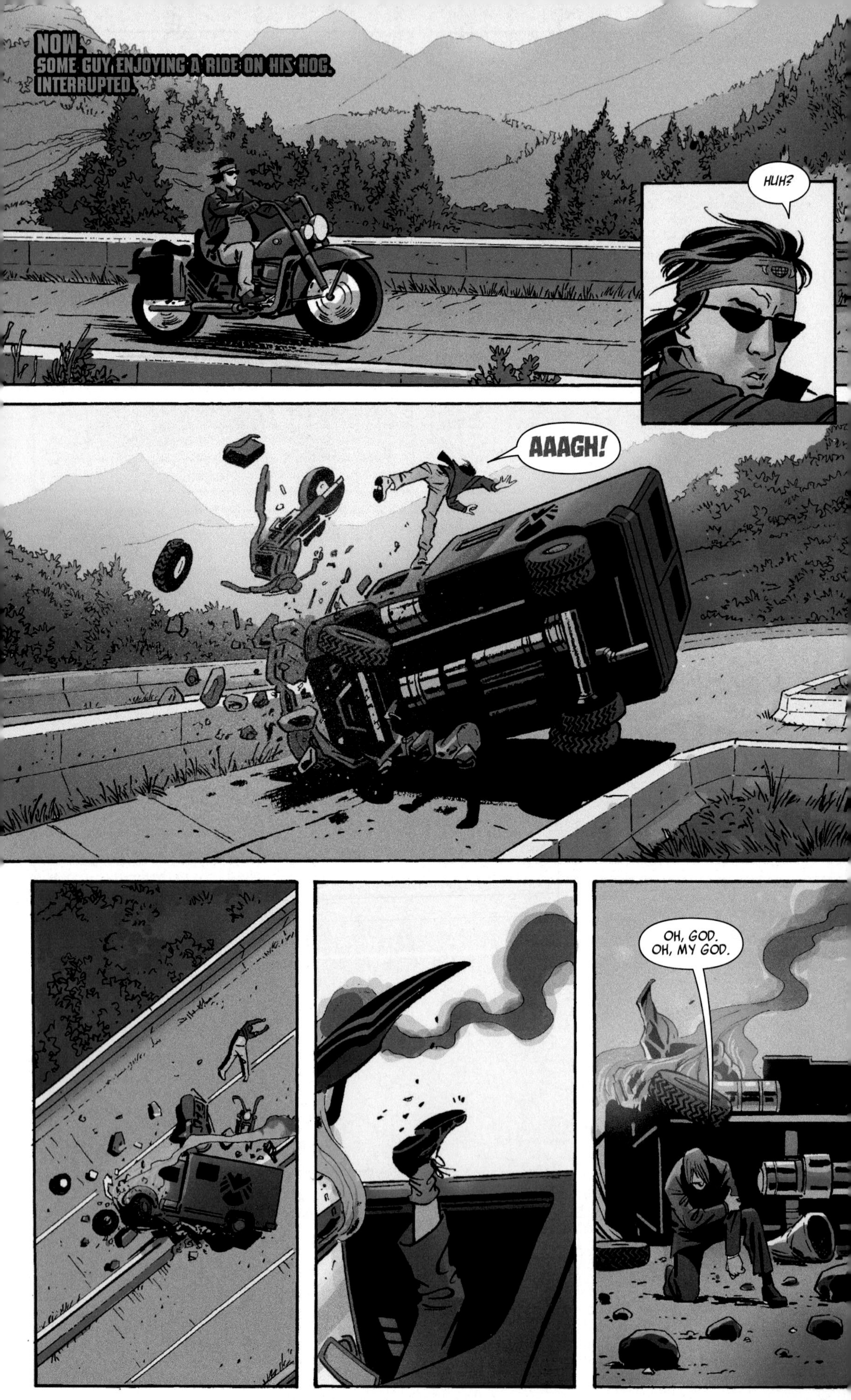
NOW.
SOME GUY ENJOYING A RIDE ON HIS HOG.
INTERRUPTED.
HUH?
AAAGH!
OH, GOD.
OH, MY GOD.

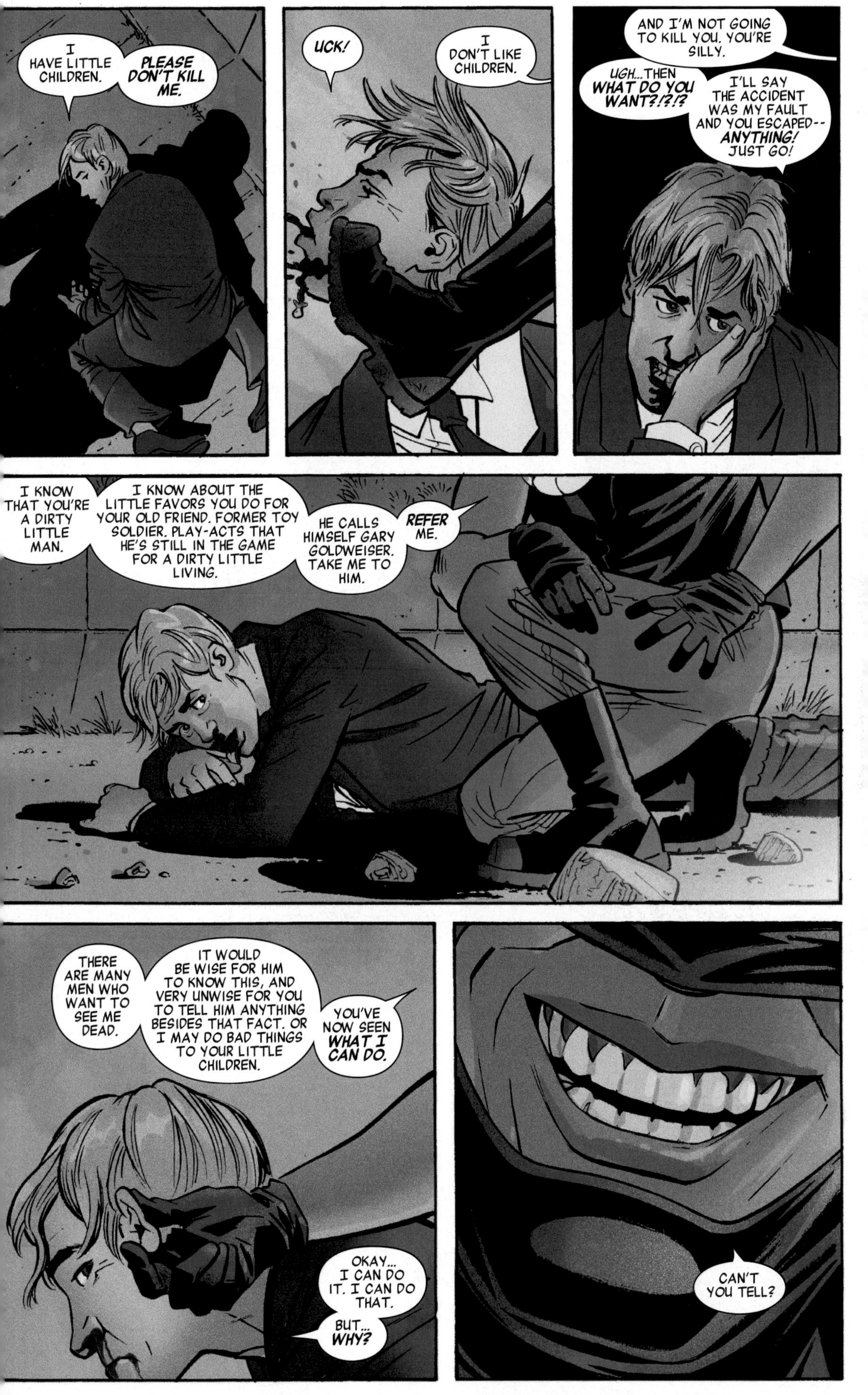
I HAVE LITTLE CHILDREN.
PLEASE DON'T KILL ME.
UCK!
I DON'T LIKE CHILDREN.
AND I'M NOT GOING TO KILL YOU. YOU'RE SILLY.
UGH...THEN WHAT DO YOU WANT?!?!?
I'LL SAY THE ACCIDENT WAS MY FAULT AND YOU ESCAPED-- ANYTHING! JUST GO!
I KNOW THAT YOU'RE A DIRTY LITTLE MAN.
I KNOW ABOUT THE LITTLE FAVORS YOU DO FOR YOUR OLD FRIEND. FORMER TOY SOLDIER. PLAY-ACTS THAT HE'S STILL IN THE GAME FOR A DIRTY LITTLE LIVING.
HE CALLS HIMSELF GARY GOLDWEISER. TAKE ME TO HIM.
REFER ME.
THERE ARE MANY MEN WHO WANT TO SEE ME DEAD.
IT WOULD BE WISE FOR HIM TO KNOW THIS, AND VERY UNWISE FOR YOU TO TELL HIM ANYTHING BESIDES THAT FACT. OR I MAY DO BAD THINGS TO YOUR LITTLE CHILDREN.
YOU'VE NOW SEEN WHAT I CAN DO.
OKAY... I CAN DO IT. I CAN DO THAT.
BUT... WHY?
CAN'T YOU TELL?

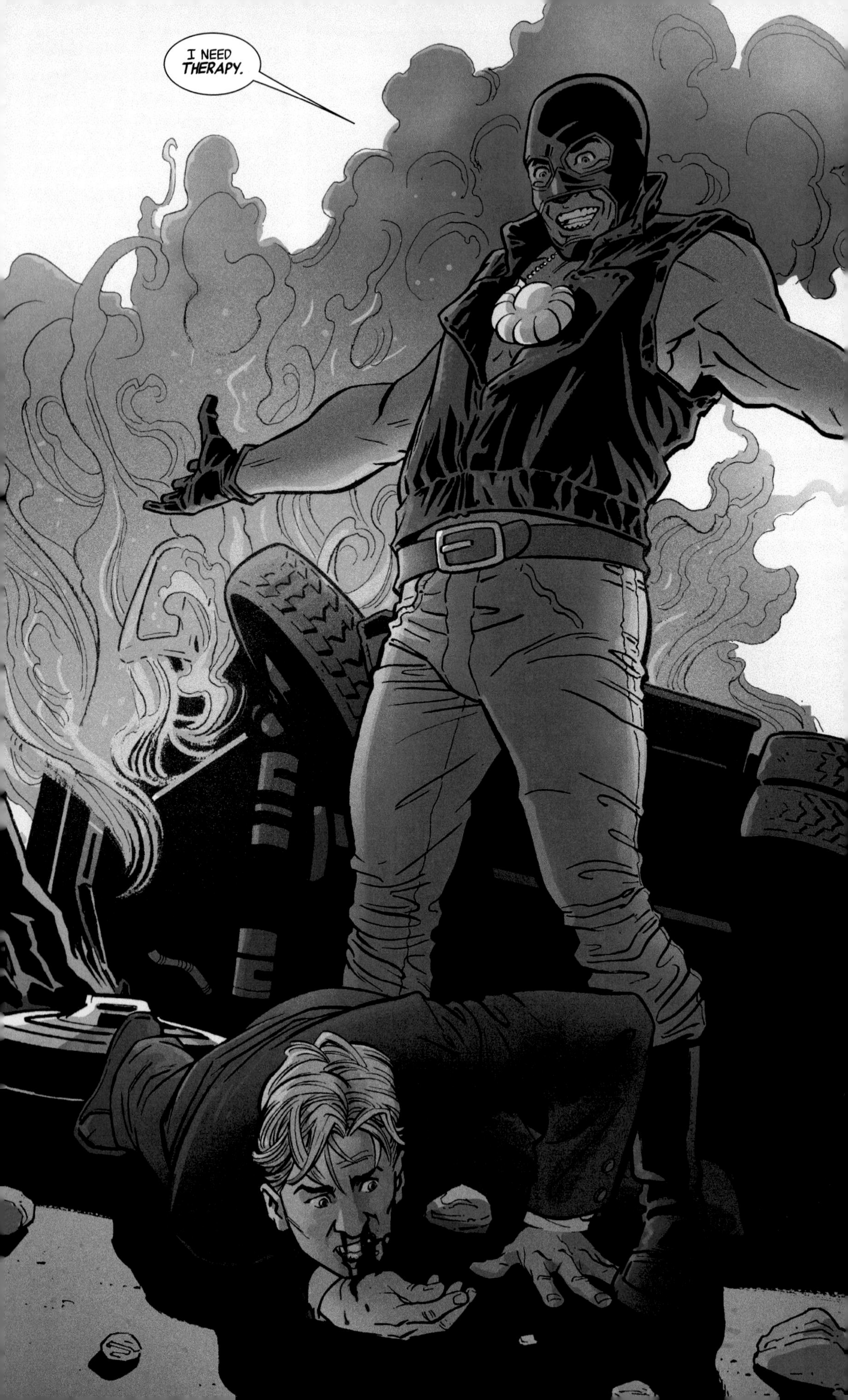
I NEED THERAPY.

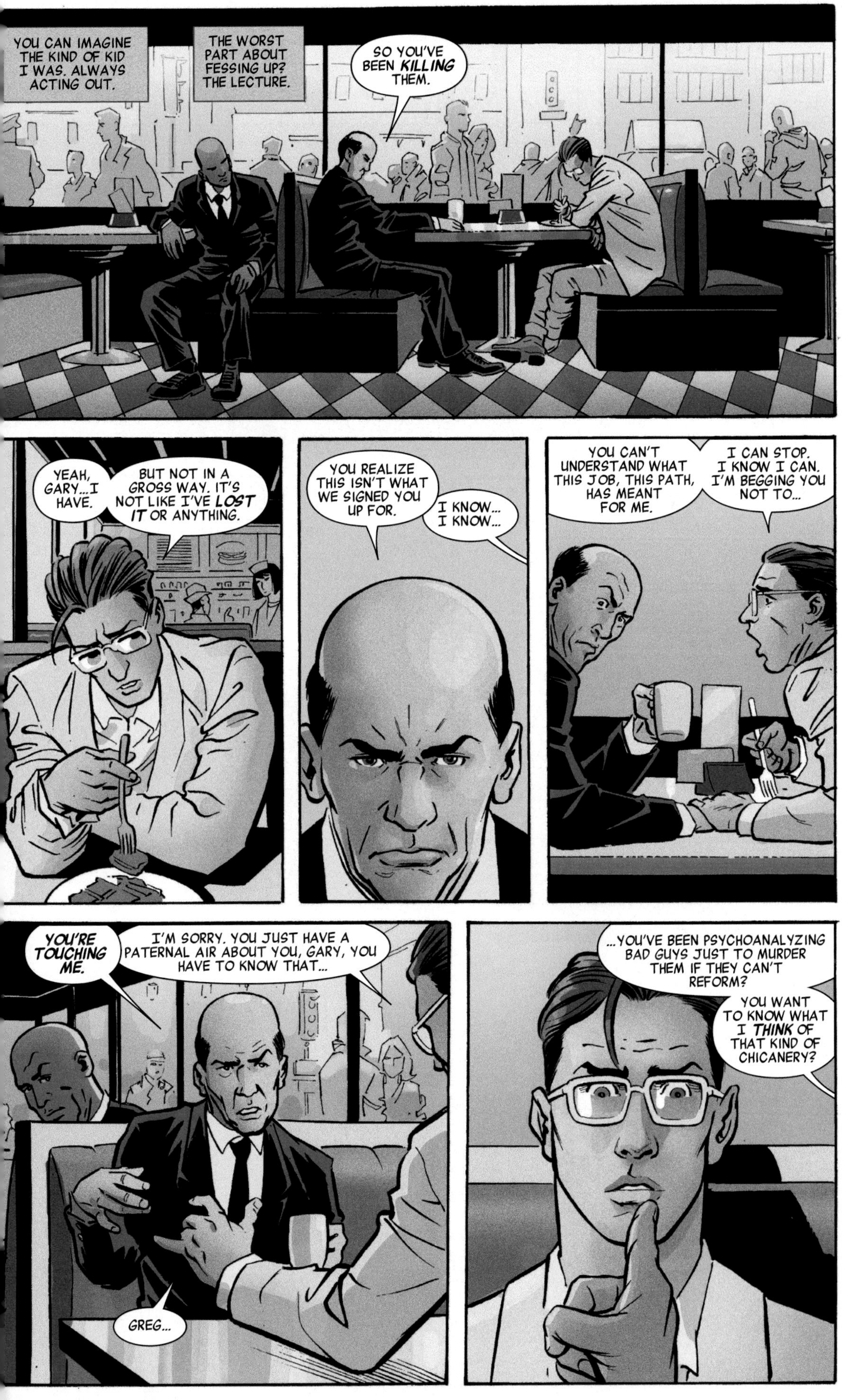

YOU CAN IMAGINE THE KIND OF KID I WAS. ALWAYS ACTING OUT.
THE WORST PART ABOUT FESSING UP? THE LECTURE.
SO YOU'VE BEEN KILLING THEM.
YEAH, GARY...I HAVE.
BUT NOT IN A GROSS WAY. IT'S NOT LIKE I'VE LOST IT OR ANYTHING.
YOU REALIZE THIS ISN'T WHAT WE SIGNED YOU UP FOR.
I KNOW... I KNOW...
YOU CAN'T UNDERSTAND WHAT THIS JOB, THIS PATH, HAS MEANT FOR ME.
I CAN STOP. I KNOW I CAN. I'M BEGGING YOU NOT TO...
YOU'RE TOUCHING ME.
I'M SORRY. YOU JUST HAVE A PATERNAL AIR ABOUT YOU, GARY, YOU HAVE TO KNOW THAT...
GREG...
...YOU'VE BEEN PSYCHOANALYZING BAD GUYS JUST TO MURDER THEM IF THEY CAN'T REFORM?
YOU WANT TO KNOW WHAT I THINK OF THAT KIND OF CHICANERY?

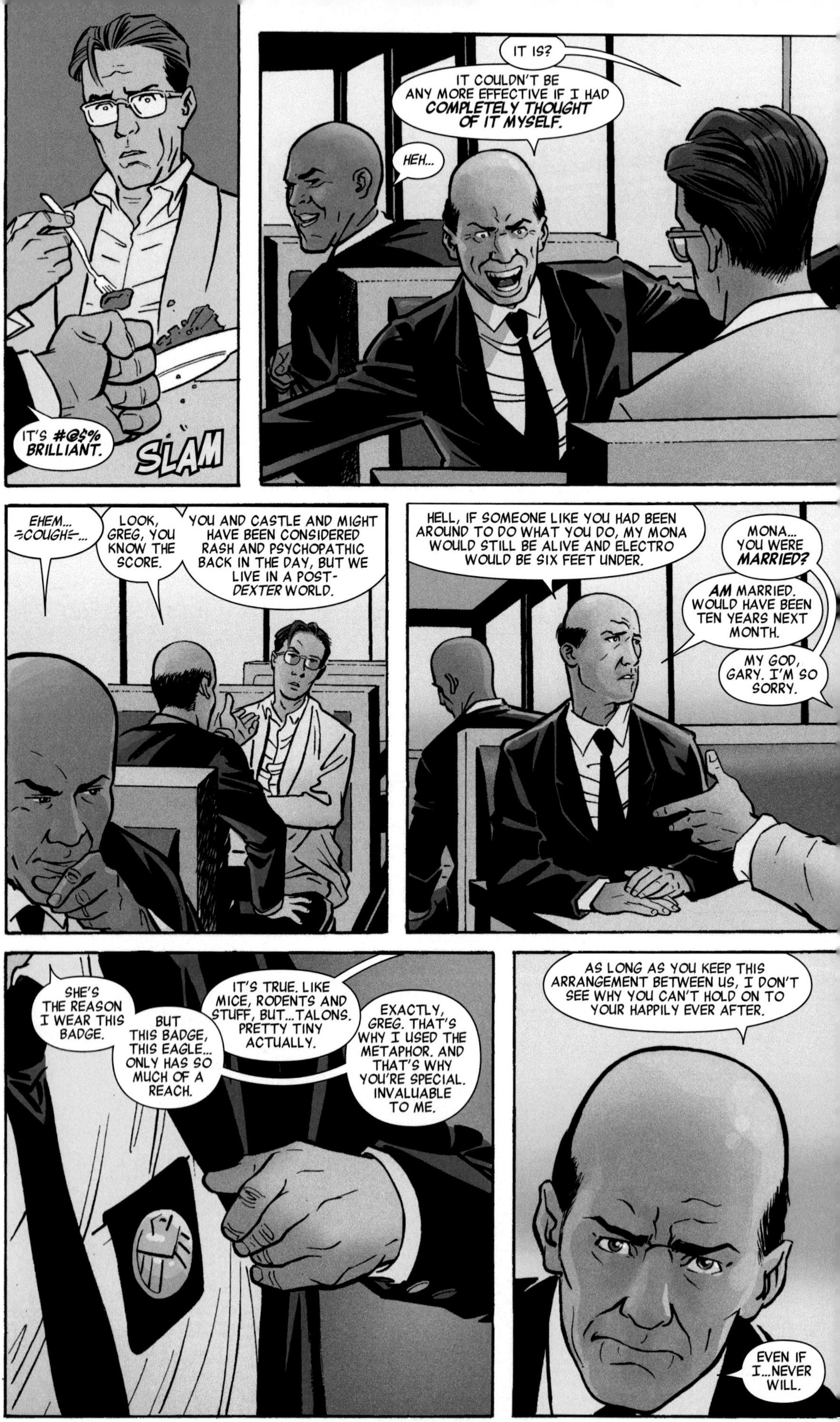

IT'S #@$% BRILLIANT.
SLAM
IT IS?
IT COULDN'T BE ANY MORE EFFECTIVE IF I HAD COMPLETELY THOUGHT OF IT MYSELF.
HEH...
EHEM... =COUGH=...
LOOK, GREG, YOU KNOW THE SCORE.
YOU AND CASTLE AND MIGHT HAVE BEEN CONSIDERED RASH AND PSYCHOPATHIC BACK IN THE DAY, BUT WE LIVE IN A POST-DEXTER WORLD.
HELL, IF SOMEONE LIKE YOU HAD BEEN AROUND TO DO WHAT YOU DO, MY MONA WOULD STILL BE ALIVE AND ELECTRO WOULD BE SIX FEET UNDER.
MONA... YOU WERE MARRIED?
AM MARRIED. WOULD HAVE BEEN TEN YEARS NEXT MONTH.
MY GOD, GARY. I'M SO SORRY.
SHE'S THE REASON I WEAR THIS BADGE.
BUT THIS BADGE, THIS EAGLE... ONLY HAS SO MUCH OF A REACH.
IT'S TRUE. LIKE MICE, RODENTS AND STUFF, BUT...TALONS. PRETTY TINY ACTUALLY.
EXACTLY, GREG. THAT'S WHY I USED THE METAPHOR. AND THAT'S WHY YOU'RE SPECIAL. INVALUABLE TO ME.
AS LONG AS YOU KEEP THIS ARRANGEMENT BETWEEN US, I DON'T SEE WHY YOU CAN'T HOLD ON TO YOUR HAPPILY EVER AFTER.
EVEN IF I...NEVER WILL.

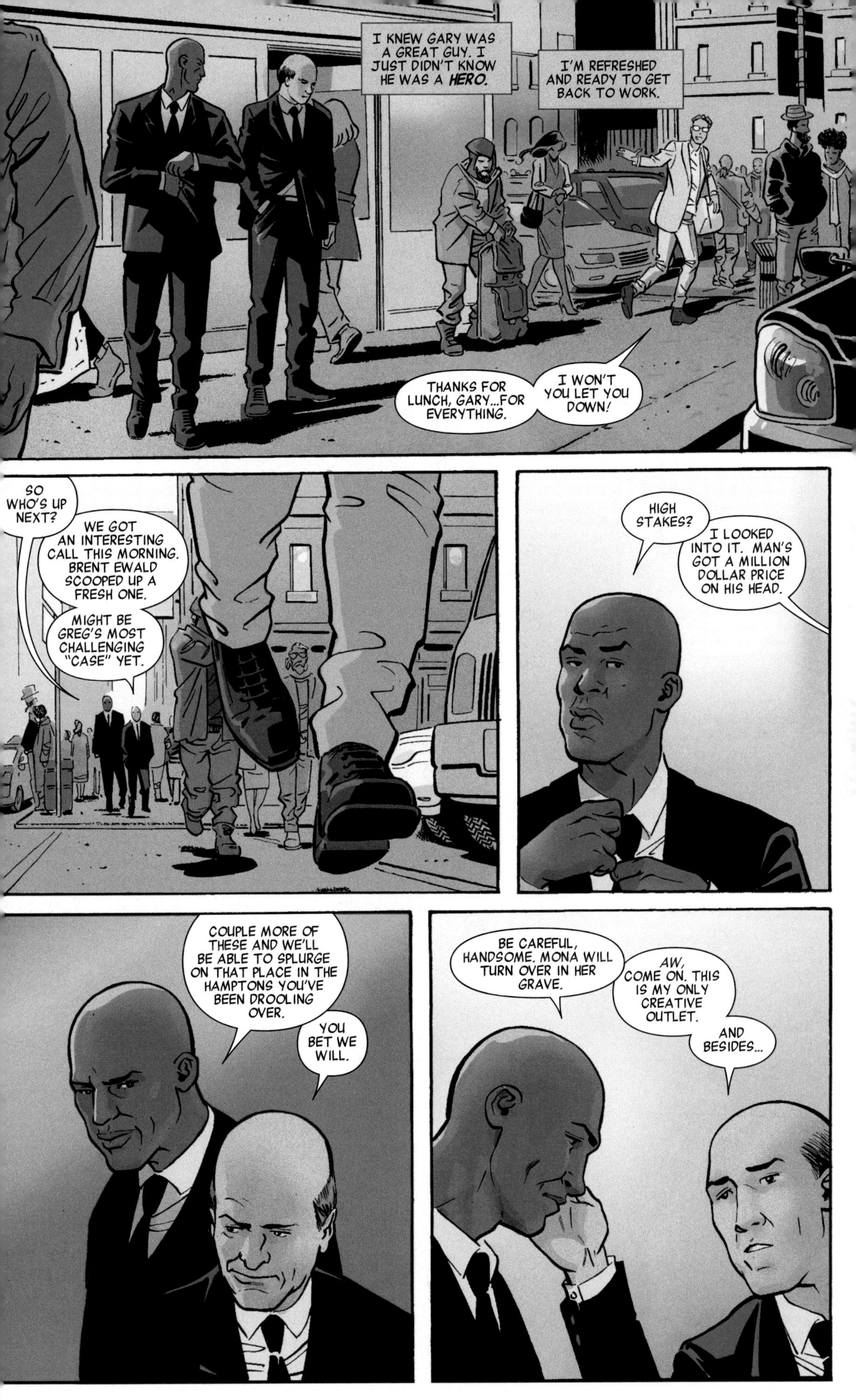
I KNEW GARY WAS A GREAT GUY. I JUST DIDN'T KNOW HE WAS A HERO.
I'M REFRESHED AND READY TO GET BACK TO WORK.
THANKS FOR LUNCH, GARY...FOR EVERYTHING.
I WON'T YOU LET YOU DOWN!
SO WHO'S UP NEXT?
WE GOT AN INTERESTING CALL THIS MORNING. BRENT EWALD SCOOPED UP A FRESH ONE.
MIGHT BE GREG'S MOST CHALLENGING "CASE" YET.
HIGH STAKES?
I LOOKED INTO IT. MAN'S GOT A MILLION DOLLAR PRICE ON HIS HEAD.
COUPLE MORE OF THESE AND WE'LL BE ABLE TO SPLURGE ON THAT PLACE IN THE HAMPTONS YOU'VE BEEN DROOLING OVER.
YOU BET WE WILL.
BE CAREFUL, HANDSOME. MONA WILL TURN OVER IN HER GRAVE.
AW, COME ON. THIS IS MY ONLY CREATIVE OUTLET.
AND BESIDES...

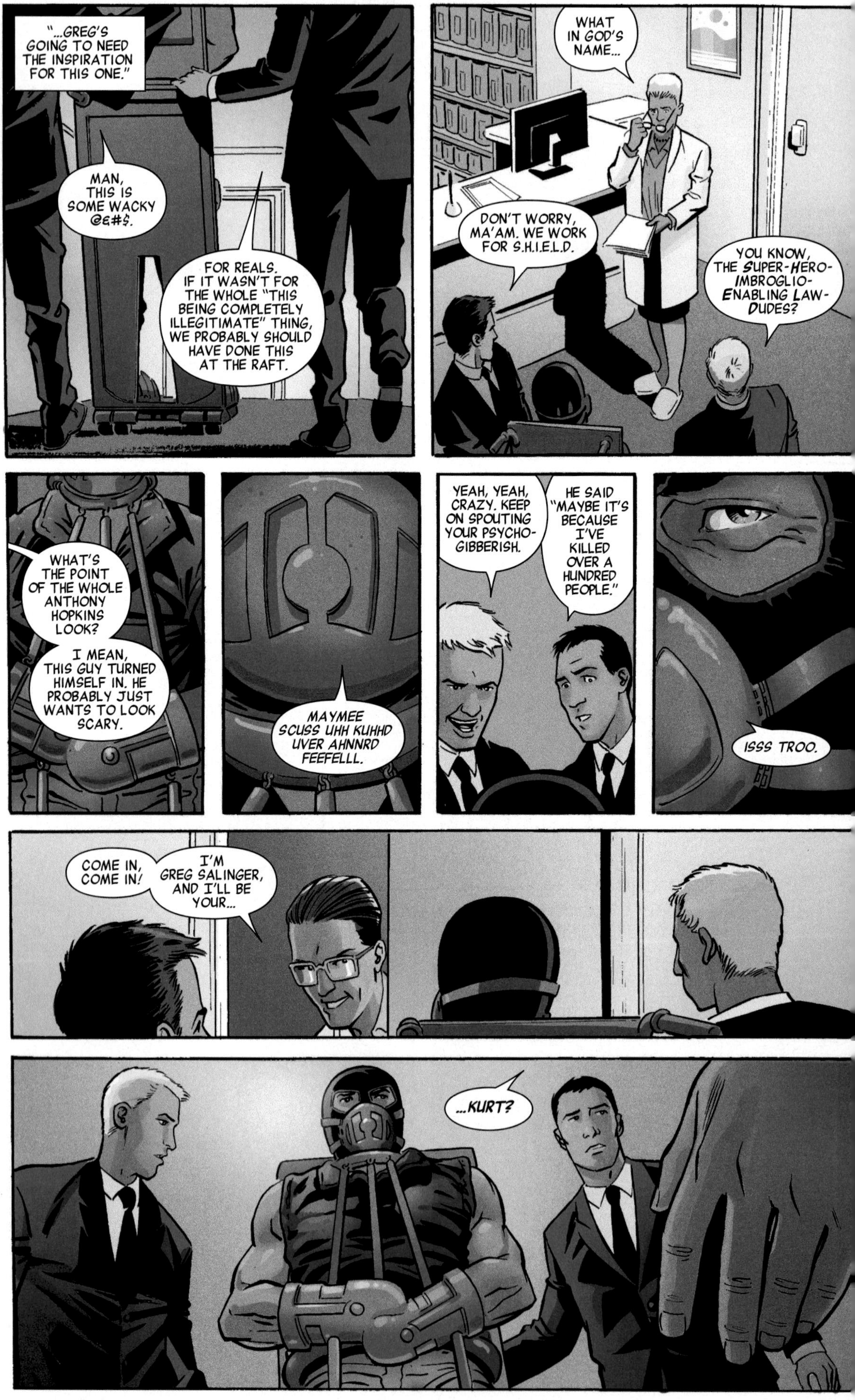
"...GREG'S GOING TO NEED THE INSPIRATION FOR THIS ONE."
MAN, THIS IS SOME WACKY @&#$.
FOR REALS. IF IT WASN'T FOR THE WHOLE "THIS BEING COMPLETELY ILLEGITIMATE" THING, WE PROBABLY SHOULD HAVE DONE THIS AT THE RAFT.
WHAT IN GOD'S NAME...
DON'T WORRY, MA'AM. WE WORK FOR S.H.I.E.L.D.
YOU KNOW, THE SUPER-HERO-IMBROGLIO-ENABLING LAW-DUDES?
WHAT'S THE POINT OF THE WHOLE ANTHONY HOPKINS LOOK?
I MEAN, THIS GUY TURNED HIMSELF IN. HE PROBABLY JUST WANTS TO LOOK SCARY.
MAYMEE SCUSS UHH KUHHD UVER AHNNRD FEEFELLL.
YEAH, YEAH, CRAZY. KEEP ON SPOUTING YOUR PSYCHO-GIBBERISH.
HE SAID "MAYBE IT'S BECAUSE I'VE KILLED OVER A HUNDRED PEOPLE."
ISSS TROO.
COME IN, COME IN!
I'M GREG SALINGER, AND I'LL BE YOUR...
...KURT?

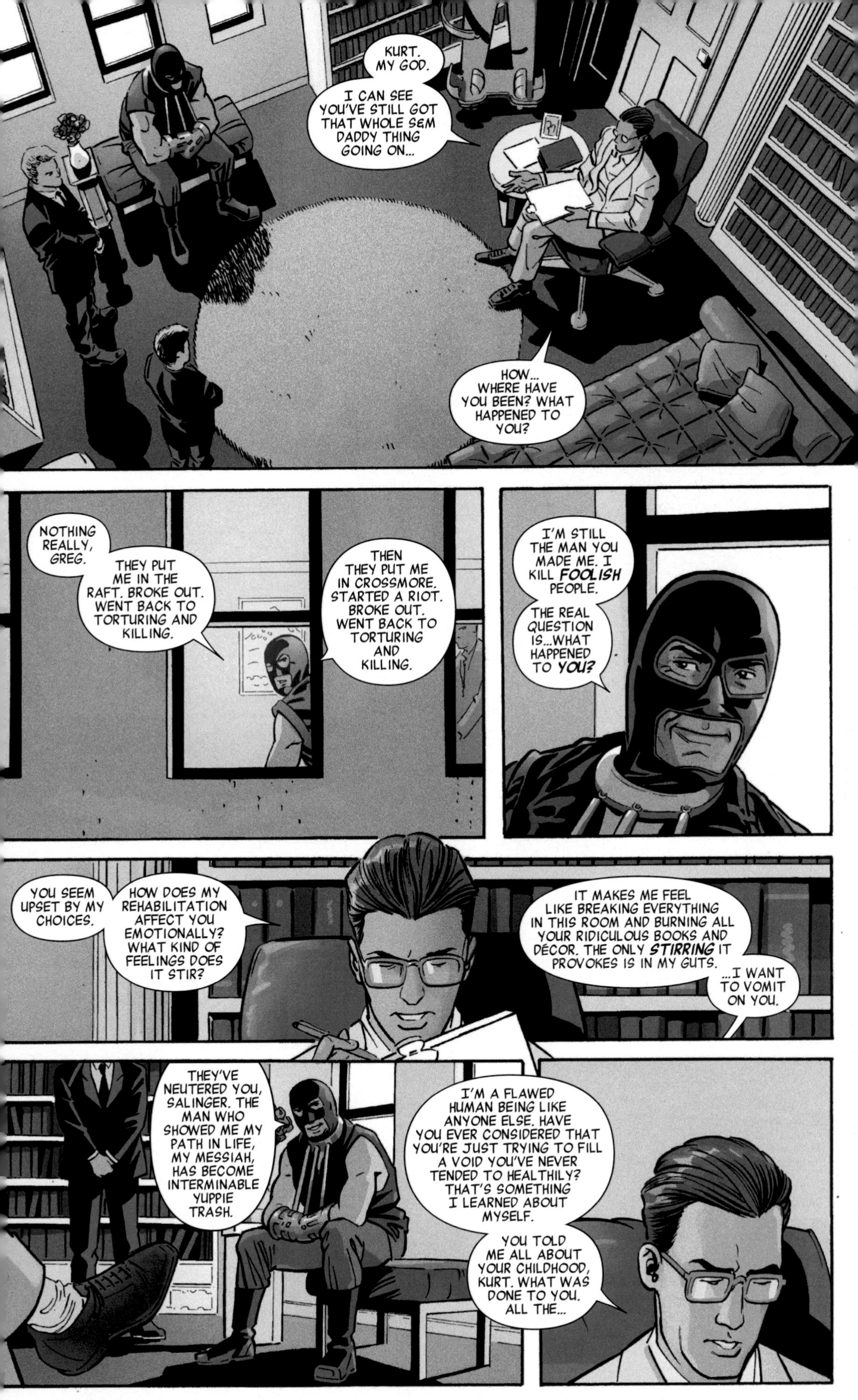
KURT. MY GOD.
I CAN SEE YOU'VE STILL GOT THAT WHOLE S&M DADDY THING GOING ON...
HOW... WHERE HAVE YOU BEEN? WHAT HAPPENED TO YOU?
NOTHING REALLY, GREG.
THEY PUT ME IN THE RAFT. BROKE OUT. WENT BACK TO TORTURING AND KILLING.
THEN THEY PUT ME IN CROSSMORE. STARTED A RIOT. BROKE OUT. WENT BACK TO TORTURING AND KILLING.
I'M STILL THE MAN YOU MADE ME. I KILL FOOLISH PEOPLE.
THE REAL QUESTION IS...WHAT HAPPENED TO YOU?
YOU SEEM UPSET BY MY CHOICES.
HOW DOES MY REHABILITATION AFFECT YOU EMOTIONALLY? WHAT KIND OF FEELINGS DOES IT STIR?
IT MAKES ME FEEL LIKE BREAKING EVERYTHING IN THIS ROOM AND BURNING ALL YOUR RIDICULOUS BOOKS AND DÉCOR. THE ONLY STIRRING IT PROVOKES IS IN MY GUTS.
...I WANT TO VOMIT ON YOU.
THEY'VE NEUTERED YOU, SALINGER. THE MAN WHO SHOWED ME MY PATH IN LIFE, MY MESSIAH, HAS BECOME INTERMINABLE YUPPIE TRASH.
I'M A FLAWED HUMAN BEING LIKE ANYONE ELSE. HAVE YOU EVER CONSIDERED THAT YOU'RE JUST TRYING TO FILL A VOID YOU'VE NEVER TENDED TO HEALTHILY? THAT'S SOMETHING I LEARNED ABOUT MYSELF.
YOU TOLD ME ALL ABOUT YOUR CHILDHOOD, KURT. WHAT WAS DONE TO YOU. ALL THE...

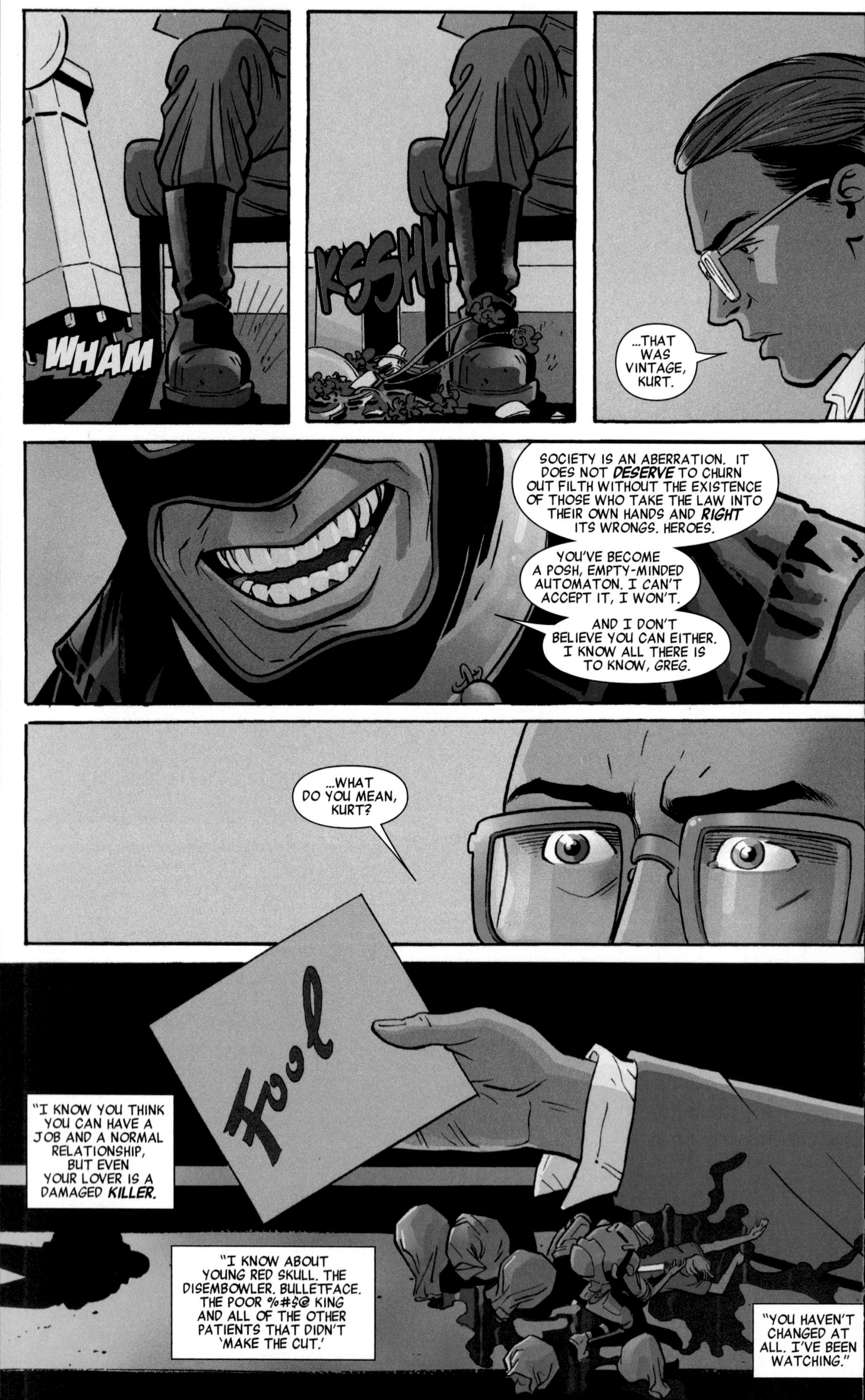
WHAM
KSSHH
...THAT WAS VINTAGE, KURT.
SOCIETY IS AN ABERRATION. IT DOES NOT DESERVE TO CHURN OUT FILTH WITHOUT THE EXISTENCE OF THOSE WHO TAKE THE LAW INTO THEIR OWN HANDS AND RIGHT ITS WRONGS. HEROES.
YOU'VE BECOME A POSH, EMPTY-MINDED AUTOMATON. I CAN'T ACCEPT IT, I WON'T.
AND I DON'T BELIEVE YOU CAN EITHER. I KNOW ALL THERE IS TO KNOW, GREG.
...WHAT DO YOU MEAN, KURT?
Fool
"I KNOW YOU THINK YOU CAN HAVE A JOB AND A NORMAL RELATIONSHIP, BUT EVEN YOUR LOVER IS A DAMAGED KILLER.
"I KNOW ABOUT YOUNG RED SKULL. THE DISEMBOWLER. BULLETFACE. THE POOR %#$@ KING AND ALL OF THE OTHER PATIENTS THAT DIDN'T 'MAKE THE CUT.'
"YOU HAVEN'T CHANGED AT ALL. I'VE BEEN WATCHING."

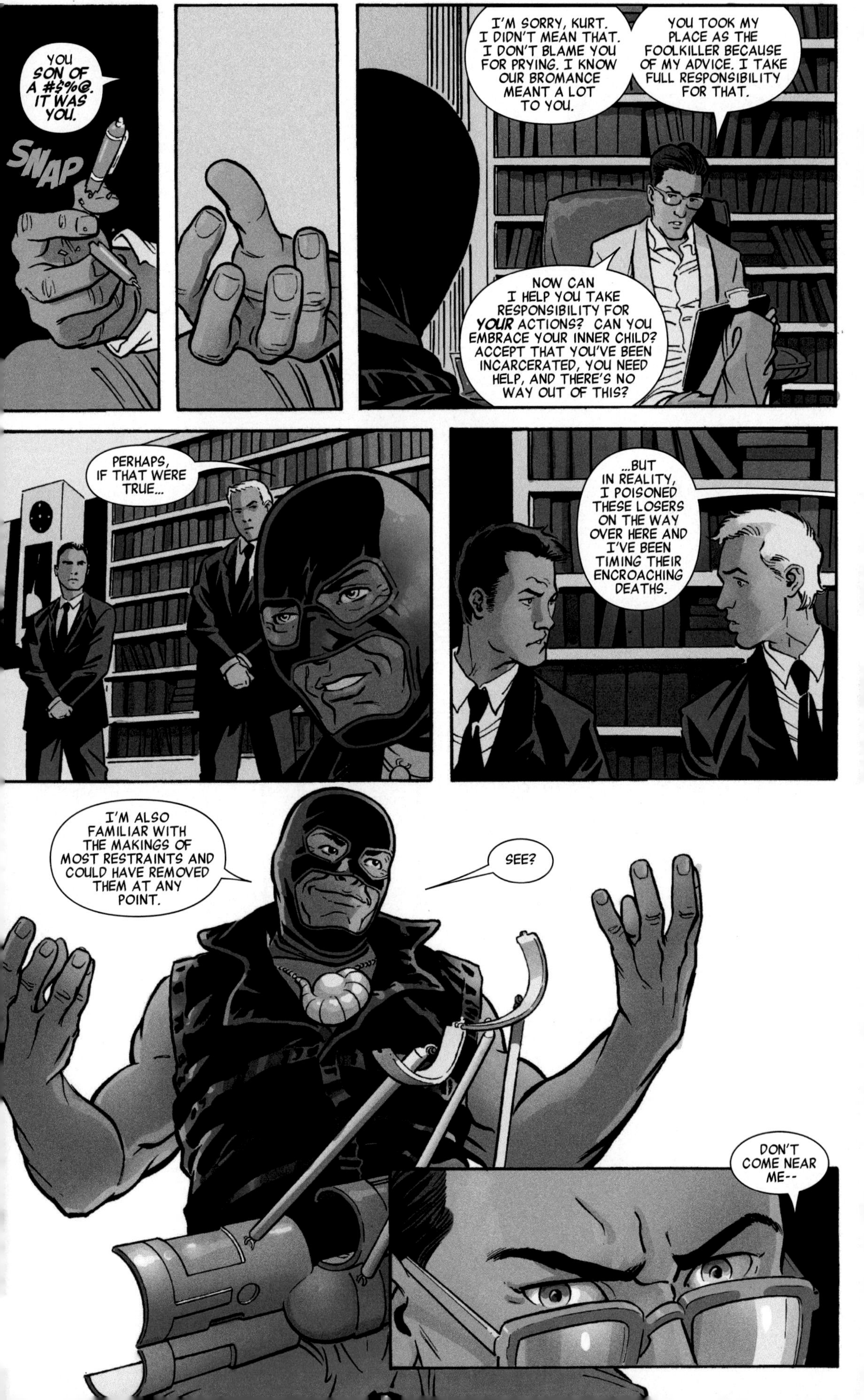
YOU SON OF A #$%@. IT WAS YOU.
SNAP
I'M SORRY, KURT. I DIDN'T MEAN THAT. I DON'T BLAME YOU FOR PRYING. I KNOW OUR BROMANCE MEANT A LOT TO YOU.
YOU TOOK MY PLACE AS THE FOOLKILLER BECAUSE OF MY ADVICE. I TAKE FULL RESPONSIBILITY FOR THAT.
NOW CAN I HELP YOU TAKE RESPONSIBILITY FOR YOUR ACTIONS? CAN YOU EMBRACE YOUR INNER CHILD? ACCEPT THAT YOU'VE BEEN INCARCERATED, YOU NEED HELP, AND THERE'S NO WAY OUT OF THIS?
PERHAPS, IF THAT WERE TRUE...
...BUT IN REALITY, I POISONED THESE LOSERS ON THE WAY OVER HERE AND I'VE BEEN TIMING THEIR ENCROACHING DEATHS.
I'M ALSO FAMILIAR WITH THE MAKINGS OF MOST RESTRAINTS AND COULD HAVE REMOVED THEM AT ANY POINT.
SEE?
DON'T COME NEAR ME--

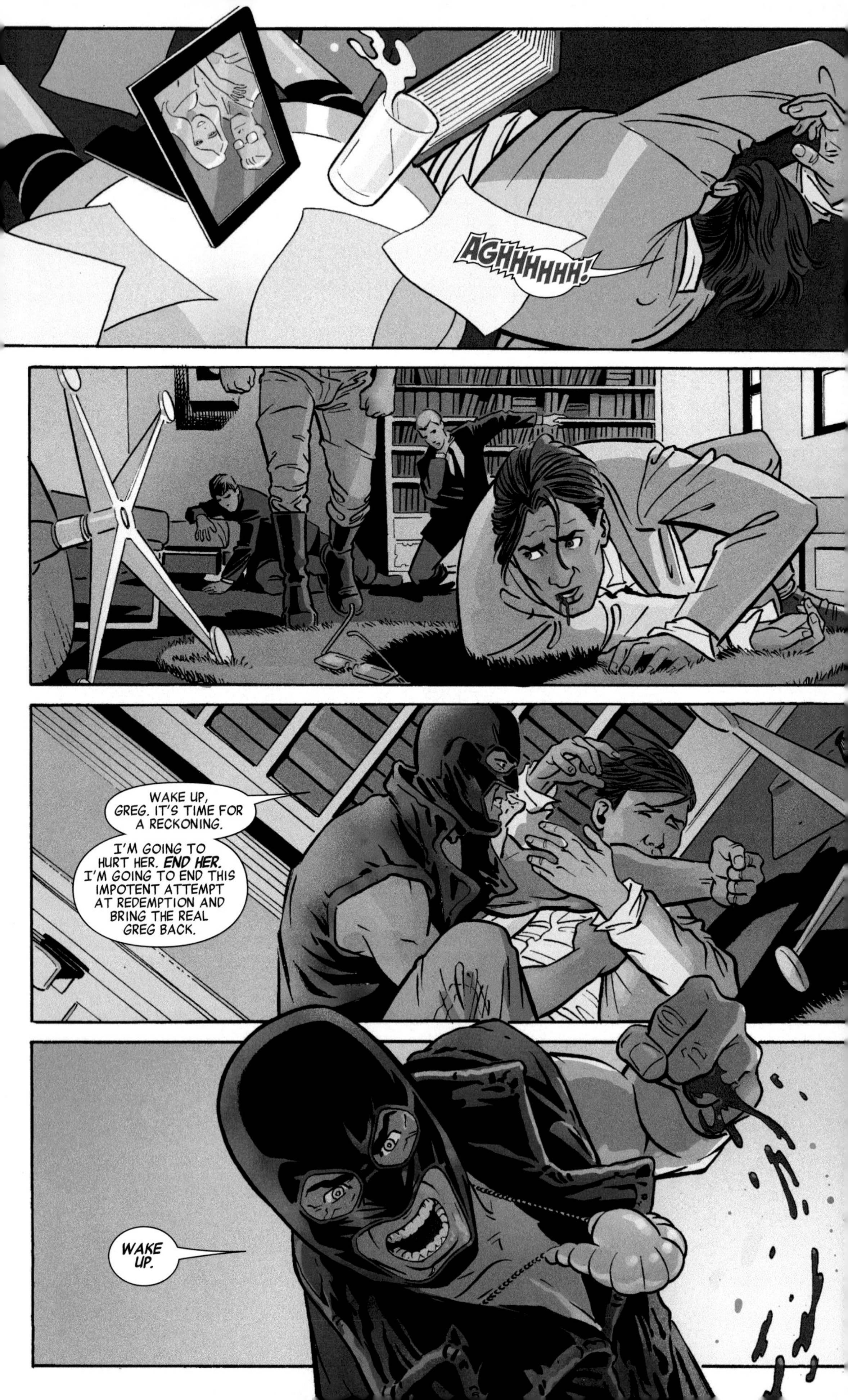
AGHHHHHH!
WAKE UP, GREG. IT'S TIME FOR A RECKONING.
I'M GOING TO HURT HER. **END HER.** I'M GOING TO END THIS IMPOTENT ATTEMPT AT REDEMPTION AND BRING THE REAL GREG BACK.
WAKE UP.

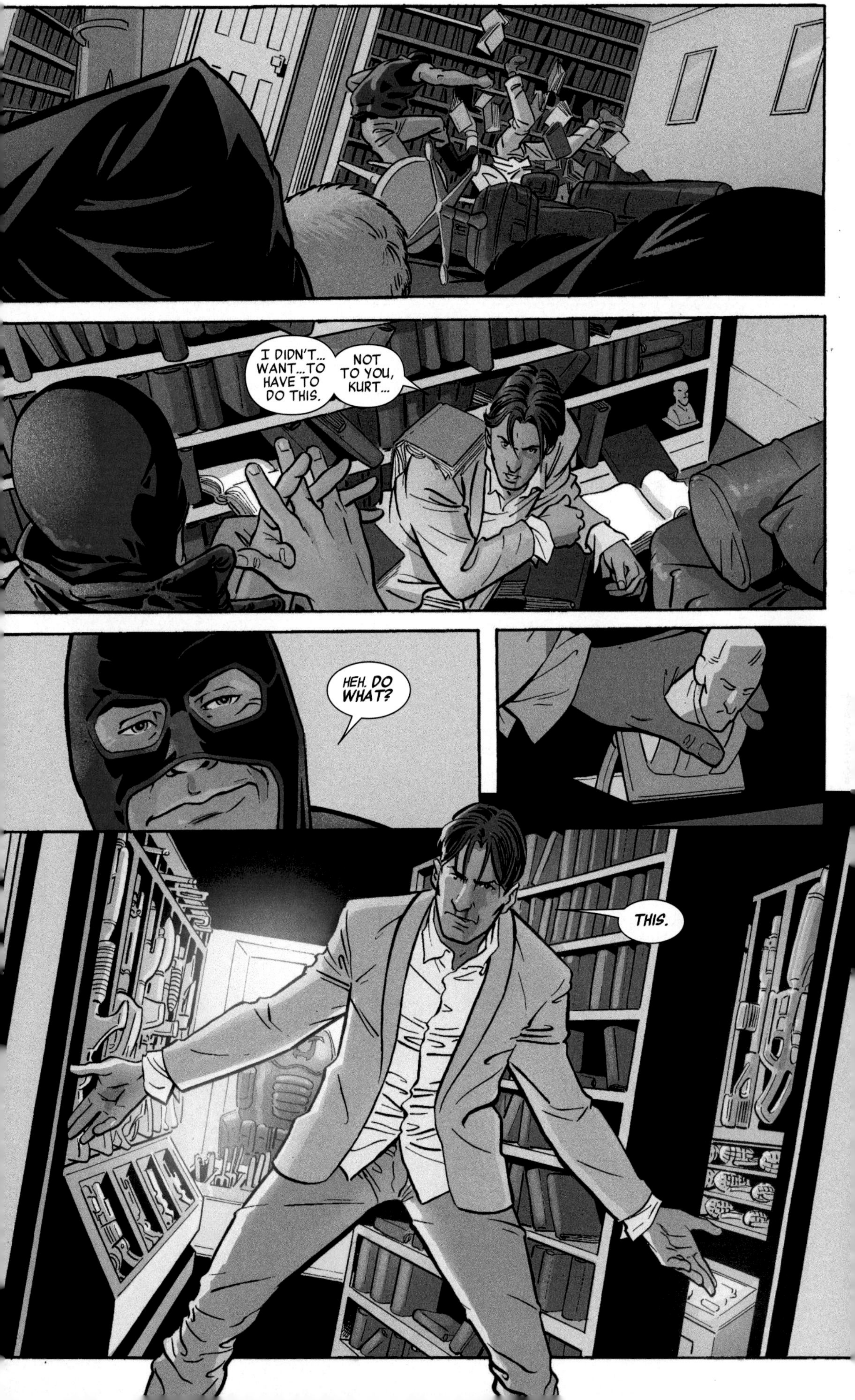
I DIDN'T... WANT...TO HAVE TO DO THIS.
NOT TO YOU, KURT...
HEH. DO WHAT?
THIS.

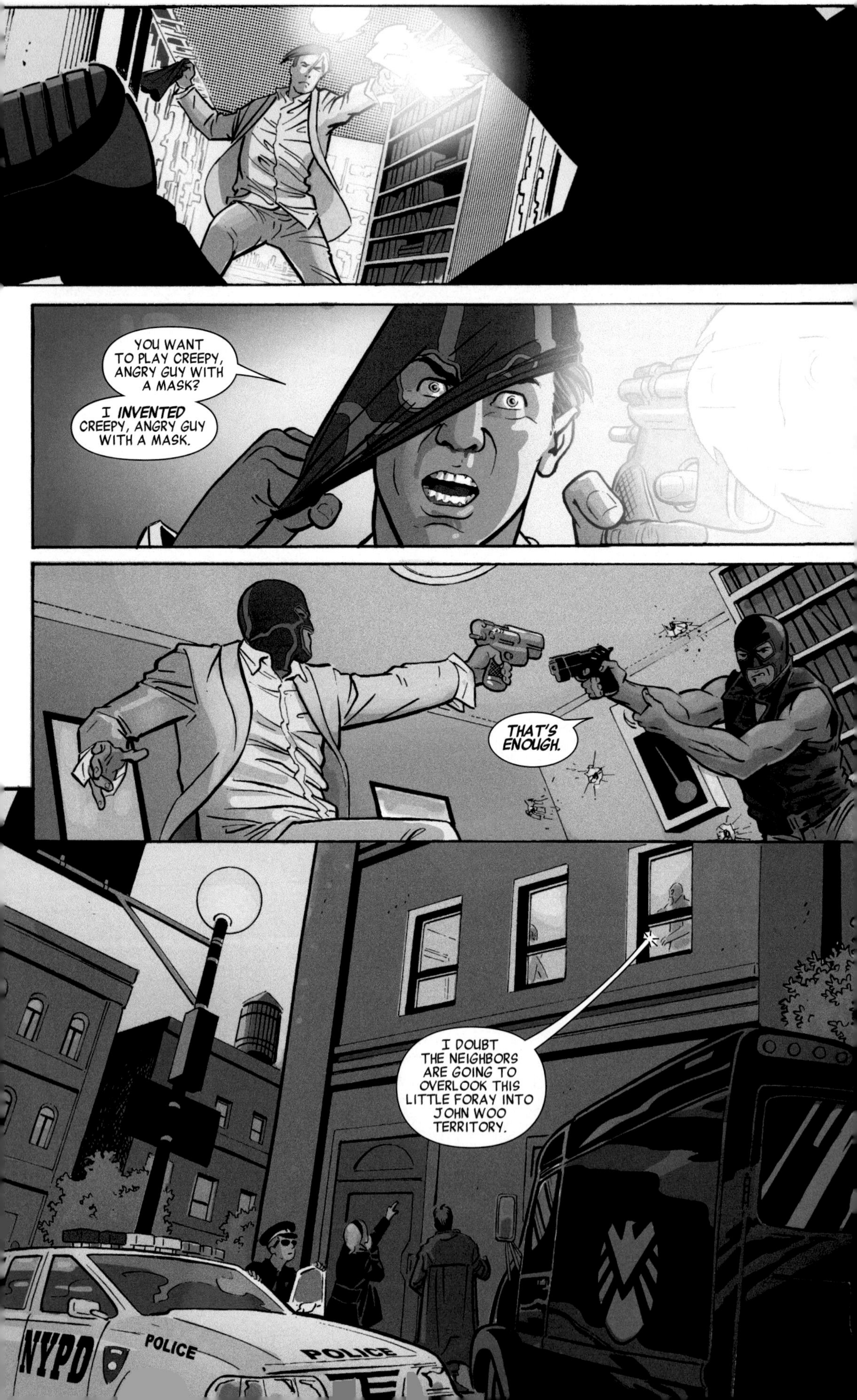

YOU WANT TO PLAY CREEPY, ANGRY GUY WITH A MASK?
I **INVENTED** CREEPY, ANGRY GUY WITH A MASK.
THAT'S ENOUGH.
I DOUBT THE NEIGHBORS ARE GOING TO OVERLOOK THIS LITTLE FORAY INTO JOHN WOO TERRITORY.
NYPD
POLICE
POLICE

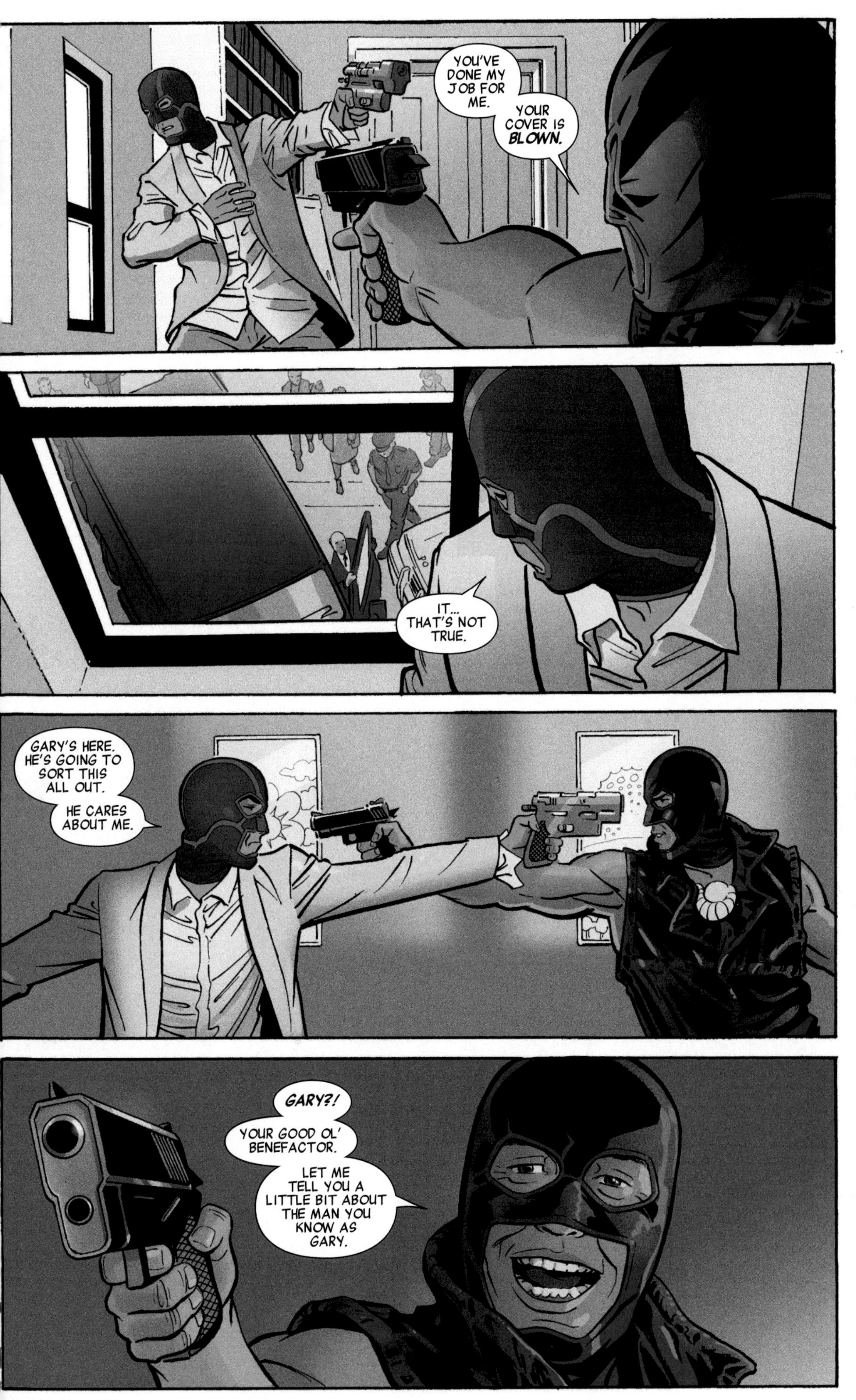
YOU'VE DONE MY JOB FOR ME.
YOUR COVER IS BLOWN.
IT... THAT'S NOT TRUE.
GARY'S HERE. HE'S GOING TO SORT THIS ALL OUT.
HE CARES ABOUT ME.
GARY?!
YOUR GOOD OL' BENEFACTOR.
LET ME TELL YOU A LITTLE BIT ABOUT THE MAN YOU KNOW AS GARY.

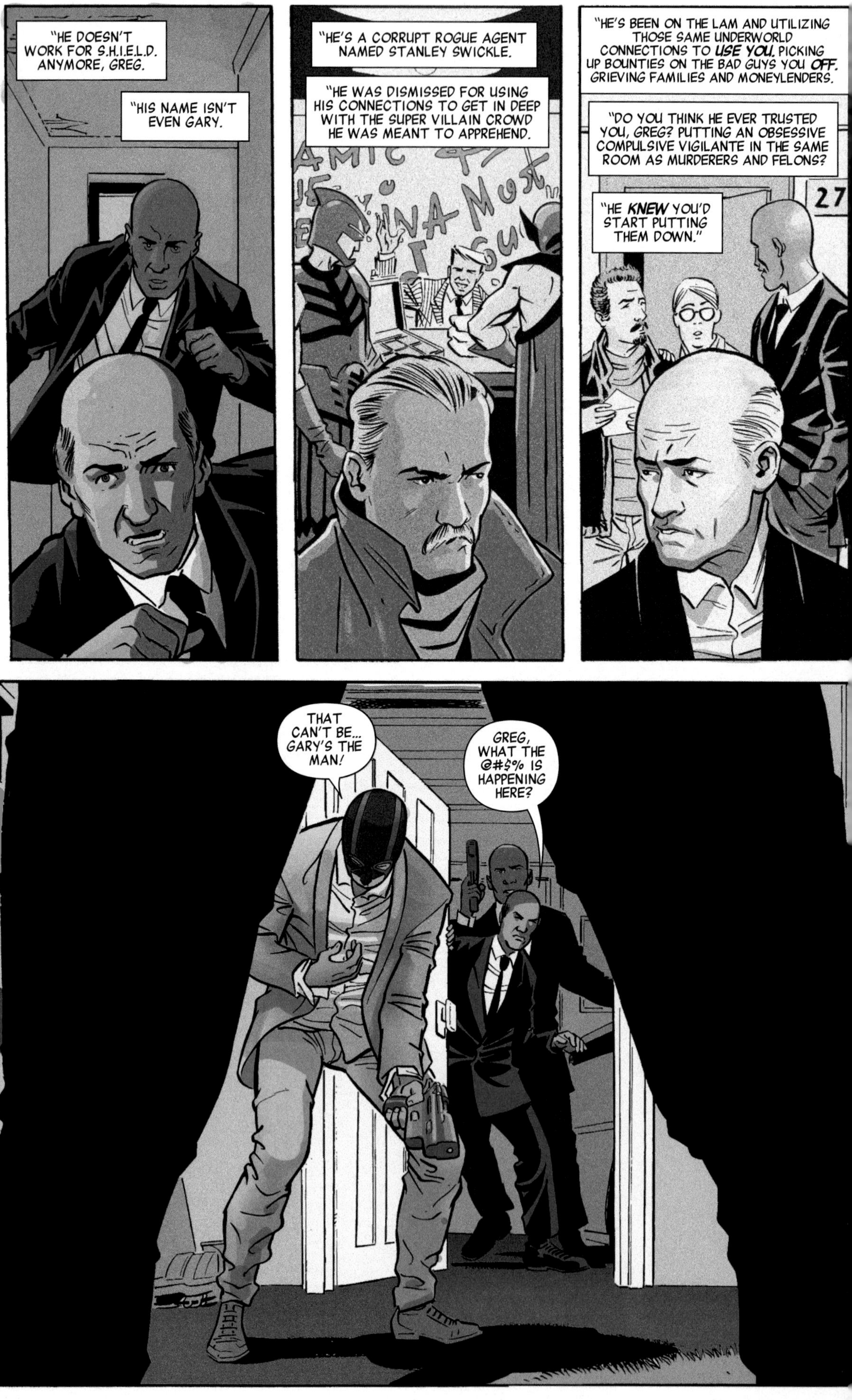
"HE DOESN'T WORK FOR S.H.I.E.L.D. ANYMORE, GREG.
"HIS NAME ISN'T EVEN GARY.
"HE'S A CORRUPT ROGUE AGENT NAMED STANLEY SWICKLE.
"HE WAS DISMISSED FOR USING HIS CONNECTIONS TO GET IN DEEP WITH THE SUPER VILLAIN CROWD HE WAS MEANT TO APPREHEND.
"HE'S BEEN ON THE LAM AND UTILIZING THOSE SAME UNDERWORLD CONNECTIONS TO USE YOU. PICKING UP BOUNTIES ON THE BAD GUYS YOU OFF. GRIEVING FAMILIES AND MONEYLENDERS.
"DO YOU THINK HE EVER TRUSTED YOU, GREG? PUTTING AN OBSESSIVE COMPULSIVE VIGILANTE IN THE SAME ROOM AS MURDERERS AND FELONS?
"HE KNEW YOU'D START PUTTING THEM DOWN."
27
THAT CAN'T BE... GARY'S THE MAN!
GREG, WHAT THE @#$% IS HAPPENING HERE?

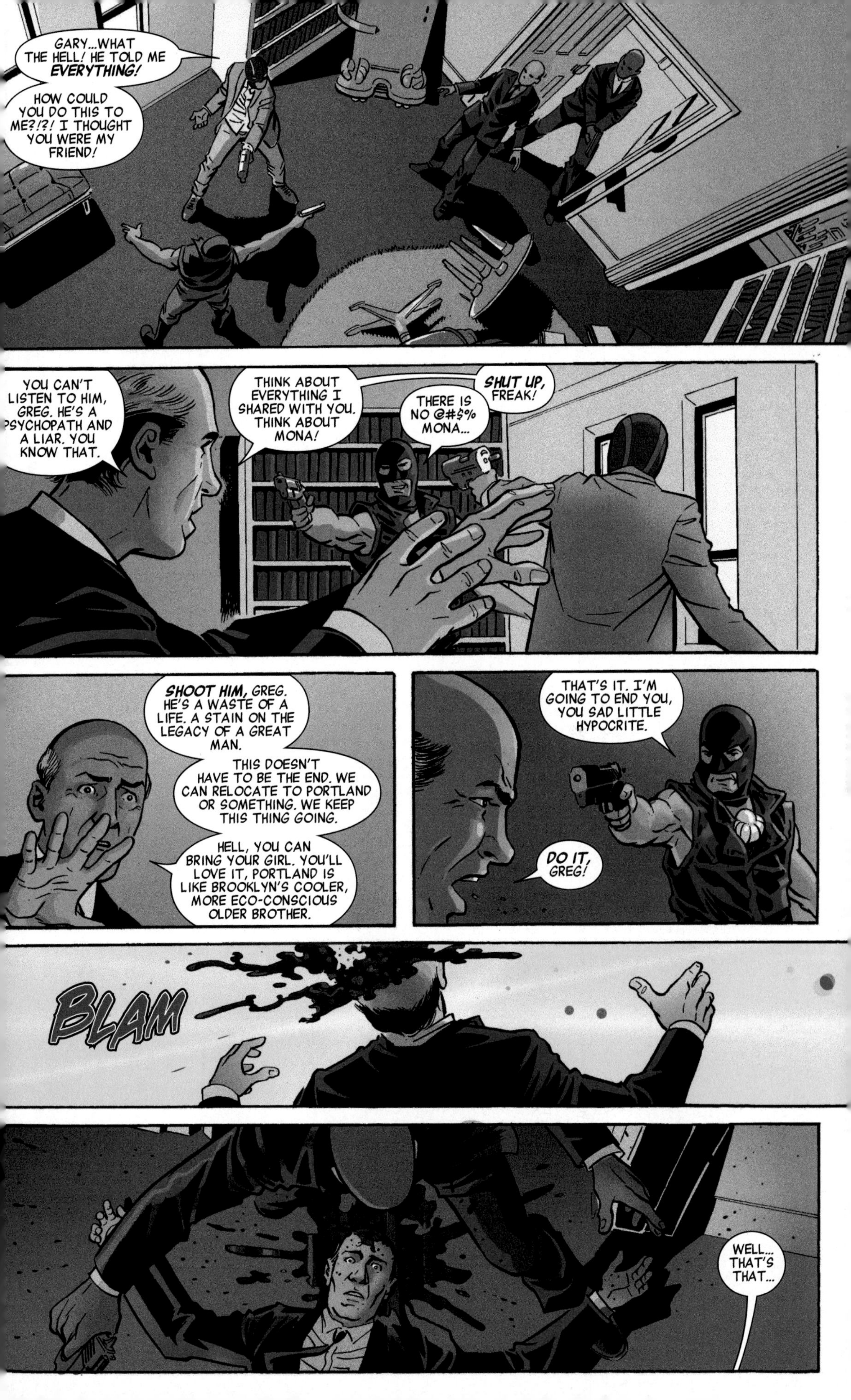
GARY...WHAT THE HELL! HE TOLD ME EVERYTHING!
HOW COULD YOU DO THIS TO ME?!?! I THOUGHT YOU WERE MY FRIEND!
YOU CAN'T LISTEN TO HIM, GREG. HE'S A PSYCHOPATH AND A LIAR. YOU KNOW THAT.
THINK ABOUT EVERYTHING I SHARED WITH YOU. THINK ABOUT MONA!
SHUT UP, FREAK!
THERE IS NO @#$% MONA...
SHOOT HIM, GREG. HE'S A WASTE OF A LIFE. A STAIN ON THE LEGACY OF A GREAT MAN.
THIS DOESN'T HAVE TO BE THE END. WE CAN RELOCATE TO PORTLAND OR SOMETHING. WE KEEP THIS THING GOING.
HELL, YOU CAN BRING YOUR GIRL. YOU'LL LOVE IT, PORTLAND IS LIKE BROOKLYN'S COOLER, MORE ECO-CONSCIOUS OLDER BROTHER.
THAT'S IT. I'M GOING TO END YOU, YOU SAD LITTLE HYPOCRITE.
DO IT, GREG!
BLAM
WELL... THAT'S THAT...

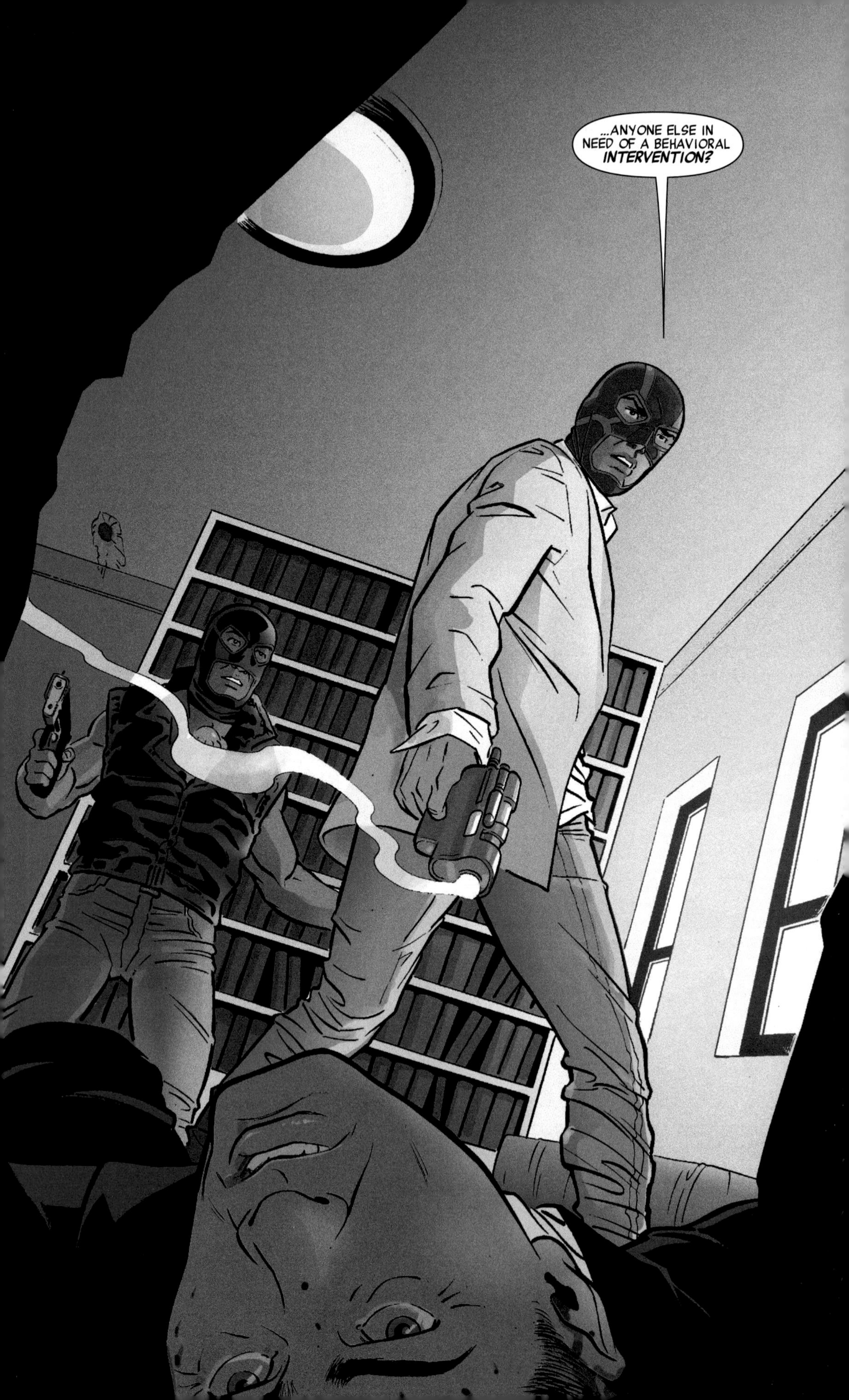
...ANYONE ELSE IN NEED OF A BEHAVIORAL INTERVENTION?

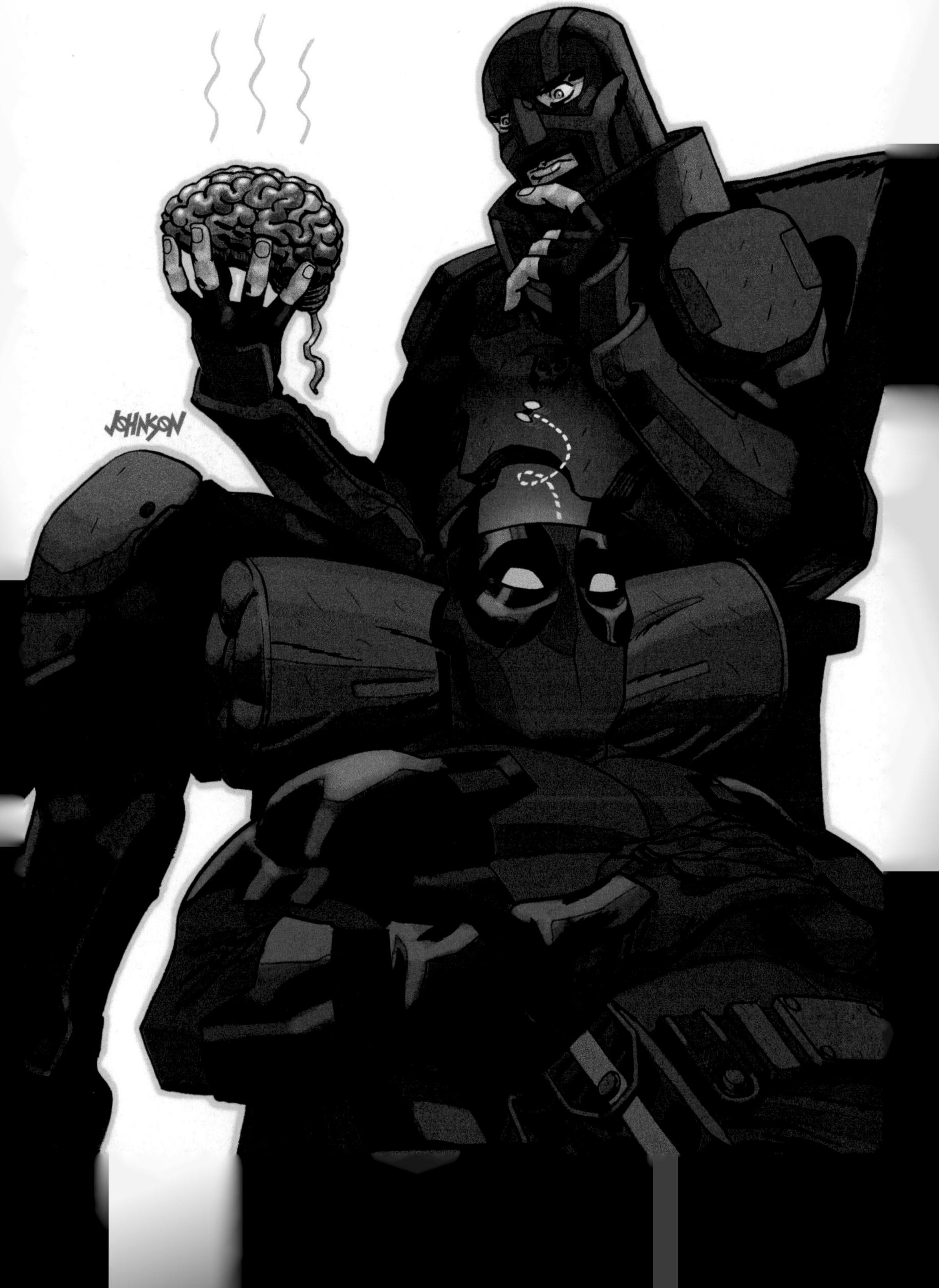
JOHNSON

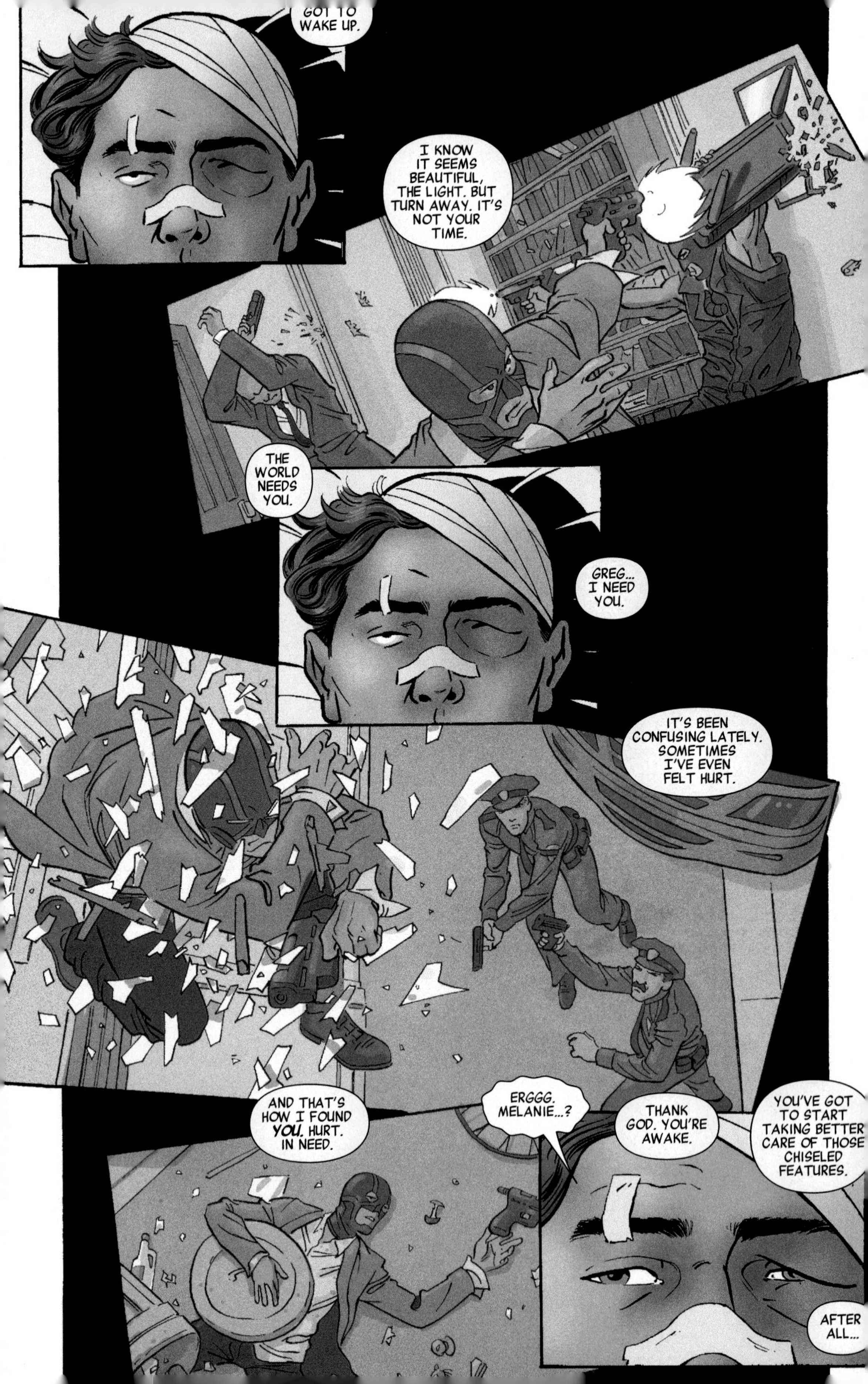
GOT TO WAKE UP.
I KNOW IT SEEMS BEAUTIFUL, THE LIGHT. BUT TURN AWAY. IT'S NOT YOUR TIME.
THE WORLD NEEDS YOU.
GREG... I NEED YOU.
IT'S BEEN CONFUSING LATELY. SOMETIMES I'VE EVEN FELT HURT.
AND THAT'S HOW I FOUND YOU. HURT. IN NEED.
ERGGG. MELANIE...?
THANK GOD. YOU'RE AWAKE.
YOU'VE GOT TO START TAKING BETTER CARE OF THOSE CHISELED FEATURES.
AFTER ALL...

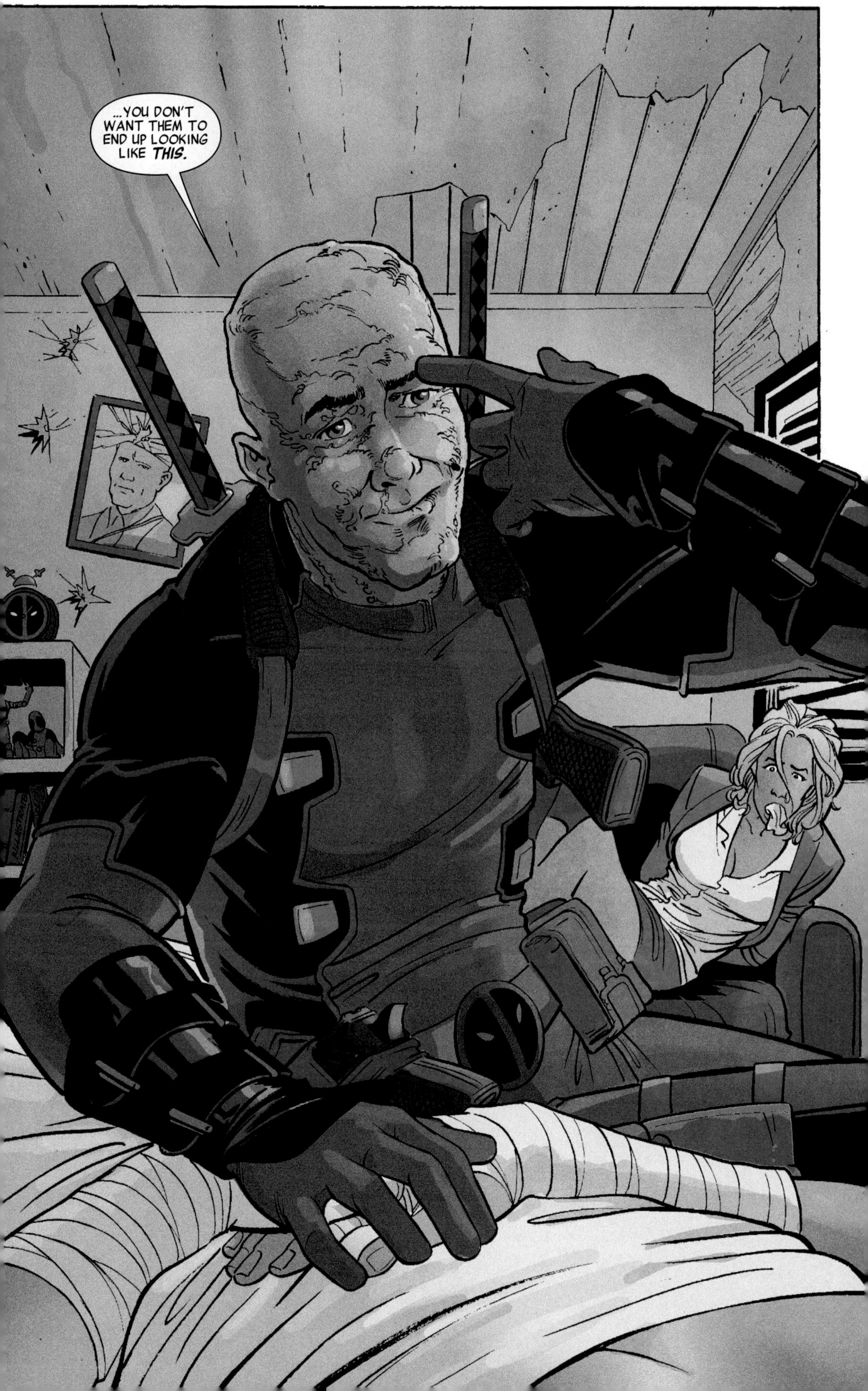
...YOU DON'T WANT THEM TO END UP LOOKING LIKE THIS.

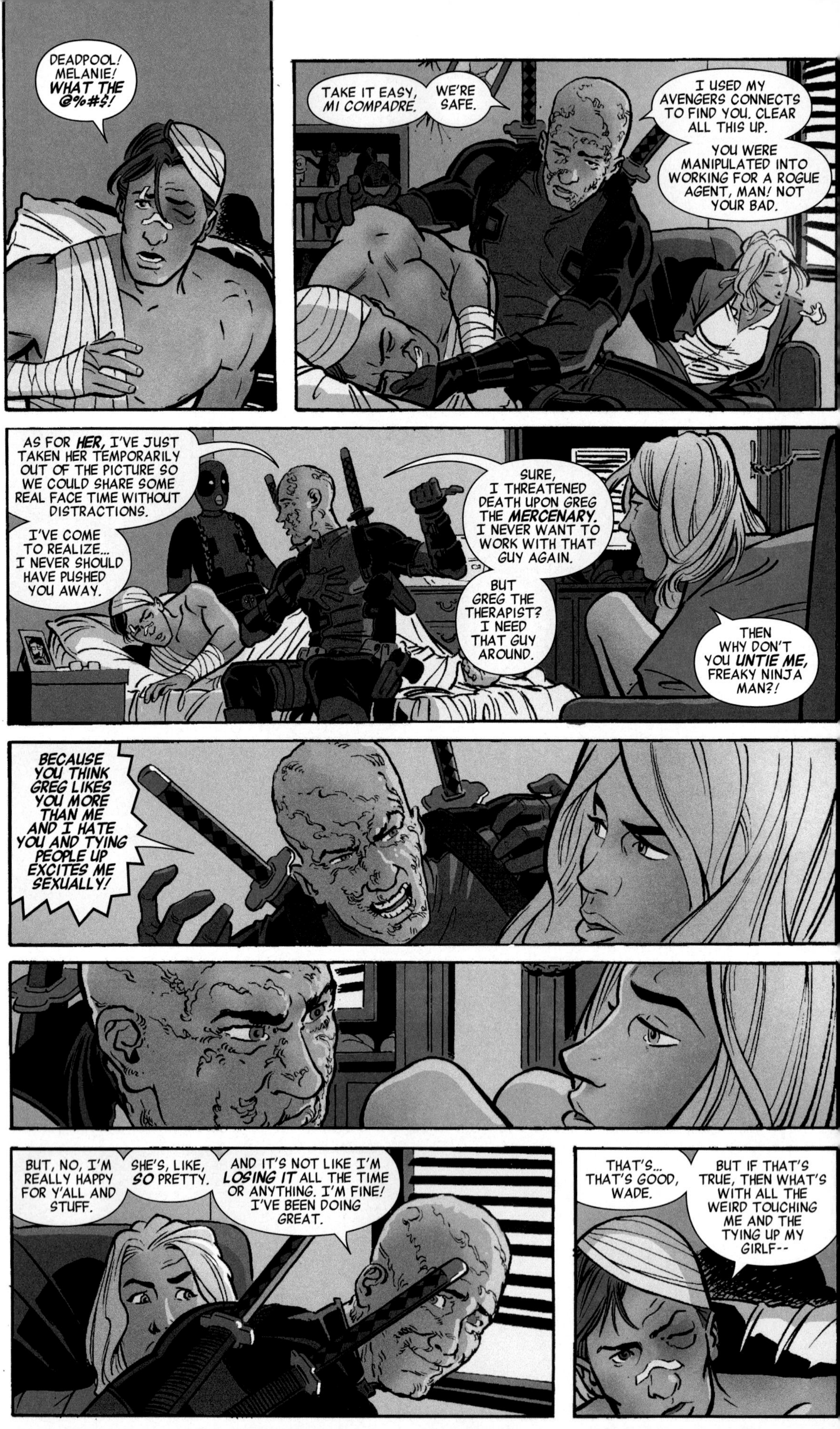

DEADPOOL! MELANIE! WHAT THE @%#$!
TAKE IT EASY, MI COMPADRE.
WE'RE SAFE.
I USED MY AVENGERS CONNECTS TO FIND YOU. CLEAR ALL THIS UP.
YOU WERE MANIPULATED INTO WORKING FOR A ROGUE AGENT, MAN! NOT YOUR BAD.
AS FOR HER, I'VE JUST TAKEN HER TEMPORARILY OUT OF THE PICTURE SO WE COULD SHARE SOME REAL FACE TIME WITHOUT DISTRACTIONS.
I'VE COME TO REALIZE... I NEVER SHOULD HAVE PUSHED YOU AWAY.
SURE, I THREATENED DEATH UPON GREG THE MERCENARY. I NEVER WANT TO WORK WITH THAT GUY AGAIN.
BUT GREG THE THERAPIST? I NEED THAT GUY AROUND.
THEN WHY DON'T YOU UNTIE ME, FREAKY NINJA MAN?!
BECAUSE YOU THINK GREG LIKES YOU MORE THAN ME AND I HATE YOU AND TYING PEOPLE UP EXCITES ME SEXUALLY!
BUT, NO, I'M REALLY HAPPY FOR Y'ALL AND STUFF.
SHE'S, LIKE, SO PRETTY.
AND IT'S NOT LIKE I'M LOSING IT ALL THE TIME OR ANYTHING. I'M FINE! I'VE BEEN DOING GREAT.
THAT'S... THAT'S GOOD, WADE.
BUT IF THAT'S TRUE, THEN WHAT'S WITH ALL THE WEIRD TOUCHING ME AND THE TYING UP MY GIRLF--

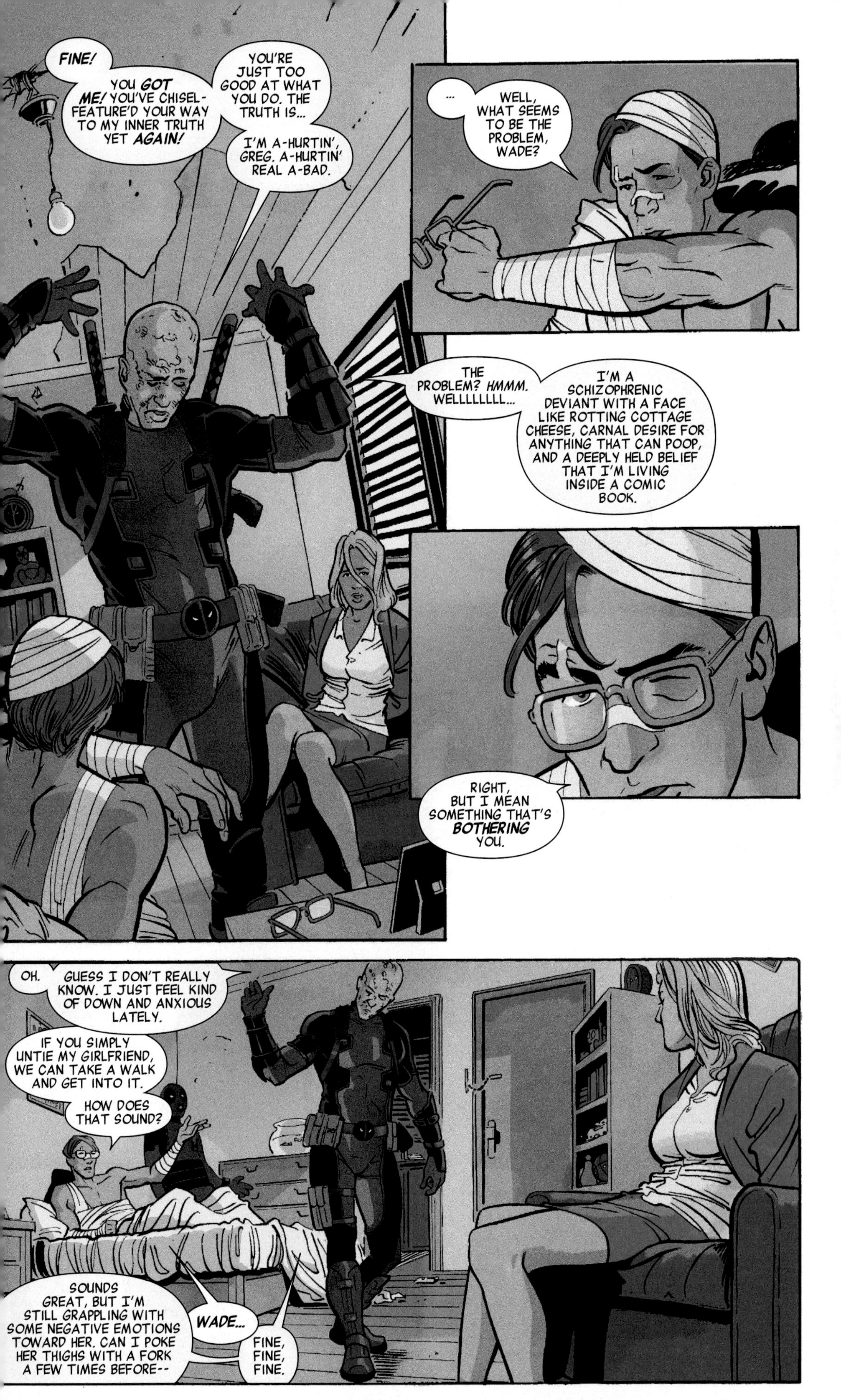
FINE!
YOU GOT ME! YOU'VE CHISEL-FEATURE'D YOUR WAY TO MY INNER TRUTH YET AGAIN!
YOU'RE JUST TOO GOOD AT WHAT YOU DO. THE TRUTH IS...
I'M A-HURTIN', GREG. A-HURTIN' REAL A-BAD.
...
WELL, WHAT SEEMS TO BE THE PROBLEM, WADE?
THE PROBLEM? HMMM. WELLLLLLLLL...
I'M A SCHIZOPHRENIC DEVIANT WITH A FACE LIKE ROTTING COTTAGE CHEESE, CARNAL DESIRE FOR ANYTHING THAT CAN POOP, AND A DEEPLY HELD BELIEF THAT I'M LIVING INSIDE A COMIC BOOK.
RIGHT, BUT I MEAN SOMETHING THAT'S BOTHERING YOU.
OH.
GUESS I DON'T REALLY KNOW. I JUST FEEL KIND OF DOWN AND ANXIOUS LATELY.
IF YOU SIMPLY UNTIE MY GIRLFRIEND, WE CAN TAKE A WALK AND GET INTO IT.
HOW DOES THAT SOUND?
SOUNDS GREAT, BUT I'M STILL GRAPPLING WITH SOME NEGATIVE EMOTIONS TOWARD HER. CAN I POKE HER THIGHS WITH A FORK A FEW TIMES BEFORE--
WADE...
FINE, FINE, FINE.

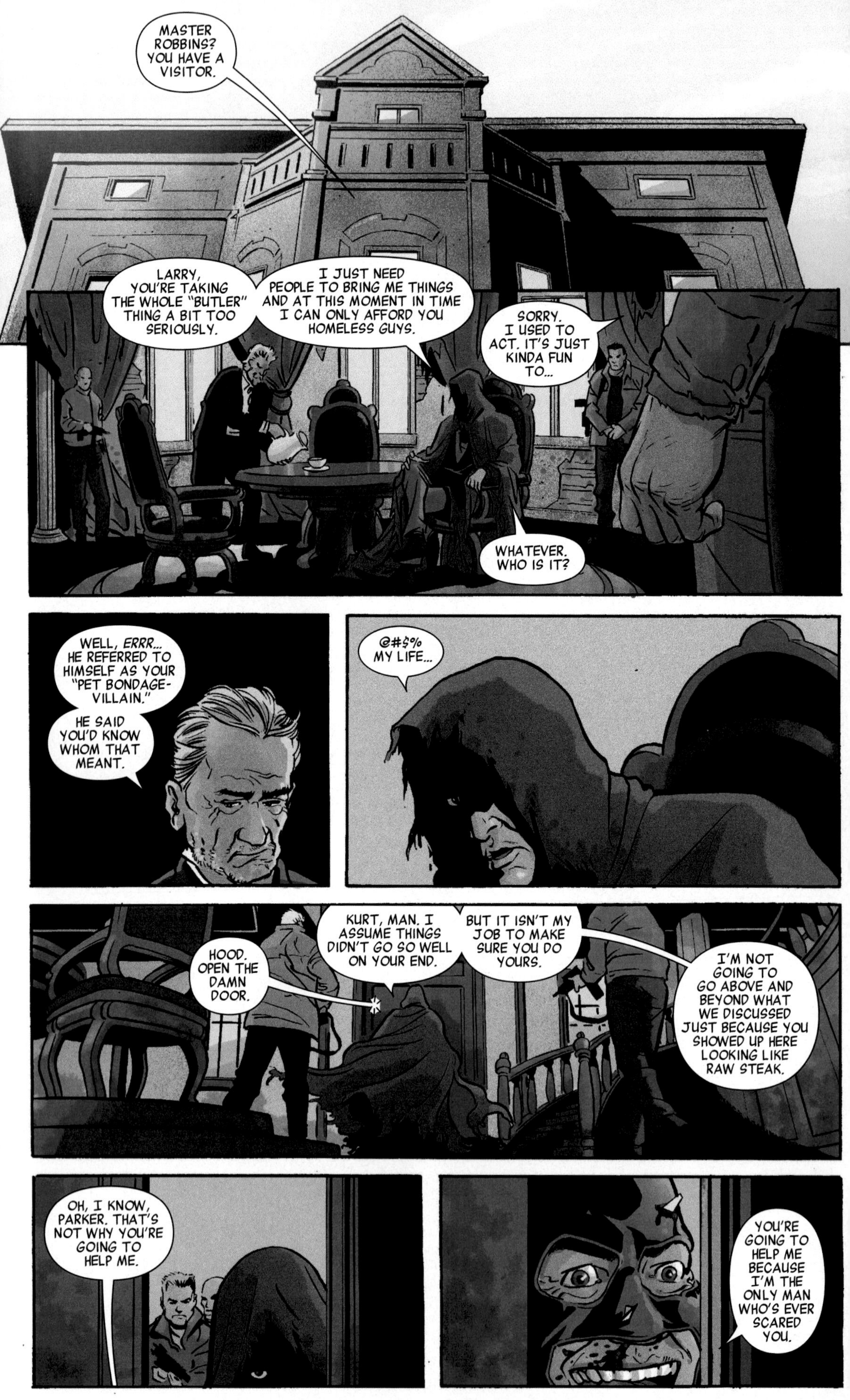
MASTER ROBBINS? YOU HAVE A VISITOR.
LARRY, YOU'RE TAKING THE WHOLE "BUTLER" THING A BIT TOO SERIOUSLY.
I JUST NEED PEOPLE TO BRING ME THINGS AND AT THIS MOMENT IN TIME I CAN ONLY AFFORD YOU HOMELESS GUYS.
SORRY. I USED TO ACT. IT'S JUST KINDA FUN TO...
WHATEVER. WHO IS IT?
WELL, *ERRR...* HE REFERRED TO HIMSELF AS YOUR "PET BONDAGE-VILLAIN."
HE SAID YOU'D KNOW WHOM THAT MEANT.
@#$% MY LIFE...
HOOD. OPEN THE DAMN DOOR.
KURT, MAN. I ASSUME THINGS DIDN'T GO SO WELL ON YOUR END.
BUT IT ISN'T MY JOB TO MAKE SURE YOU DO YOURS.
I'M NOT GOING TO GO ABOVE AND BEYOND WHAT WE DISCUSSED JUST BECAUSE YOU SHOWED UP HERE LOOKING LIKE RAW STEAK.
OH, I KNOW, PARKER. THAT'S NOT WHY YOU'RE GOING TO HELP ME.
YOU'RE GOING TO HELP ME BECAUSE I'M THE ONLY MAN WHO'S EVER SCARED YOU.

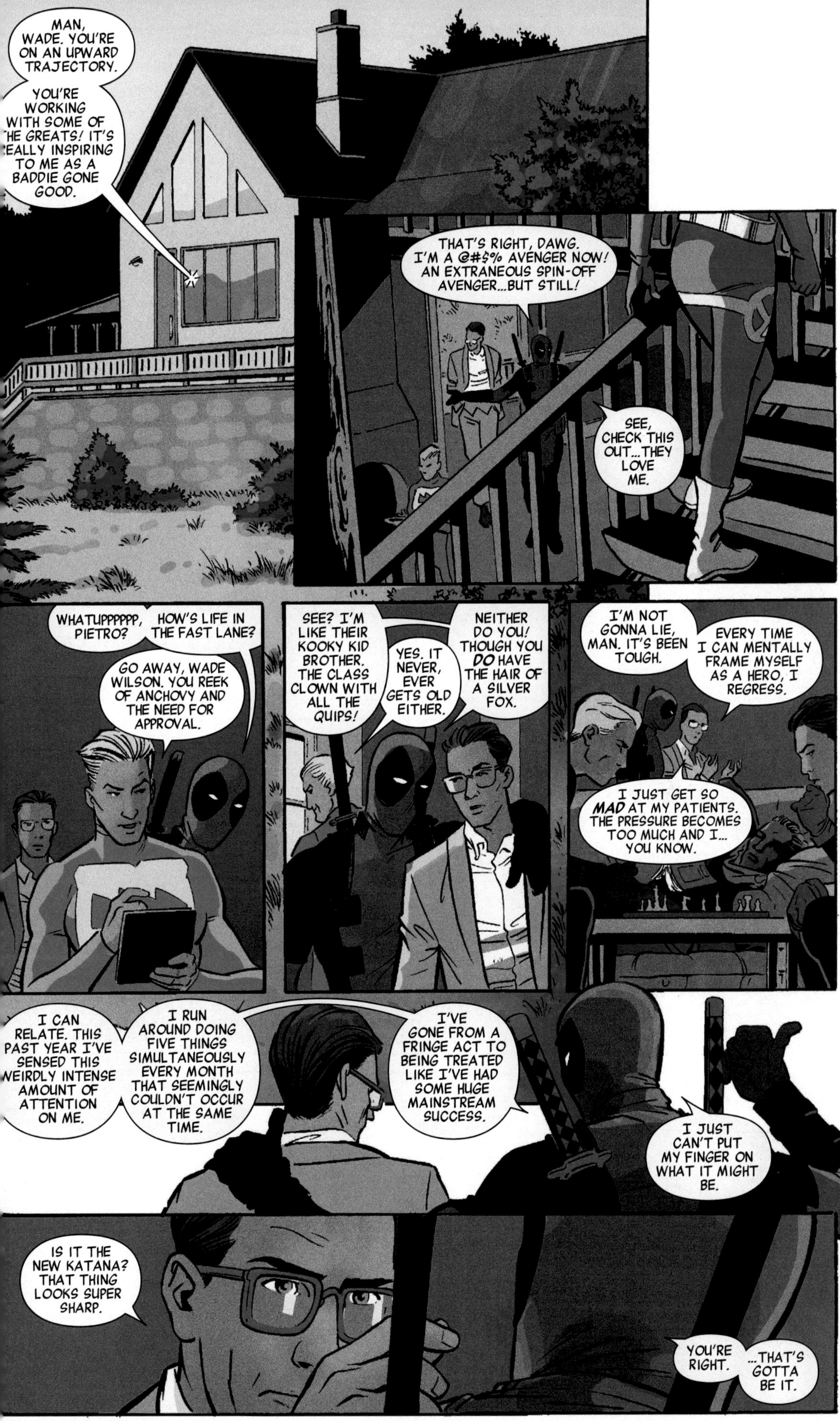
MAN, WADE. YOU'RE ON AN UPWARD TRAJECTORY.
YOU'RE WORKING WITH SOME OF HE GREATS! IT'S EALLY INSPIRING TO ME AS A BADDIE GONE GOOD.
THAT'S RIGHT, DAWG. I'M A @#$% AVENGER NOW! AN EXTRANEOUS SPIN-OFF AVENGER...BUT STILL!
SEE, CHECK THIS OUT...THEY LOVE ME.
WHATUPPPPPP, PIETRO?
HOW'S LIFE IN THE FAST LANE?
GO AWAY, WADE WILSON. YOU REEK OF ANCHOVY AND THE NEED FOR APPROVAL.
SEE? I'M LIKE THEIR KOOKY KID BROTHER. THE CLASS CLOWN WITH ALL THE QUIPS!
YES. IT NEVER, EVER GETS OLD EITHER.
NEITHER DO YOU! THOUGH YOU DO HAVE THE HAIR OF A SILVER FOX.
I'M NOT GONNA LIE, MAN. IT'S BEEN TOUGH.
EVERY TIME I CAN MENTALLY FRAME MYSELF AS A HERO, I REGRESS.
I JUST GET SO MAD AT MY PATIENTS. THE PRESSURE BECOMES TOO MUCH AND I... YOU KNOW.
I CAN RELATE. THIS PAST YEAR I'VE SENSED THIS EIRDLY INTENSE AMOUNT OF ATTENTION ON ME.
I RUN AROUND DOING FIVE THINGS SIMULTANEOUSLY EVERY MONTH THAT SEEMINGLY COULDN'T OCCUR AT THE SAME TIME.
I'VE GONE FROM A FRINGE ACT TO BEING TREATED LIKE I'VE HAD SOME HUGE MAINSTREAM SUCCESS.
I JUST CAN'T PUT MY FINGER ON WHAT IT MIGHT BE.
IS IT THE NEW KATANA? THAT THING LOOKS SUPER SHARP.
YOU'RE RIGHT.
...THAT'S GOTTA BE IT.

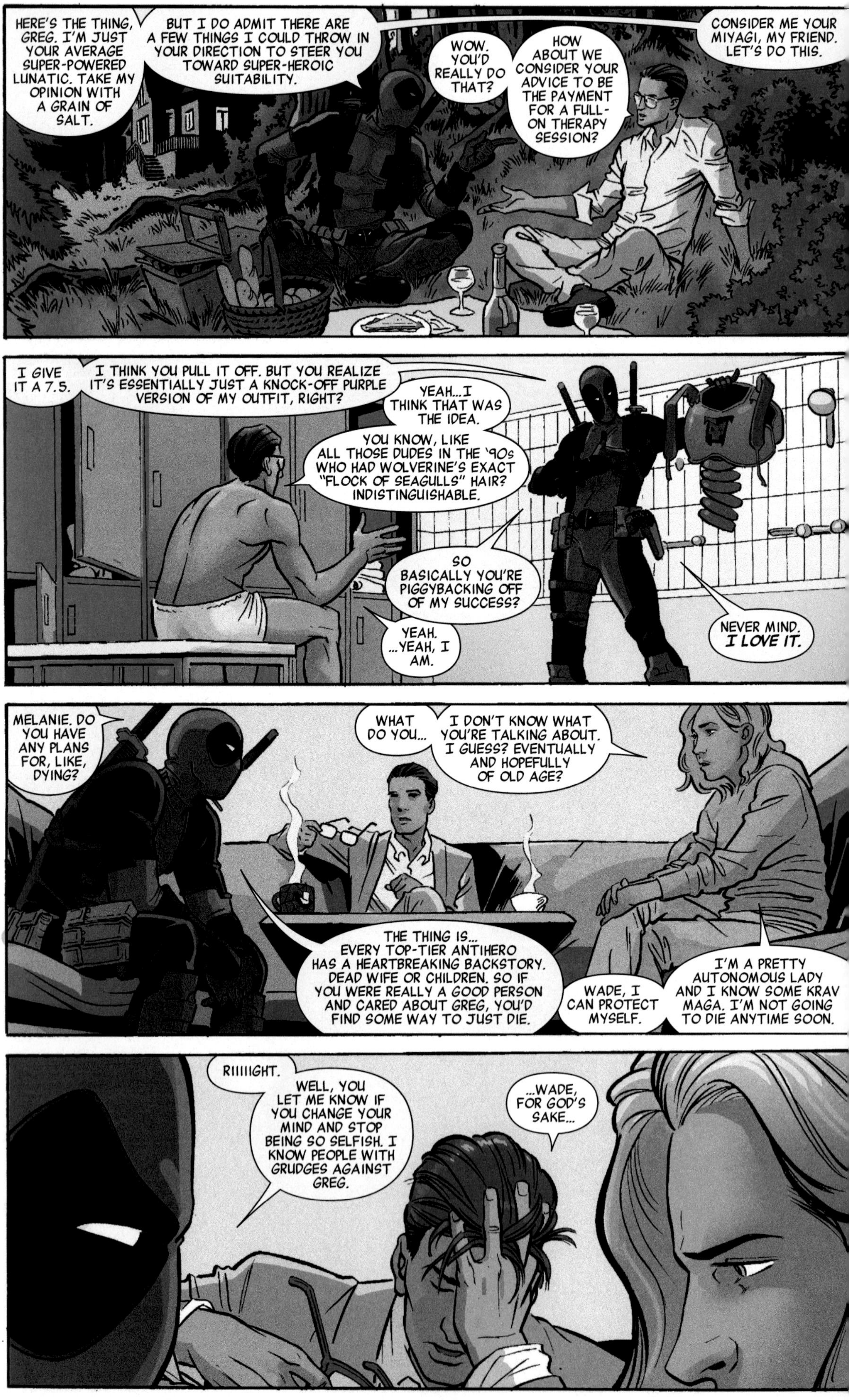
HERE'S THE THING, GREG. I'M JUST YOUR AVERAGE SUPER-POWERED LUNATIC. TAKE MY OPINION WITH A GRAIN OF SALT.
BUT I DO ADMIT THERE ARE A FEW THINGS I COULD THROW IN YOUR DIRECTION TO STEER YOU TOWARD SUPER-HEROIC SUITABILITY.
WOW. YOU'D REALLY DO THAT?
HOW ABOUT WE CONSIDER YOUR ADVICE TO BE THE PAYMENT FOR A FULL-ON THERAPY SESSION?
CONSIDER ME YOUR MIYAGI, MY FRIEND. LET'S DO THIS.
I GIVE IT A 7.5.
I THINK YOU PULL IT OFF. BUT YOU REALIZE IT'S ESSENTIALLY JUST A KNOCK-OFF PURPLE VERSION OF MY OUTFIT, RIGHT?
YEAH...I THINK THAT WAS THE IDEA.
YOU KNOW, LIKE ALL THOSE DUDES IN THE '90s WHO HAD WOLVERINE'S EXACT "FLOCK OF SEAGULLS" HAIR? INDISTINGUISHABLE.
SO BASICALLY YOU'RE PIGGYBACKING OFF OF MY SUCCESS?
YEAH. ...YEAH, I AM.
NEVER MIND. I LOVE IT.
MELANIE. DO YOU HAVE ANY PLANS FOR, LIKE, DYING?
WHAT DO YOU...
I DON'T KNOW WHAT YOU'RE TALKING ABOUT. I GUESS? EVENTUALLY AND HOPEFULLY OF OLD AGE?
THE THING IS... EVERY TOP-TIER ANTIHERO HAS A HEARTBREAKING BACKSTORY. DEAD WIFE OR CHILDREN. SO IF YOU WERE REALLY A GOOD PERSON AND CARED ABOUT GREG, YOU'D FIND SOME WAY TO JUST DIE.
WADE, I CAN PROTECT MYSELF.
I'M A PRETTY AUTONOMOUS LADY AND I KNOW SOME KRAV MAGA. I'M NOT GOING TO DIE ANYTIME SOON.
RIIIIIGHT.
WELL, YOU LET ME KNOW IF YOU CHANGE YOUR MIND AND STOP BEING SO SELFISH. I KNOW PEOPLE WITH GRUDGES AGAINST GREG.
...WADE, FOR GOD'S SAKE...

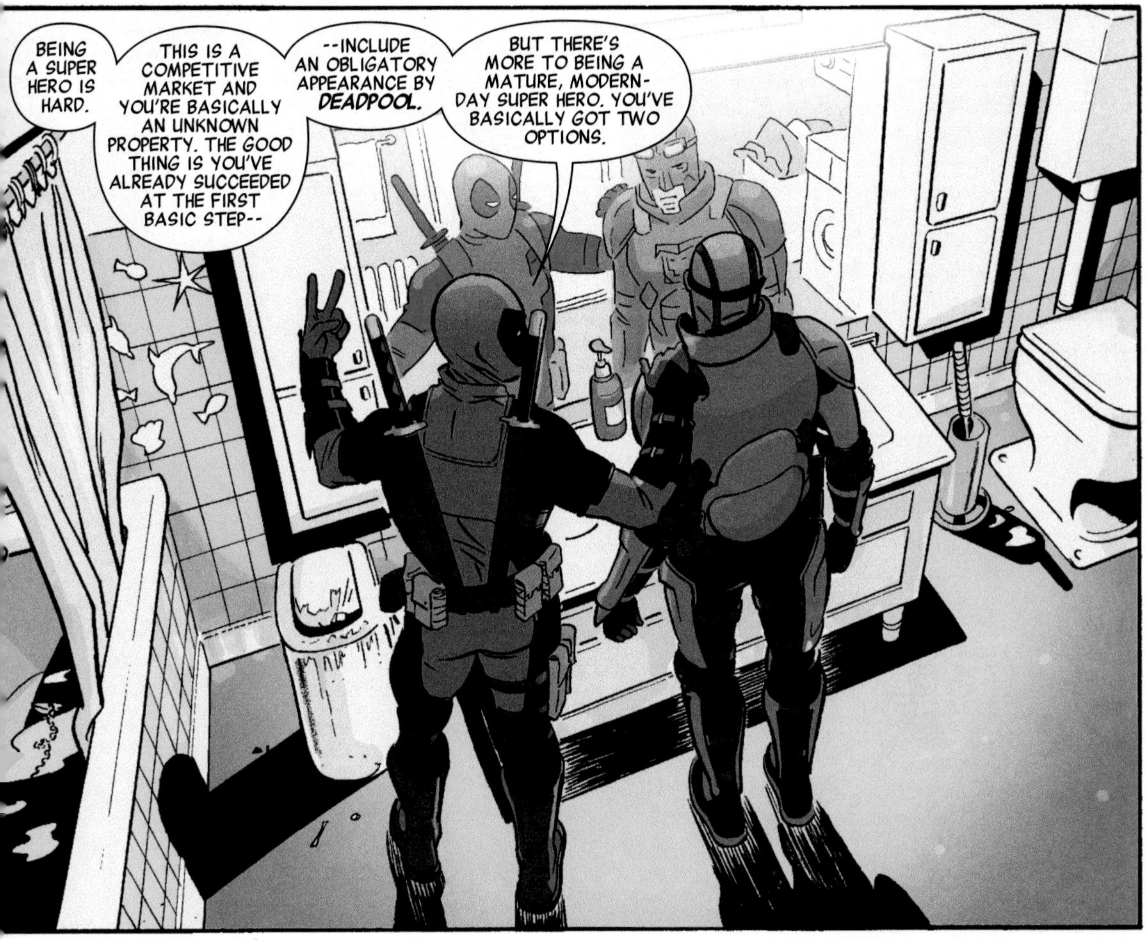

BEING A SUPER HERO IS HARD.
THIS IS A COMPETITIVE MARKET AND YOU'RE BASICALLY AN UNKNOWN PROPERTY. THE GOOD THING IS YOU'VE ALREADY SUCCEEDED AT THE FIRST BASIC STEP--
--INCLUDE AN OBLIGATORY APPEARANCE BY DEADPOOL.
BUT THERE'S MORE TO BEING A MATURE, MODERN-DAY SUPER HERO. YOU'VE BASICALLY GOT TWO OPTIONS.

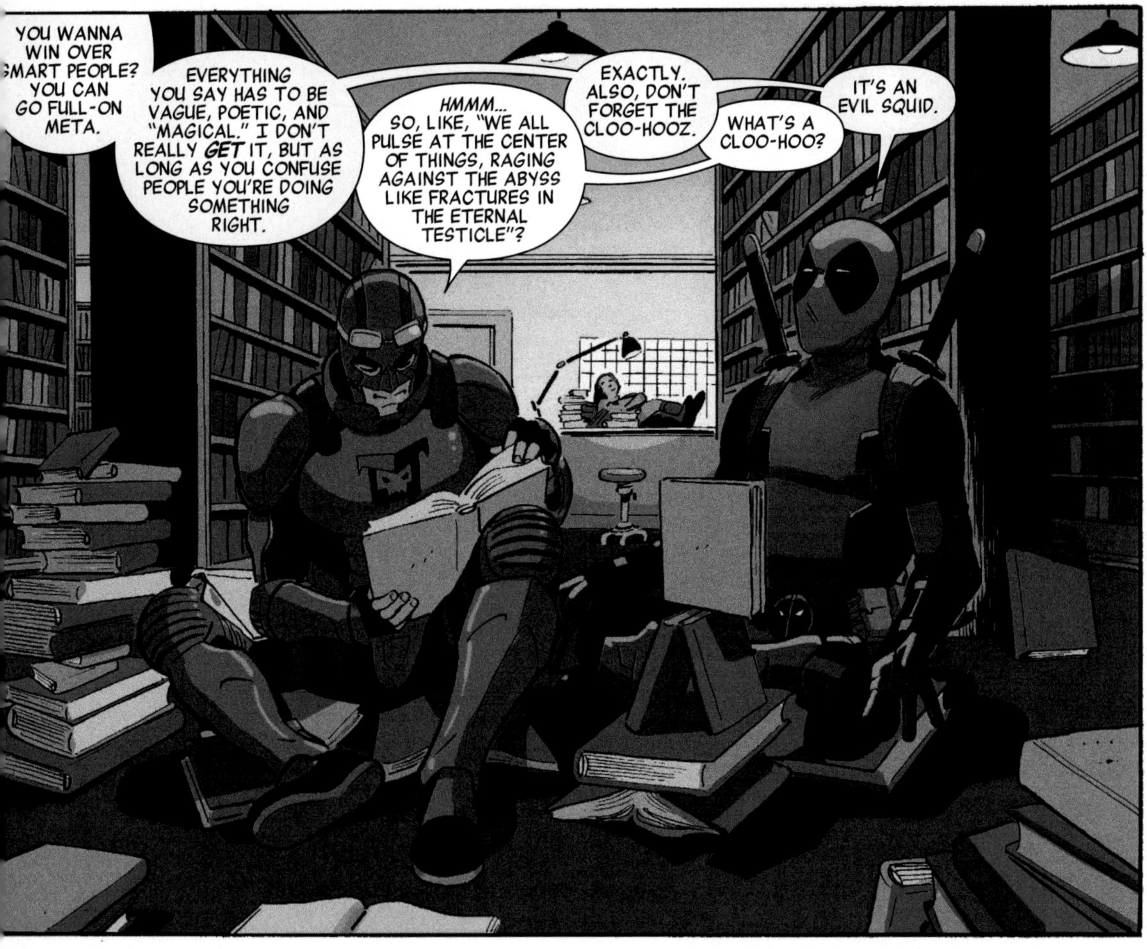

YOU WANNA WIN OVER SMART PEOPLE? YOU CAN GO FULL-ON META.
EVERYTHING YOU SAY HAS TO BE VAGUE, POETIC, AND "MAGICAL." I DON'T REALLY GET IT, BUT AS LONG AS YOU CONFUSE PEOPLE YOU'RE DOING SOMETHING RIGHT.
HMMM... SO, LIKE, "WE ALL PULSE AT THE CENTER OF THINGS, RAGING AGAINST THE ABYSS LIKE FRACTURES IN THE ETERNAL TESTICLE"?
EXACTLY. ALSO, DON'T FORGET THE CLOO-HOOZ.
WHAT'S A CLOO-HOO?
IT'S AN EVIL SQUID.

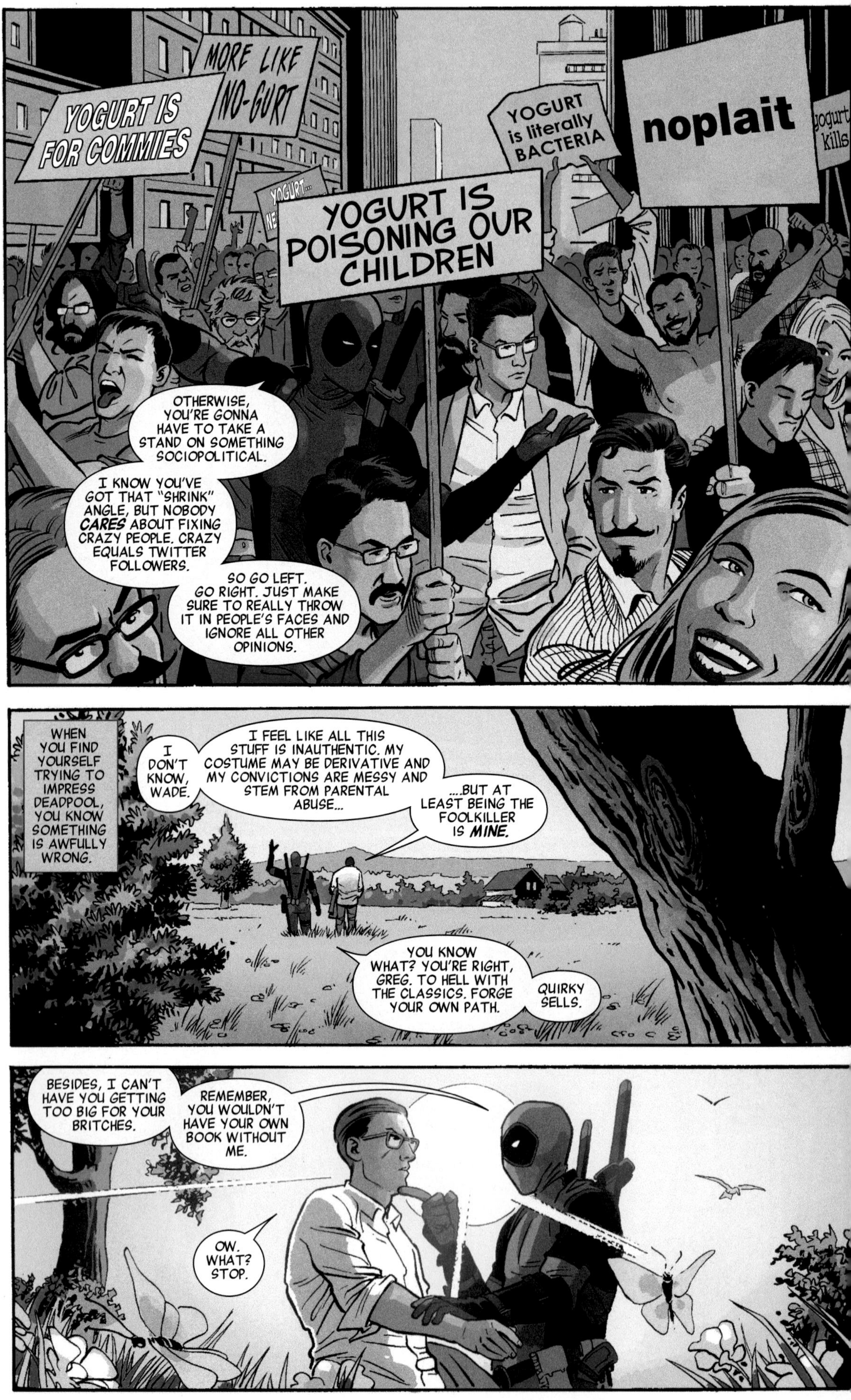
MORE LIKE NO-GURT
YOGURT IS FOR COMMIES
YOGURT...
YOGURT IS POISONING OUR CHILDREN
YOGURT is literally BACTERIA
noplait
yogurt kills
OTHERWISE, YOU'RE GONNA HAVE TO TAKE A STAND ON SOMETHING SOCIOPOLITICAL.
I KNOW YOU'VE GOT THAT "SHRINK" ANGLE, BUT NOBODY CARES ABOUT FIXING CRAZY PEOPLE. CRAZY EQUALS TWITTER FOLLOWERS.
SO GO LEFT. GO RIGHT. JUST MAKE SURE TO REALLY THROW IT IN PEOPLE'S FACES AND IGNORE ALL OTHER OPINIONS.
WHEN YOU FIND YOURSELF TRYING TO IMPRESS DEADPOOL, YOU KNOW SOMETHING IS AWFULLY WRONG.
I DON'T KNOW, WADE.
I FEEL LIKE ALL THIS STUFF IS INAUTHENTIC. MY COSTUME MAY BE DERIVATIVE AND MY CONVICTIONS ARE MESSY AND STEM FROM PARENTAL ABUSE...
....BUT AT LEAST BEING THE FOOLKILLER IS MINE.
YOU KNOW WHAT? YOU'RE RIGHT, GREG. TO HELL WITH THE CLASSICS. FORGE YOUR OWN PATH.
QUIRKY SELLS.
BESIDES, I CAN'T HAVE YOU GETTING TOO BIG FOR YOUR BRITCHES.
REMEMBER, YOU WOULDN'T HAVE YOUR OWN BOOK WITHOUT ME.
OW. WHAT? STOP.

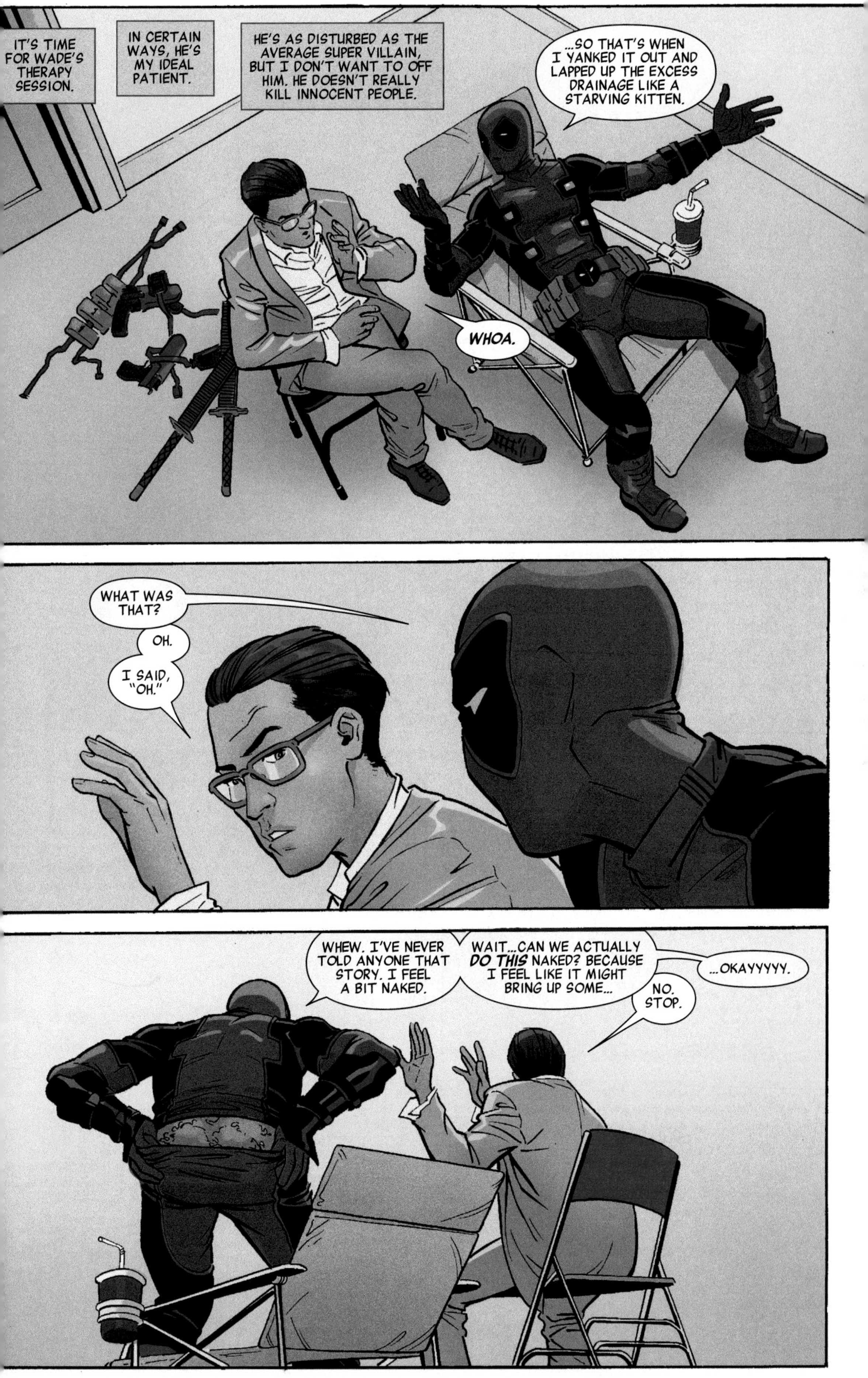

IT'S TIME FOR WADE'S THERAPY SESSION.
IN CERTAIN WAYS, HE'S MY IDEAL PATIENT.
HE'S AS DISTURBED AS THE AVERAGE SUPER VILLAIN, BUT I DON'T WANT TO OFF HIM. HE DOESN'T REALLY KILL INNOCENT PEOPLE.
...SO THAT'S WHEN I YANKED IT OUT AND LAPPED UP THE EXCESS DRAINAGE LIKE A STARVING KITTEN.
WHOA.
WHAT WAS THAT?
OH.
I SAID, "OH."
WHEW. I'VE NEVER TOLD ANYONE THAT STORY. I FEEL A BIT NAKED.
WAIT...CAN WE ACTUALLY DO THIS NAKED? BECAUSE I FEEL LIKE IT MIGHT BRING UP SOME...
...OKAYYYYY.
NO. STOP.

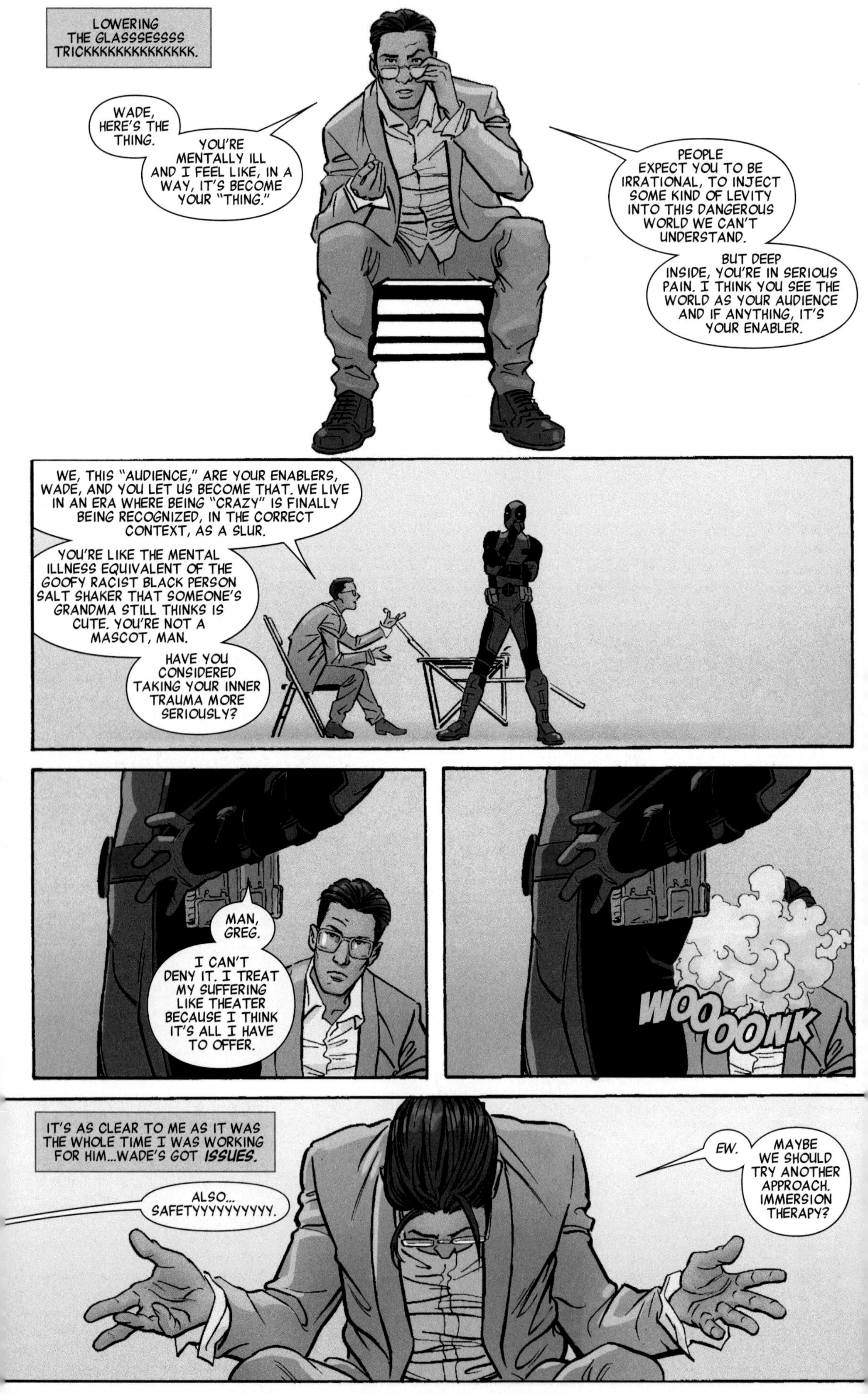
LOWERING THE GLASSSESSSS TRICKKKKKKKKKKKKK.
WADE, HERE'S THE THING.
YOU'RE MENTALLY ILL AND I FEEL LIKE, IN A WAY, IT'S BECOME YOUR "THING."
PEOPLE EXPECT YOU TO BE IRRATIONAL, TO INJECT SOME KIND OF LEVITY INTO THIS DANGEROUS WORLD WE CAN'T UNDERSTAND.
BUT DEEP INSIDE, YOU'RE IN SERIOUS PAIN. I THINK YOU SEE THE WORLD AS YOUR AUDIENCE AND IF ANYTHING, IT'S YOUR ENABLER.
WE, THIS "AUDIENCE," ARE YOUR ENABLERS, WADE, AND YOU LET US BECOME THAT. WE LIVE IN AN ERA WHERE BEING "CRAZY" IS FINALLY BEING RECOGNIZED, IN THE CORRECT CONTEXT, AS A SLUR.
YOU'RE LIKE THE MENTAL ILLNESS EQUIVALENT OF THE GOOFY RACIST BLACK PERSON SALT SHAKER THAT SOMEONE'S GRANDMA STILL THINKS IS CUTE. YOU'RE NOT A MASCOT, MAN.
HAVE YOU CONSIDERED TAKING YOUR INNER TRAUMA MORE SERIOUSLY?
MAN, GREG.
I CAN'T DENY IT. I TREAT MY SUFFERING LIKE THEATER BECAUSE I THINK IT'S ALL I HAVE TO OFFER.
WOOOONK
IT'S AS CLEAR TO ME AS IT WAS THE WHOLE TIME I WAS WORKING FOR HIM...WADE'S GOT ISSUES.
ALSO... SAFETYYYYYYYYYYY.
EW.
MAYBE WE SHOULD TRY ANOTHER APPROACH. IMMERSION THERAPY?

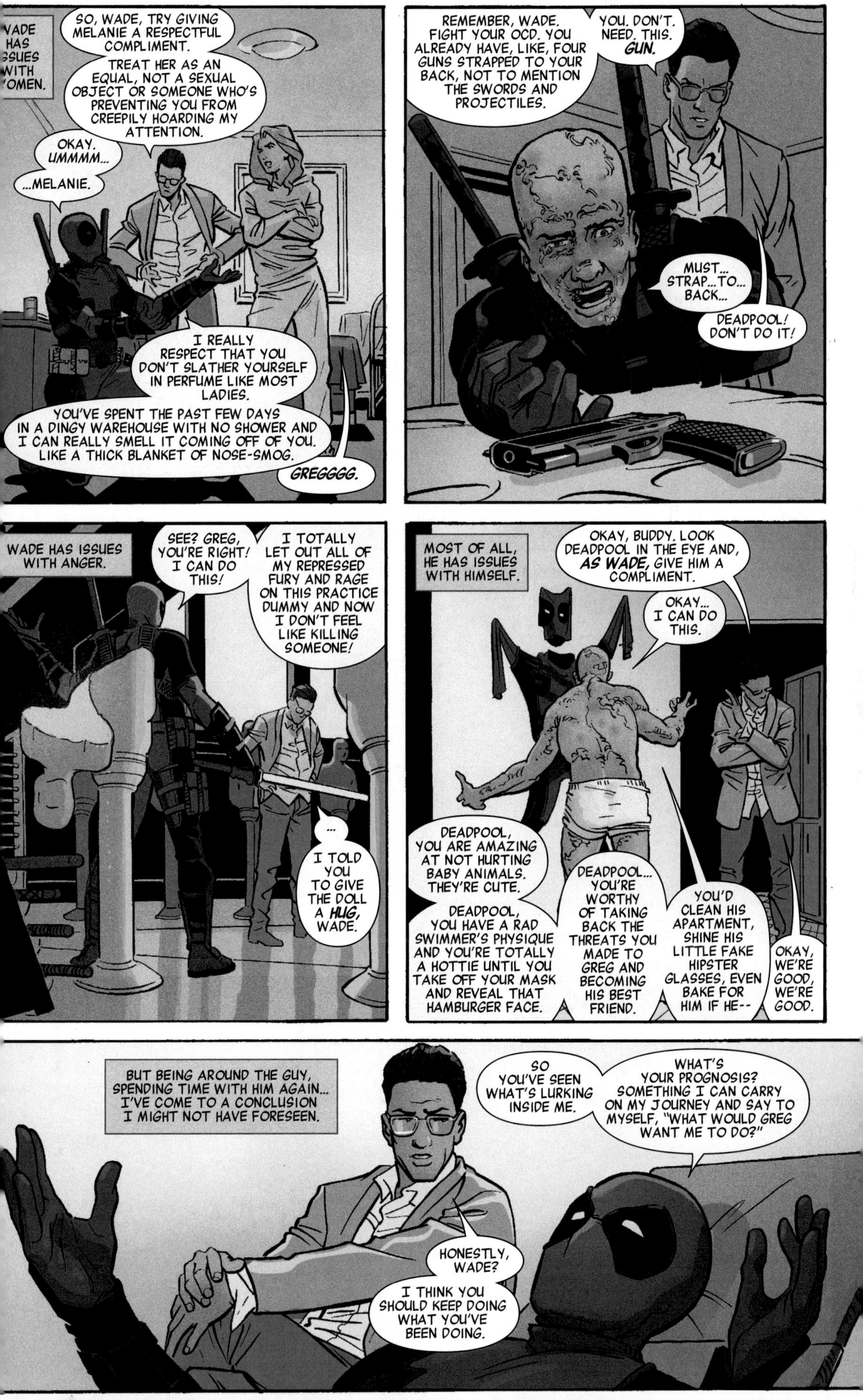
WADE HAS ISSUES WITH WOMEN.
SO, WADE, TRY GIVING MELANIE A RESPECTFUL COMPLIMENT.
TREAT HER AS AN EQUAL, NOT A SEXUAL OBJECT OR SOMEONE WHO'S PREVENTING YOU FROM CREEPILY HOARDING MY ATTENTION.
OKAY. UMMMM...
...MELANIE.
I REALLY RESPECT THAT YOU DON'T SLATHER YOURSELF IN PERFUME LIKE MOST LADIES.
YOU'VE SPENT THE PAST FEW DAYS IN A DINGY WAREHOUSE WITH NO SHOWER AND I CAN REALLY SMELL IT COMING OFF OF YOU. LIKE A THICK BLANKET OF NOSE-SMOG.
GREGGGG.
REMEMBER, WADE. FIGHT YOUR OCD. YOU ALREADY HAVE, LIKE, FOUR GUNS STRAPPED TO YOUR BACK, NOT TO MENTION THE SWORDS AND PROJECTILES.
YOU. DON'T. NEED. THIS. GUN.
MUST... STRAP...TO... BACK...
DEADPOOL! DON'T DO IT!
WADE HAS ISSUES WITH ANGER.
SEE? GREG, YOU'RE RIGHT! I CAN DO THIS!
I TOTALLY LET OUT ALL OF MY REPRESSED FURY AND RAGE ON THIS PRACTICE DUMMY AND NOW I DON'T FEEL LIKE KILLING SOMEONE!
...
I TOLD YOU TO GIVE THE DOLL A HUG, WADE.
MOST OF ALL, HE HAS ISSUES WITH HIMSELF.
OKAY, BUDDY. LOOK DEADPOOL IN THE EYE AND, AS WADE, GIVE HIM A COMPLIMENT.
OKAY... I CAN DO THIS.
DEADPOOL, YOU ARE AMAZING AT NOT HURTING BABY ANIMALS. THEY'RE CUTE.
DEADPOOL, YOU HAVE A RAD SWIMMER'S PHYSIQUE AND YOU'RE TOTALLY A HOTTIE UNTIL YOU TAKE OFF YOUR MASK AND REVEAL THAT HAMBURGER FACE.
DEADPOOL... YOU'RE WORTHY OF TAKING BACK THE THREATS YOU MADE TO GREG AND BECOMING HIS BEST FRIEND.
YOU'D CLEAN HIS APARTMENT, SHINE HIS LITTLE FAKE HIPSTER GLASSES, EVEN BAKE FOR HIM IF HE--
OKAY, WE'RE GOOD, WE'RE GOOD.
BUT BEING AROUND THE GUY, SPENDING TIME WITH HIM AGAIN... I'VE COME TO A CONCLUSION I MIGHT NOT HAVE FORESEEN.
SO YOU'VE SEEN WHAT'S LURKING INSIDE ME.
WHAT'S YOUR PROGNOSIS? SOMETHING I CAN CARRY ON MY JOURNEY AND SAY TO MYSELF, "WHAT WOULD GREG WANT ME TO DO?"
HONESTLY, WADE?
I THINK YOU SHOULD KEEP DOING WHAT YOU'VE BEEN DOING.

LOOK, WE BOTH KNOW IF IT WERE UP TO ME YOU WOULD BE TAKING A FISTFUL OF PILLS EVERY DAY AND ATTENDING ABOUT...WELL, TWELVE TWELVE-STEP GROUPS. BUT WE BOTH KNOW THAT'S NOT GOING TO HAPPEN.

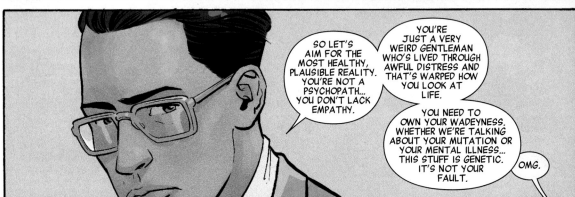

SO LET'S AIM FOR THE MOST HEALTHY, PLAUSIBLE REALITY. YOU'RE NOT A PSYCHOPATH... YOU DON'T LACK EMPATHY.

YOU'RE JUST A VERY WEIRD GENTLEMAN WHO'S LIVED THROUGH AWFUL DISTRESS AND THAT'S WARPED HOW YOU LOOK AT LIFE.

YOU NEED TO OWN YOUR WADEYNESS. WHETHER WE'RE TALKING ABOUT YOUR MUTATION OR YOUR MENTAL ILLNESS... THIS STUFF IS GENETIC. IT'S NOT YOUR FAULT.

OMG.

THIS IS OUR GOOD WILL HUNTING MOMENT. CAN I WEEP INTO YOUR ARMS?

I DON'T KNOW, DO YOU FEEL LIKE CRYING?

NOT REALLY, BUT IF I THINK ABOUT PUPPIES DYING I CAN PROBABLY...

NO, THEN. NO, YOU CAN'T WEEP INTO MY ARMS.

I GUESS YOU'RE RIGHT. AS LONG AS I'M NOT HURTING BYSTANDERS, IT'S ALL SOMEWHAT LEGIT.

THAT'S RIGHT. POINT IN FACT, YOU'RE THE FIRST OFFICIAL PATIENT I'VE HAD THAT I DIDN'T THINK DESERVED TO DIE.

THAT'S AN HONOR. THANK YOU, GREG.

BUT I HAVE TO ASK...

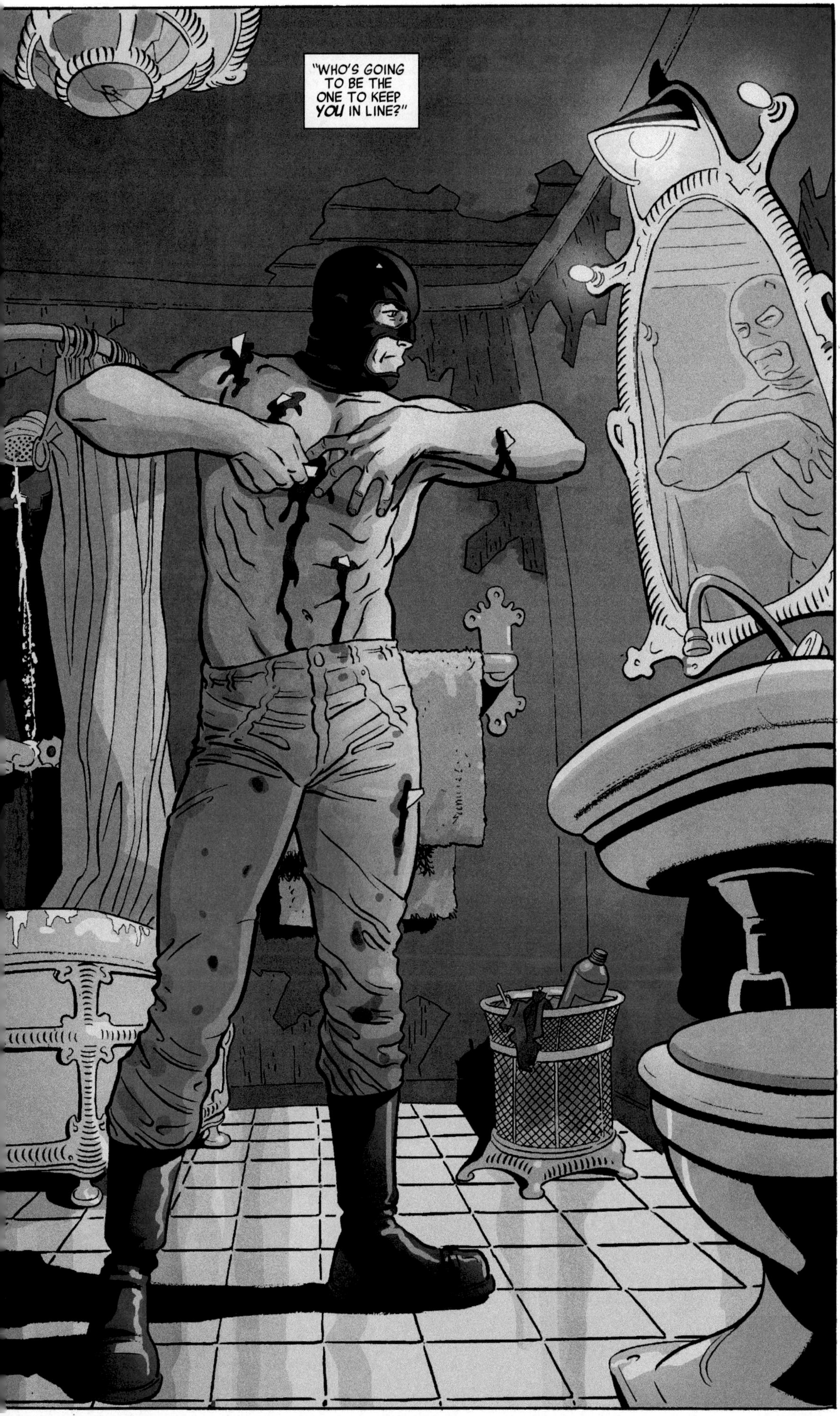
"WHO'S GOING TO BE THE ONE TO KEEP *YOU* IN LINE?"

I'M GLAD YOU AND WADE GOT TO DO THE WHOLE MALE-BONDING THING.

THE GUY CLEARLY NEEDED IT.

I'M SORRY HE'S UNKIND TO YOU. WADE JUST CHERISHES HIS FRIENDSHIPS, THAT'S ALL.

GREG, HE WANTS YOU TO BECOME HIS SIDEKICK AND ABSCOND WITH HIM TO A EUROPEAN COUNTRY.

...I KNOW.

EITHER WAY, I CAN'T THANK YOU ENOUGH FOR STICKING WITH ME THROUGH ALL OF THIS. MELANIE, YOU'RE THE MOST LOYAL, AMAZING...

I'M NOT.

...TRUSTWORTHY, BEAUTIFUL...

GREG... I'M NOT.

WHAT'S A GREGIMNOT?

I'M NOT GOING TO STICK BY YOU.

I DO LOVE YOU, GREG. I DO.

AND I'M SURE IT'LL BE EASY TO COMPARTMENTALIZE ME AS THE "GIRL WHO WASN'T COOL ENOUGH FOR YOUR VIGILANTE LIFESTYLE."

BUT I GOT KIDNAPPED TODAY. PEOPLE ARE DIGGING INTO MY DARKEST SECRETS AND THREATENING TO EXPOSE THEM. THESE ARE THINGS I'VE PUT BEHIND ME. FOR GOOD REASON, TOO.

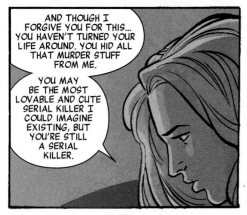

AND THOUGH I FORGIVE YOU FOR THIS... YOU HAVEN'T TURNED YOUR LIFE AROUND. YOU HID ALL THAT MURDER STUFF FROM ME.

YOU MAY BE THE MOST LOVABLE AND CUTE SERIAL KILLER I COULD IMAGINE EXISTING, BUT YOU'RE STILL A SERIAL KILLER.

IN THE WRONG CONTEXT, SERIAL KILLER CAN BE A PEJORATIVE TERM FOR A GOOD OL' FASHIONED VIGILANTE...

THAT'S GOBBLEDYGOOK COMIC BOOK SPEECH, GREG.

I'M LEAVING TOMORROW, GOING BACK TO MY MOM'S. BEING WITH YOU IS...*MORALLY IRRESPONSIBLE.*

YOU'LL FIND YOUR MATCH ONE DAY, GREG. I BELIEVE THAT.

DESPITE WHAT YOU'VE DONE, YOU'RE A GOOD GUY. THROUGH AND THROUGH.

AND THIS WAS ONE HELL OF AN ADVENTURE. THANK YOU FOR THAT.

YOU'RE WELCOME, MEL.

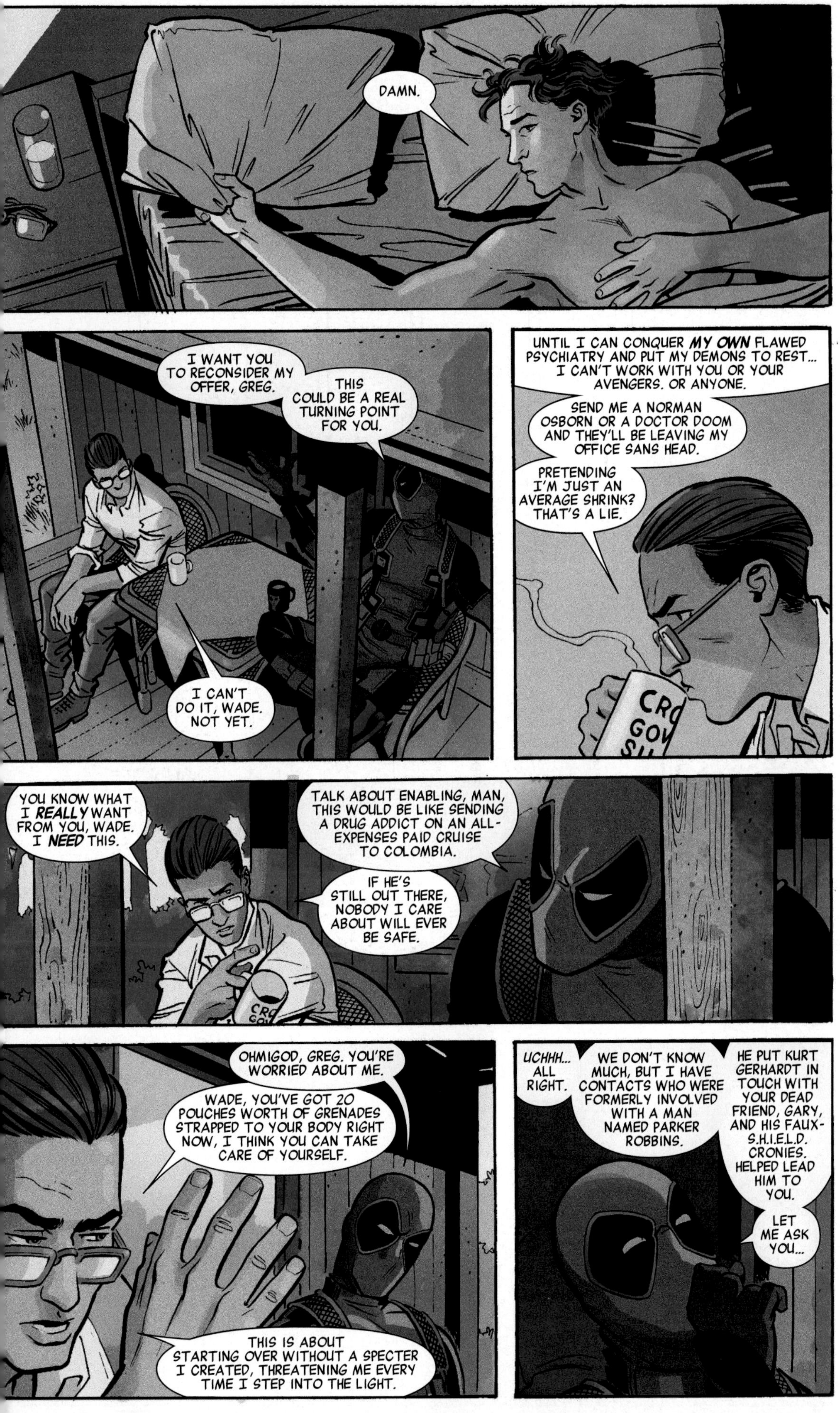
DAMN.
I WANT YOU TO RECONSIDER MY OFFER, GREG.
THIS COULD BE A REAL TURNING POINT FOR YOU.
I CAN'T DO IT, WADE. NOT YET.
UNTIL I CAN CONQUER MY OWN FLAWED PSYCHIATRY AND PUT MY DEMONS TO REST... I CAN'T WORK WITH YOU OR YOUR AVENGERS. OR ANYONE.
SEND ME A NORMAN OSBORN OR A DOCTOR DOOM AND THEY'LL BE LEAVING MY OFFICE SANS HEAD.
PRETENDING I'M JUST AN AVERAGE SHRINK? THAT'S A LIE.
YOU KNOW WHAT I REALLY WANT FROM YOU, WADE. I NEED THIS.
TALK ABOUT ENABLING, MAN, THIS WOULD BE LIKE SENDING A DRUG ADDICT ON AN ALL-EXPENSES PAID CRUISE TO COLOMBIA.
IF HE'S STILL OUT THERE, NOBODY I CARE ABOUT WILL EVER BE SAFE.
OHMIGOD, GREG. YOU'RE WORRIED ABOUT ME.
WADE, YOU'VE GOT 20 POUCHES WORTH OF GRENADES STRAPPED TO YOUR BODY RIGHT NOW, I THINK YOU CAN TAKE CARE OF YOURSELF.
THIS IS ABOUT STARTING OVER WITHOUT A SPECTER I CREATED, THREATENING ME EVERY TIME I STEP INTO THE LIGHT.
UCHHH... ALL RIGHT.
WE DON'T KNOW MUCH, BUT I HAVE CONTACTS WHO WERE FORMERLY INVOLVED WITH A MAN NAMED PARKER ROBBINS.
HE PUT KURT GERHARDT IN TOUCH WITH YOUR DEAD FRIEND, GARY, AND HIS FAUX-S.H.I.E.L.D. CRONIES. HELPED LEAD HIM TO YOU.
LET ME ASK YOU...

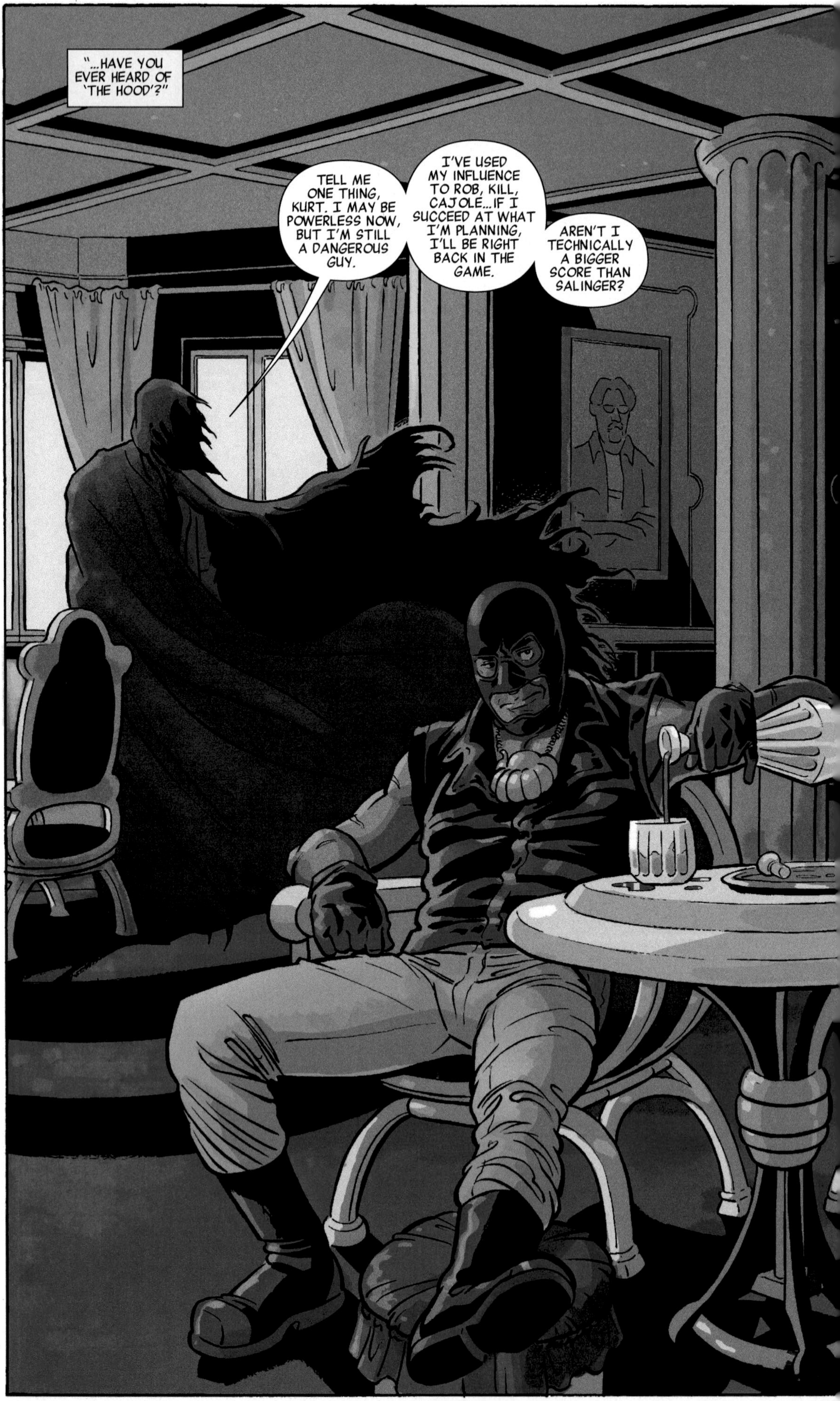
"...HAVE YOU EVER HEARD OF 'THE HOOD'?"
TELL ME ONE THING, KURT. I MAY BE POWERLESS NOW, BUT I'M STILL A DANGEROUS GUY.
I'VE USED MY INFLUENCE TO ROB, KILL, CAJOLE...IF I SUCCEED AT WHAT I'M PLANNING, I'LL BE RIGHT BACK IN THE GAME.
AREN'T I TECHNICALLY A BIGGER SCORE THAN SALINGER?

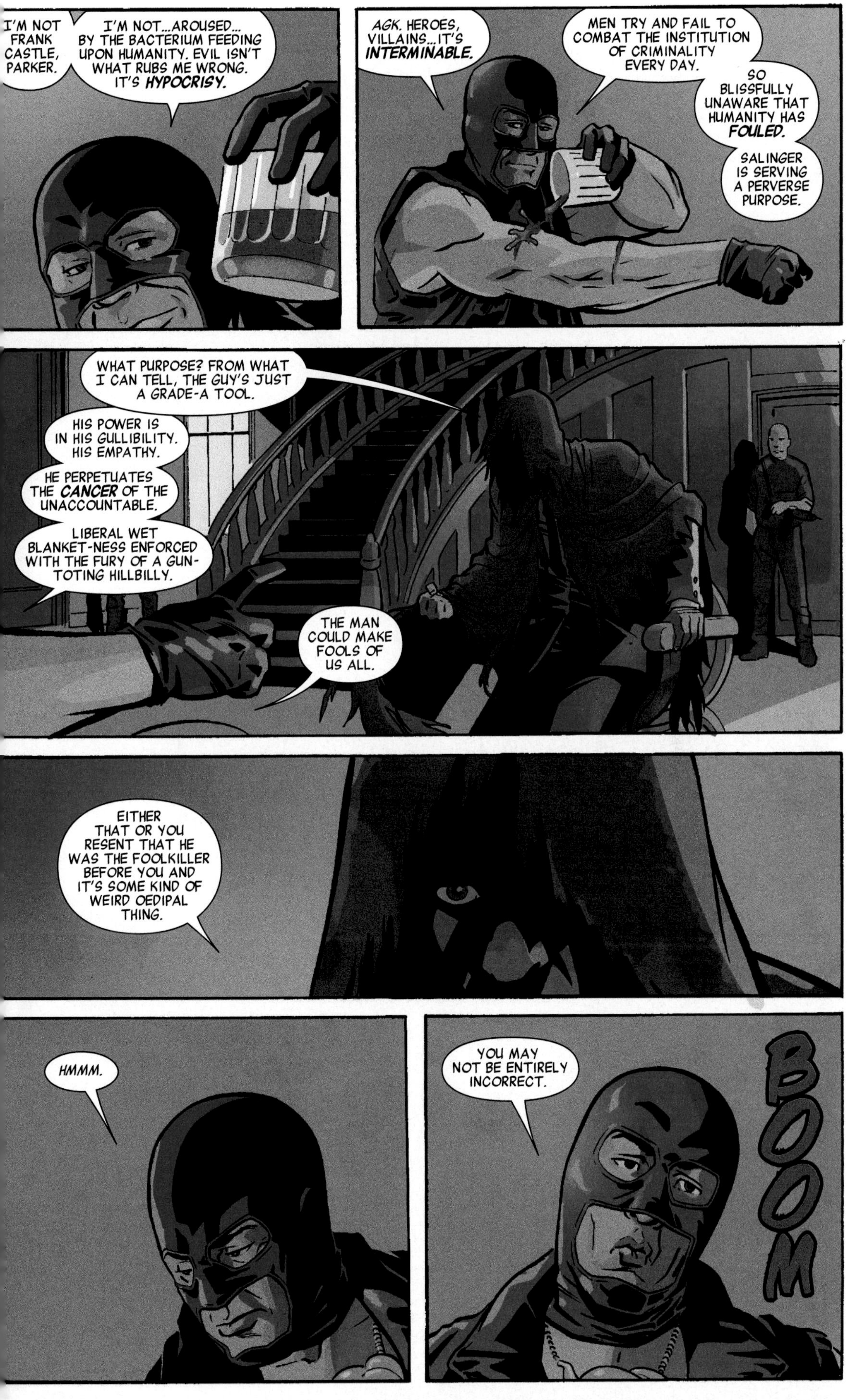
I'M NOT FRANK CASTLE, PARKER.
I'M NOT...AROUSED... BY THE BACTERIUM FEEDING UPON HUMANITY. EVIL ISN'T WHAT RUBS ME WRONG. IT'S HYPOCRISY.
AGK. HEROES, VILLAINS...IT'S INTERMINABLE.
MEN TRY AND FAIL TO COMBAT THE INSTITUTION OF CRIMINALITY EVERY DAY.
SO BLISSFULLY UNAWARE THAT HUMANITY HAS FOULED.
SALINGER IS SERVING A PERVERSE PURPOSE.
WHAT PURPOSE? FROM WHAT I CAN TELL, THE GUY'S JUST A GRADE-A TOOL.
HIS POWER IS IN HIS GULLIBILITY. HIS EMPATHY.
HE PERPETUATES THE CANCER OF THE UNACCOUNTABLE.
LIBERAL WET BLANKET-NESS ENFORCED WITH THE FURY OF A GUN-TOTING HILLBILLY.
THE MAN COULD MAKE FOOLS OF US ALL.
EITHER THAT OR YOU RESENT THAT HE WAS THE FOOLKILLER BEFORE YOU AND IT'S SOME KIND OF WEIRD OEDIPAL THING.
HMMM.
YOU MAY NOT BE ENTIRELY INCORRECT.
BOOOOM

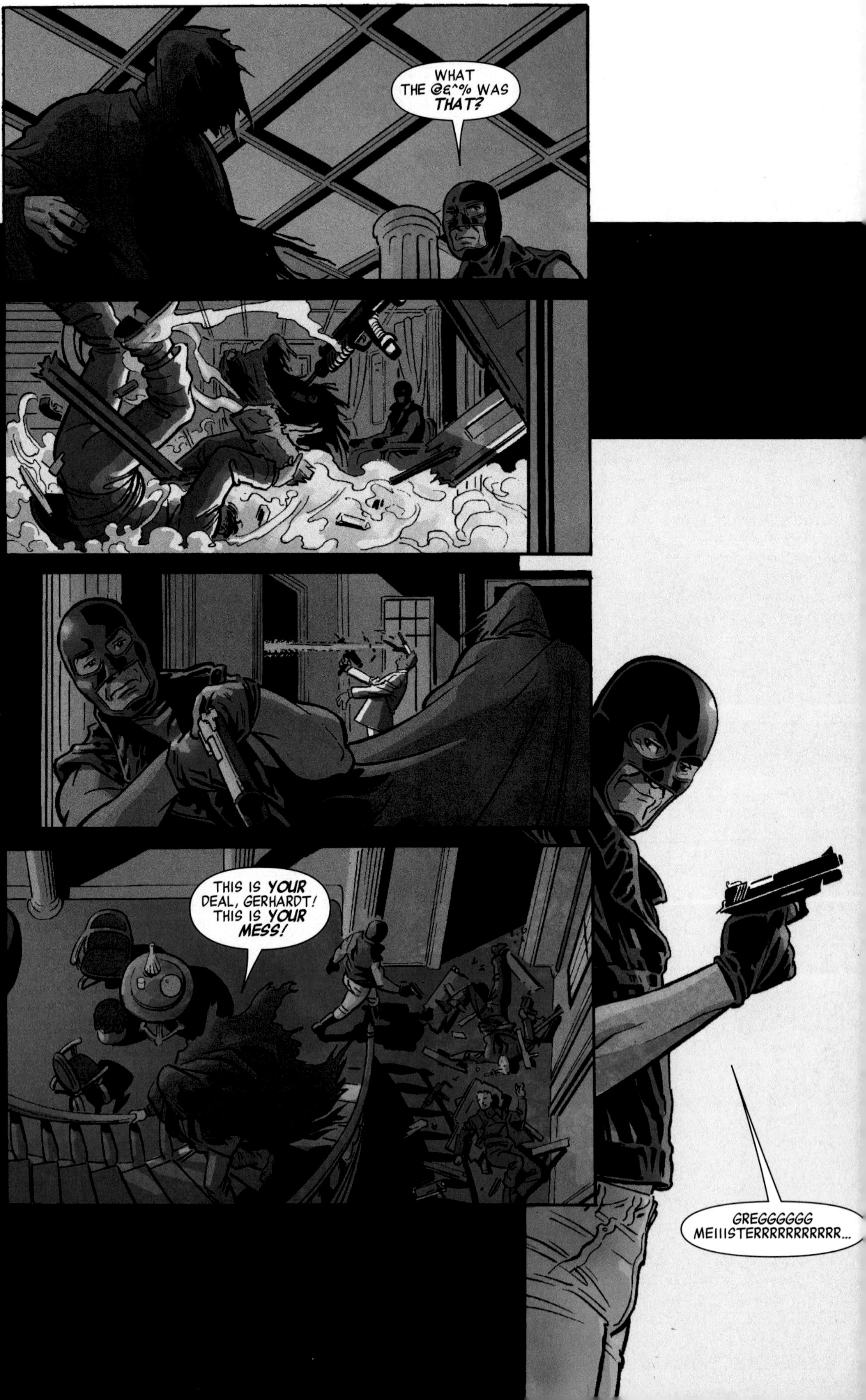

WHAT THE @ε^% WAS THAT?
THIS IS YOUR DEAL, GERHARDT! THIS IS YOUR MESS!
GREGGGGGG MEIIISTERRRRRRRRRR...

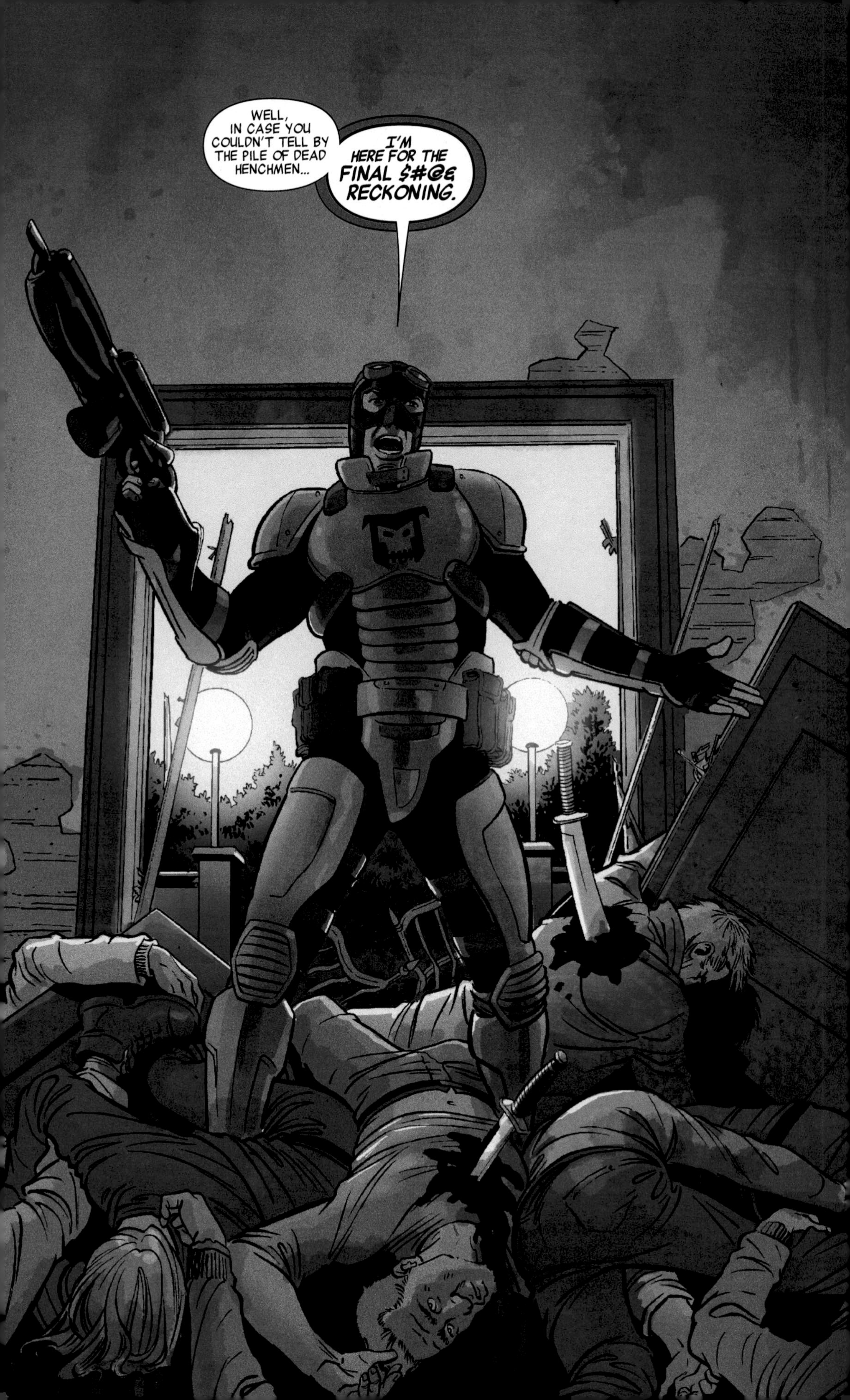
WELL, IN CASE YOU COULDN'T TELL BY THE PILE OF DEAD HENCHMEN...
I'M HERE FOR THE FINAL $#@& RECKONING.

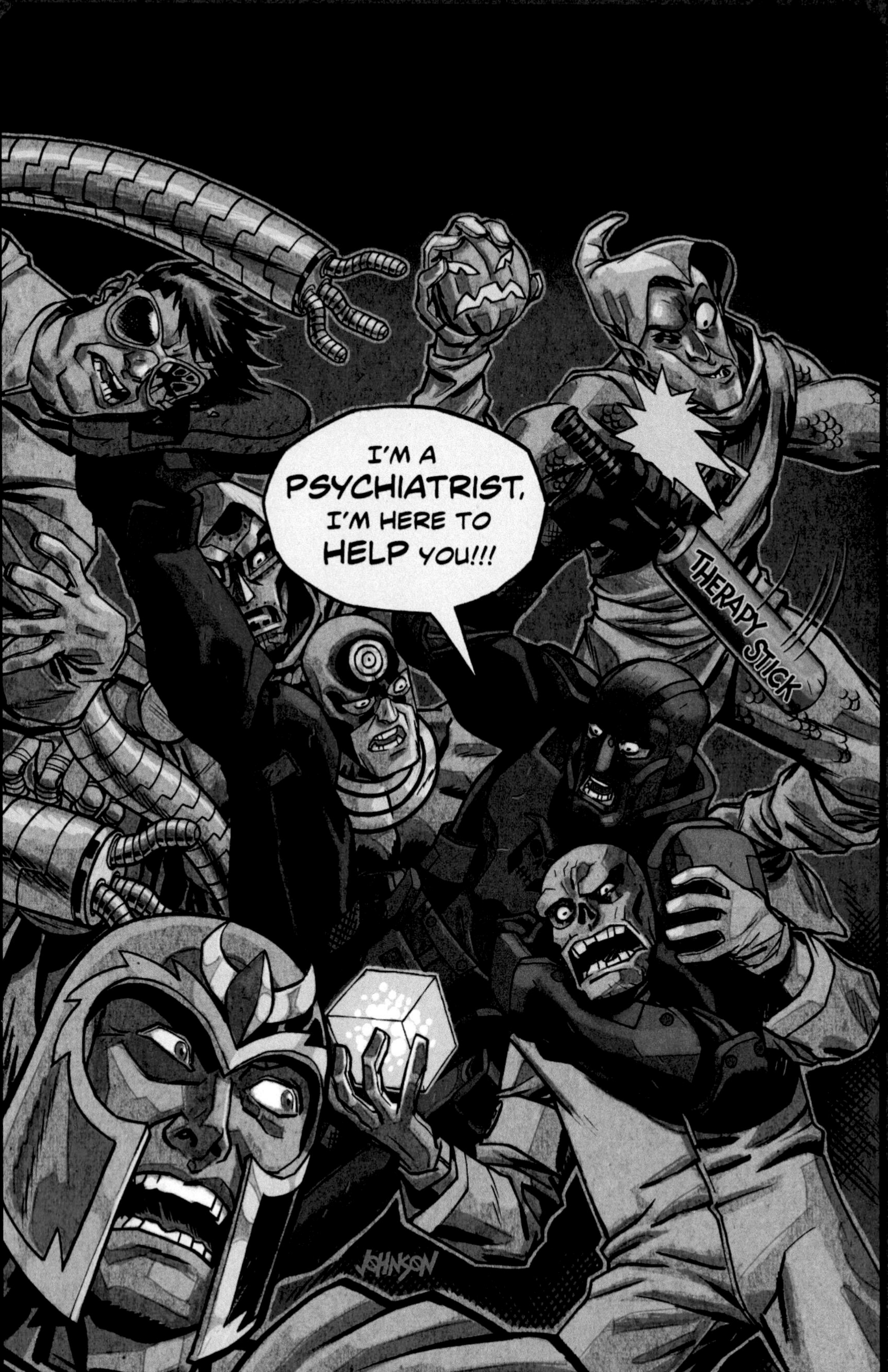
I'M A PSYCHIATRIST, I'M HERE TO HELP YOU!!!
THERAPY STICK
JOHNSON

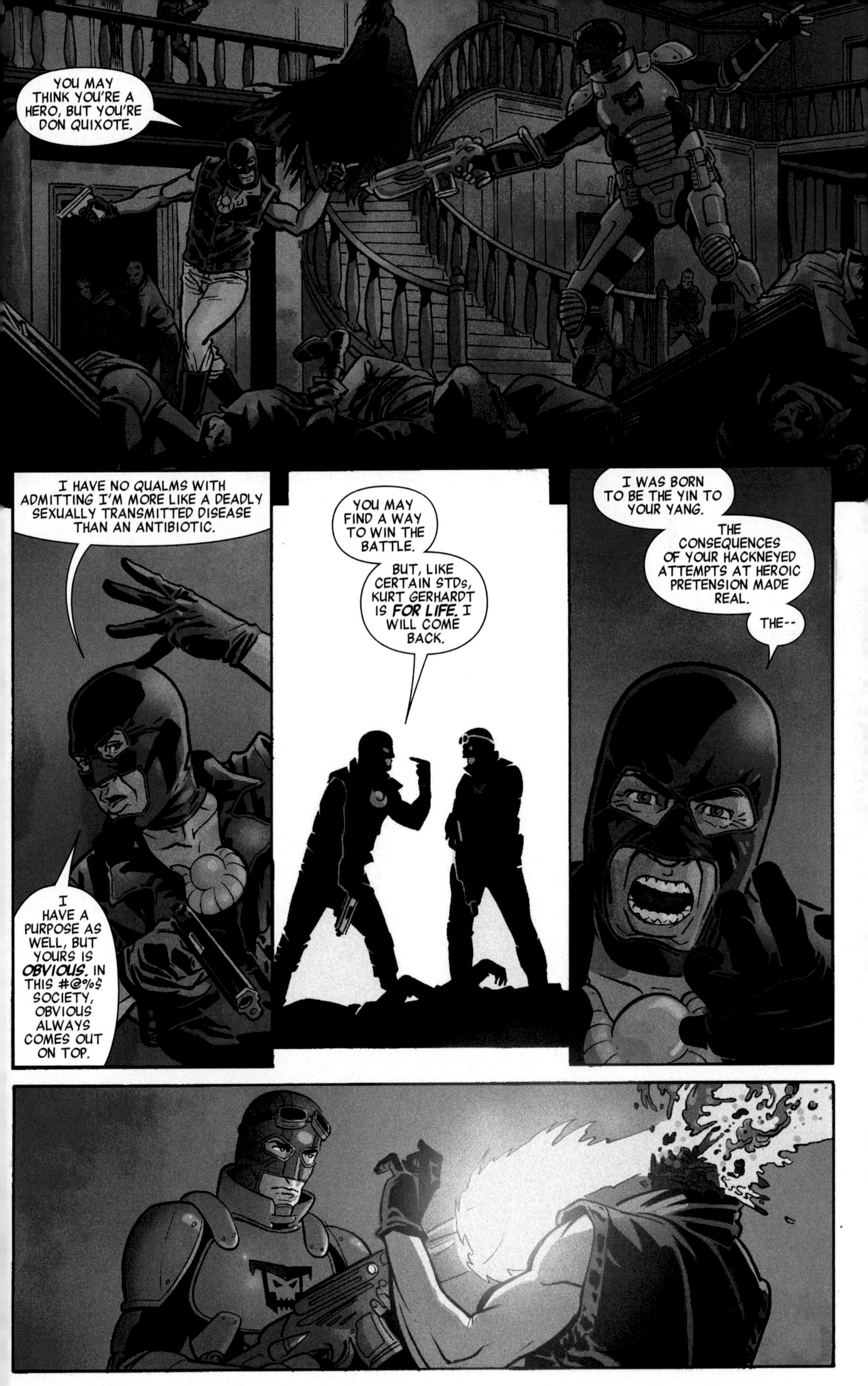
YOU MAY THINK YOU'RE A HERO, BUT YOU'RE DON QUIXOTE.
I HAVE NO QUALMS WITH ADMITTING I'M MORE LIKE A DEADLY SEXUALLY TRANSMITTED DISEASE THAN AN ANTIBIOTIC.
I HAVE A PURPOSE AS WELL, BUT YOURS IS OBVIOUS. IN THIS #@%$ SOCIETY, OBVIOUS ALWAYS COMES OUT ON TOP.
YOU MAY FIND A WAY TO WIN THE BATTLE.
BUT, LIKE CERTAIN STDs, KURT GERHARDT IS FOR LIFE. I WILL COME BACK.
I WAS BORN TO BE THE YIN TO YOUR YANG.
THE CONSEQUENCES OF YOUR HACKNEYED ATTEMPTS AT HEROIC PRETENSION MADE REAL.
THE--

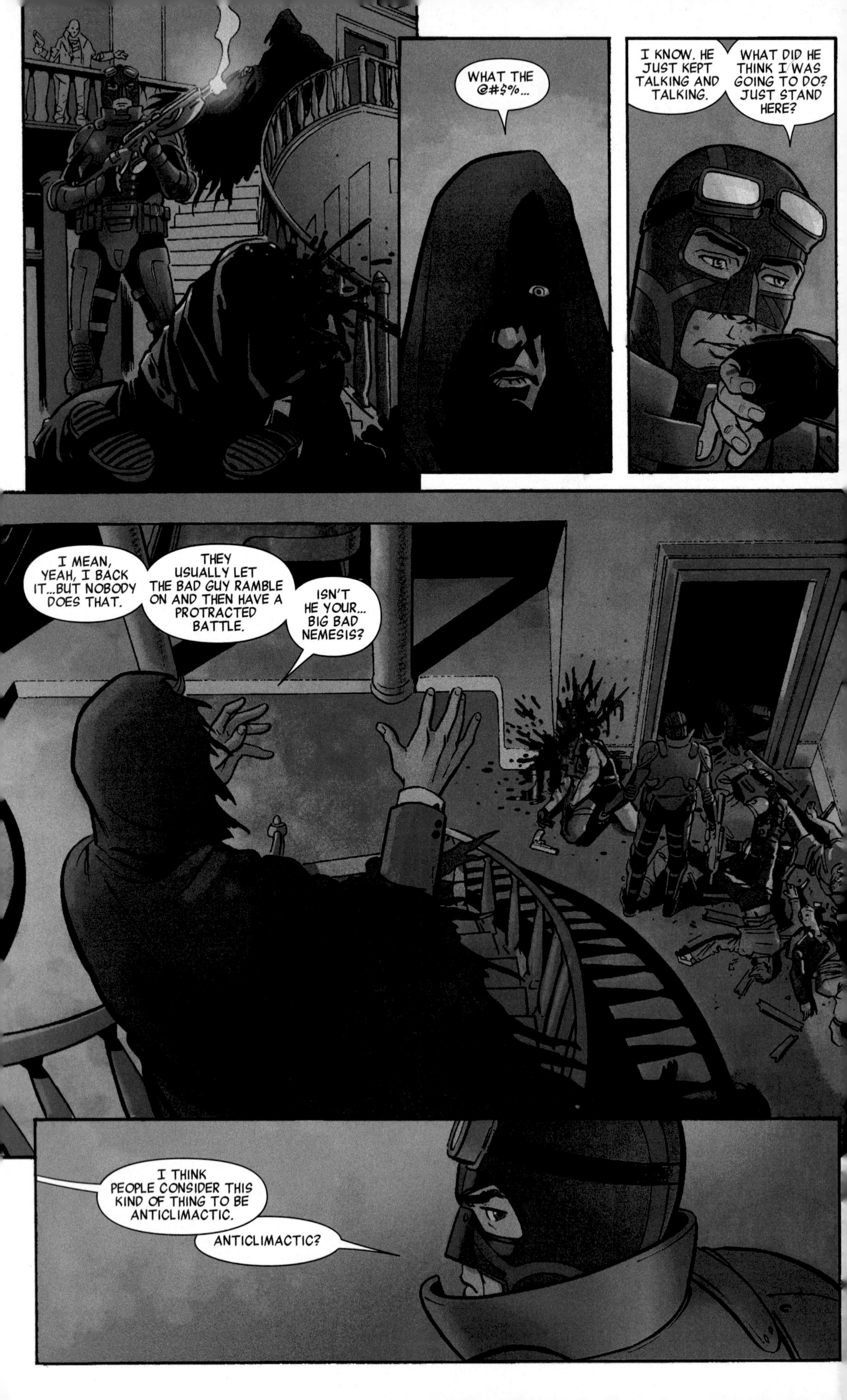
WHAT THE @#$%...
I KNOW. HE JUST KEPT TALKING AND TALKING.
WHAT DID HE THINK I WAS GOING TO DO? JUST STAND HERE?
I MEAN, YEAH, I BACK IT...BUT NOBODY DOES THAT.
THEY USUALLY LET THE BAD GUY RAMBLE ON AND THEN HAVE A PROTRACTED BATTLE.
ISN'T HE YOUR... BIG BAD NEMESIS?
I THINK PEOPLE CONSIDER THIS KIND OF THING TO BE ANTICLIMACTIC.
ANTICLIMACTIC?

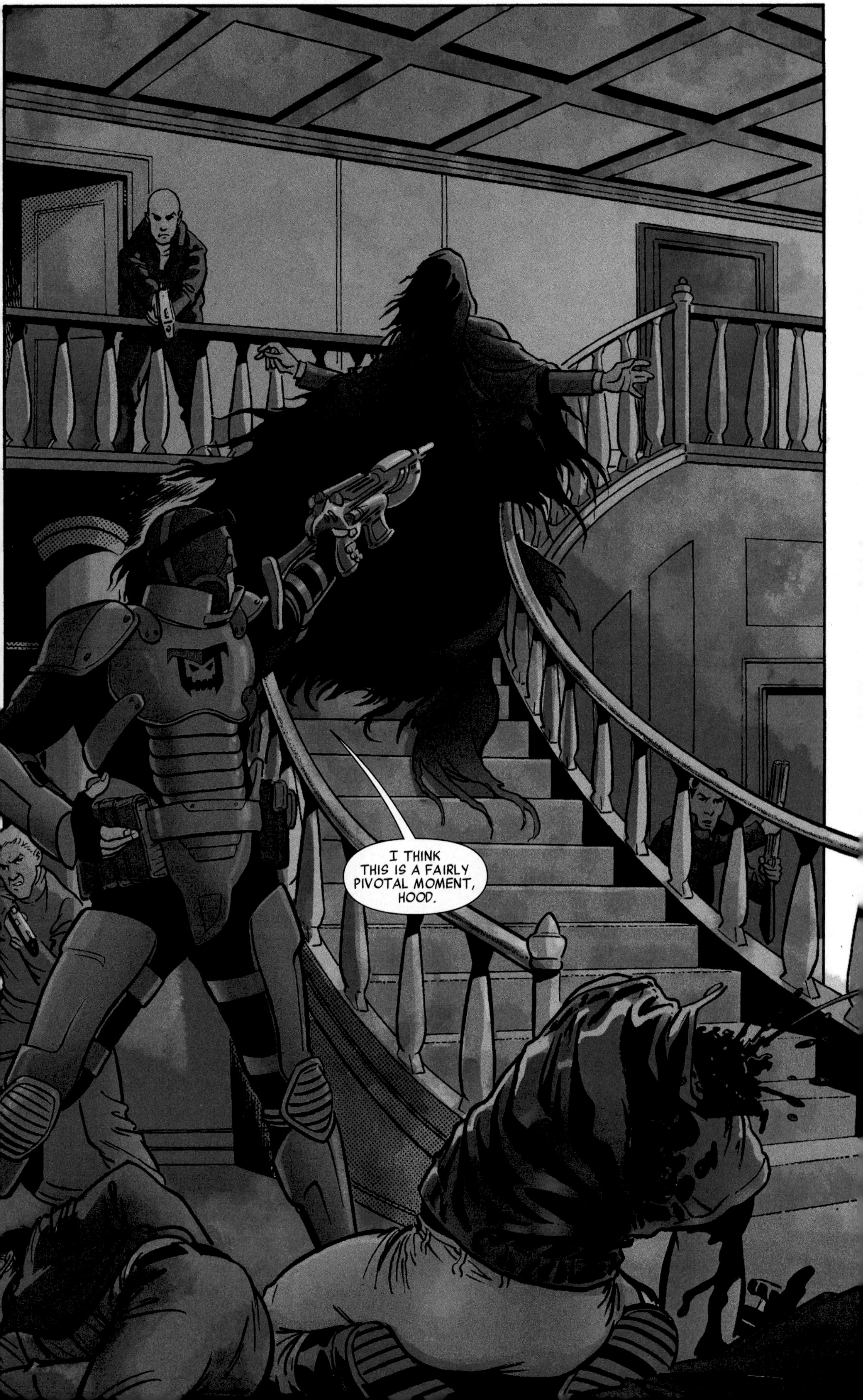
I THINK THIS IS A FAIRLY PIVOTAL MOMENT, HOOD.

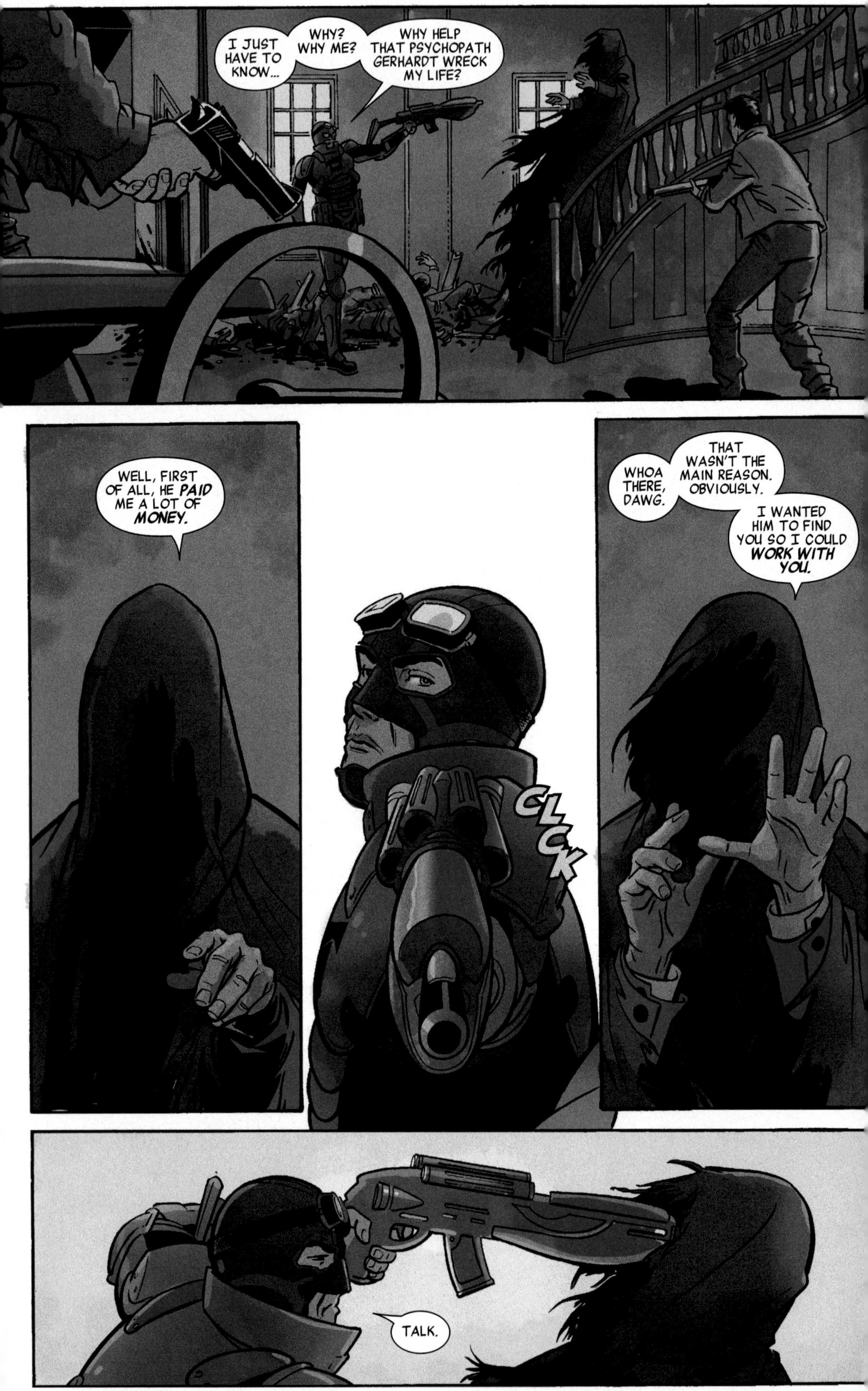

I JUST HAVE TO KNOW...
WHY? WHY ME?
WHY HELP THAT PSYCHOPATH GERHARDT WRECK MY LIFE?
WELL, FIRST OF ALL, HE **PAID** ME A LOT OF **MONEY.**
CLCK
WHOA THERE, DAWG.
THAT WASN'T THE MAIN REASON. OBVIOUSLY.
I WANTED HIM TO FIND YOU SO I COULD **WORK WITH YOU.**
TALK.

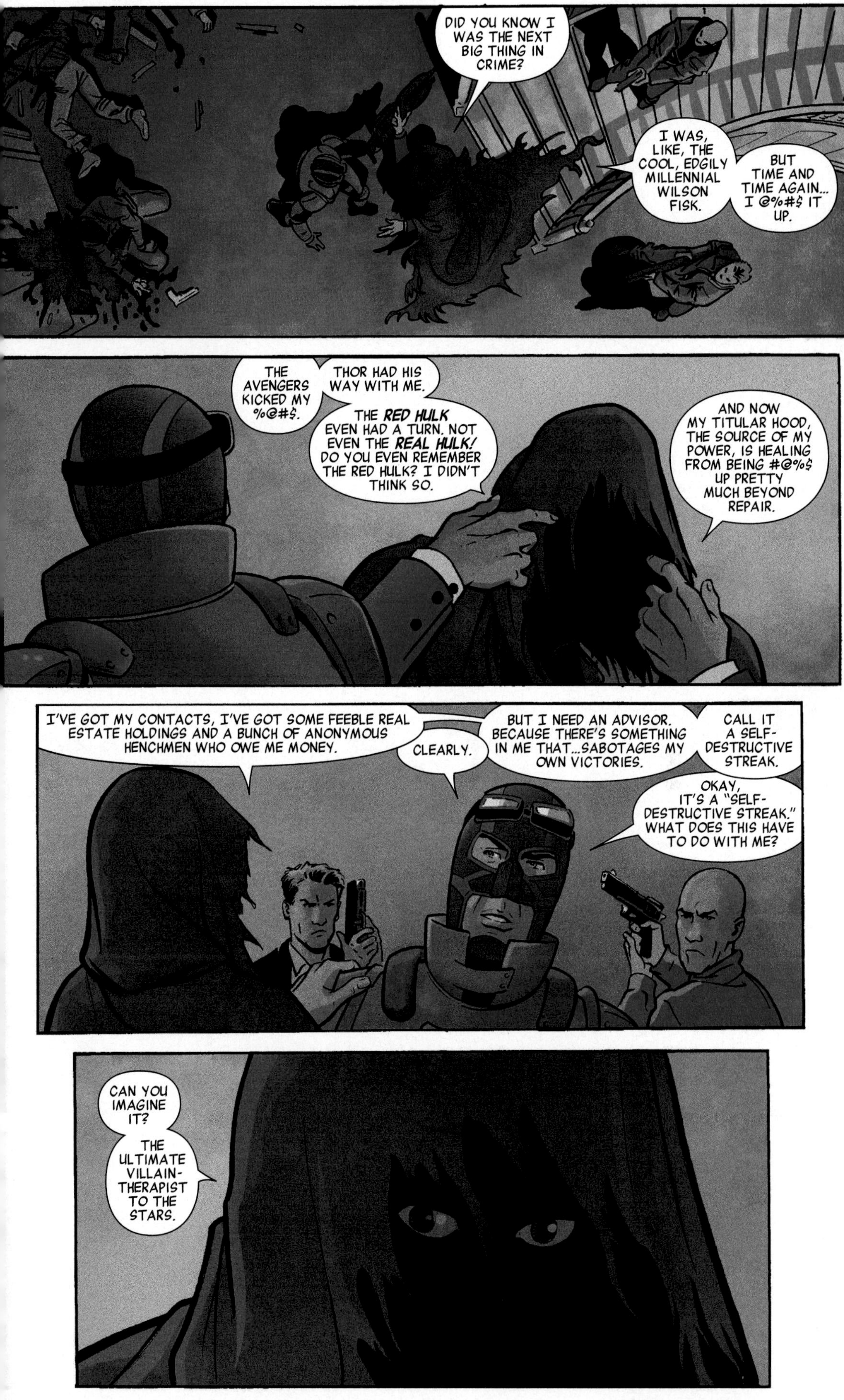
DID YOU KNOW I WAS THE NEXT BIG THING IN CRIME?
I WAS, LIKE, THE COOL, EDGILY MILLENNIAL WILSON FISK.
BUT TIME AND TIME AGAIN... I @%#$ IT UP.
THE AVENGERS KICKED MY %@#$.
THOR HAD HIS WAY WITH ME.
THE RED HULK EVEN HAD A TURN. NOT EVEN THE REAL HULK! DO YOU EVEN REMEMBER THE RED HULK? I DIDN'T THINK SO.
AND NOW MY TITULAR HOOD, THE SOURCE OF MY POWER, IS HEALING FROM BEING #@%$ UP PRETTY MUCH BEYOND REPAIR.
I'VE GOT MY CONTACTS, I'VE GOT SOME FEEBLE REAL ESTATE HOLDINGS AND A BUNCH OF ANONYMOUS HENCHMEN WHO OWE ME MONEY.
CLEARLY.
BUT I NEED AN ADVISOR. BECAUSE THERE'S SOMETHING IN ME THAT...SABOTAGES MY OWN VICTORIES.
CALL IT A SELF-DESTRUCTIVE STREAK.
OKAY, IT'S A "SELF-DESTRUCTIVE STREAK." WHAT DOES THIS HAVE TO DO WITH ME?
CAN YOU IMAGINE IT?
THE ULTIMATE VILLAIN-THERAPIST TO THE STARS.

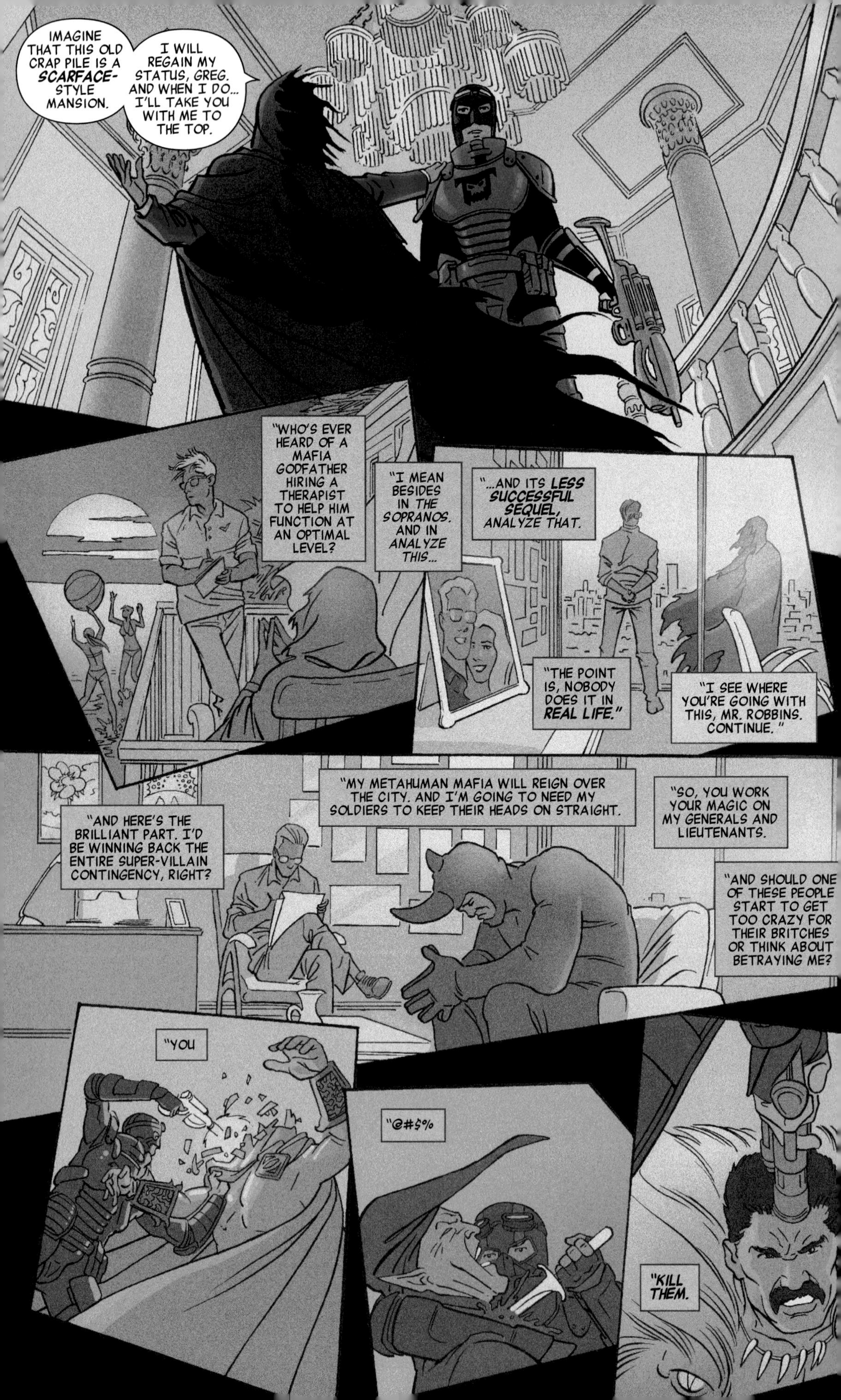
IMAGINE THAT THIS OLD CRAP PILE IS A SCARFACE-STYLE MANSION.
I WILL REGAIN MY STATUS, GREG. AND WHEN I DO... I'LL TAKE YOU WITH ME TO THE TOP.
"WHO'S EVER HEARD OF A MAFIA GODFATHER HIRING A THERAPIST TO HELP HIM FUNCTION AT AN OPTIMAL LEVEL?
"I MEAN BESIDES IN THE SOPRANOS. AND IN ANALYZE THIS...
"...AND ITS LESS SUCCESSFUL SEQUEL, ANALYZE THAT.
"THE POINT IS, NOBODY DOES IT IN REAL LIFE."
"I SEE WHERE YOU'RE GOING WITH THIS, MR. ROBBINS. CONTINUE."
"AND HERE'S THE BRILLIANT PART. I'D BE WINNING BACK THE ENTIRE SUPER-VILLAIN CONTINGENCY, RIGHT?
"MY METAHUMAN MAFIA WILL REIGN OVER THE CITY. AND I'M GOING TO NEED MY SOLDIERS TO KEEP THEIR HEADS ON STRAIGHT.
"SO, YOU WORK YOUR MAGIC ON MY GENERALS AND LIEUTENANTS.
"AND SHOULD ONE OF THESE PEOPLE START TO GET TOO CRAZY FOR THEIR BRITCHES OR THINK ABOUT BETRAYING ME?
"YOU
"@#$%
"KILL THEM.

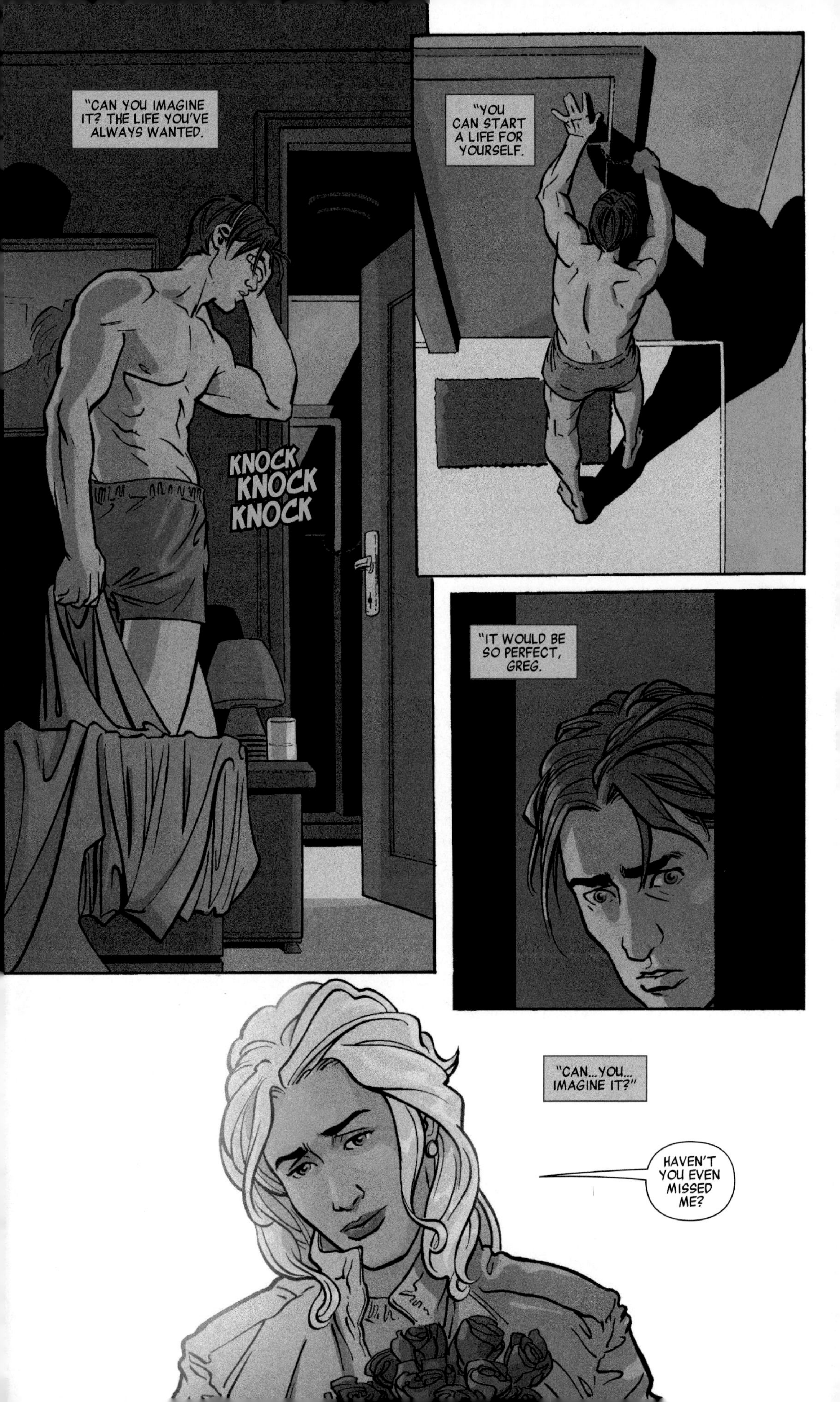
"CAN YOU IMAGINE IT? THE LIFE YOU'VE ALWAYS WANTED.
KNOCK KNOCK KNOCK
"YOU CAN START A LIFE FOR YOURSELF.
"IT WOULD BE SO PERFECT, GREG.
"CAN... YOU... IMAGINE IT?"
HAVEN'T YOU EVEN MISSED ME?

YOU'RE SIMULTANEOUSLY RUBBING IN MY FAILURES AND TOTALLY LYING TO ME.

I'M NOT MESSING WITH YOU, GREG.

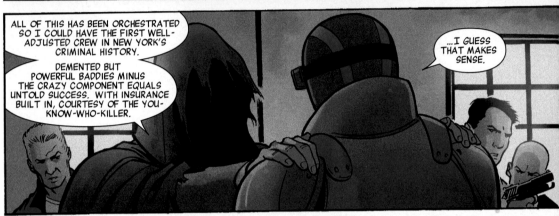

ALL OF THIS HAS BEEN ORCHESTRATED SO I COULD HAVE THE FIRST WELL-ADJUSTED CREW IN NEW YORK'S CRIMINAL HISTORY.

DEMENTED BUT POWERFUL BADDIES MINUS THE CRAZY COMPONENT EQUALS UNTOLD SUCCESS. WITH INSURANCE BUILT IN, COURTESY OF THE YOU-KNOW-WHO-KILLER.

...I GUESS THAT MAKES SENSE.

AND WHAT IF I'M DONE KILLING? DONE WORKING FOR SHADY, EGOMANIACAL JERKS WHO JUST WANT TO USE ME AS SOME KIND OF SICK WEAPON?

WELL, UNFORTUNATELY, GREG, YOU WOULDN'T BE ALLOWED TO LIVE.

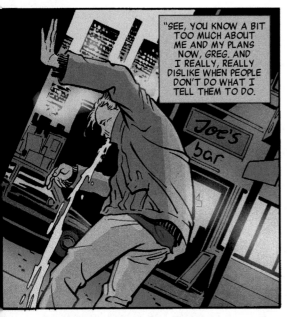

"SEE, YOU KNOW A BIT TOO MUCH ABOUT ME AND MY PLANS NOW, GREG. AND I REALLY, REALLY DISLIKE WHEN PEOPLE DON'T DO WHAT I TELL THEM TO DO.

"LIKE I SAID, I STILL HAVE MY CONTACTS. ONE OF THEM IS A CERTAIN STOOLIE.

"GUILTY OF THE CARDINAL SIN OF INFORMING TO A CERTAIN VIGILANTE. HE KNOWS I CAN EXPOSE HIM AT ANY TIME, SO HE WORKS MY ANGLES. I CAN FEED HIM INFORMATION ABOUT MY RIVALS.

"THE VIGILANTE TAKES OUT THE RIVAL, AND BLISSFULLY UNBEKNOWNST TO HIM, MAKES ME A VERY HAPPY HOOD.

"NOW, YOU MAY FANCY YOURSELF A 'GOOD GUY,' BUT YOU'VE MURDERED THE HELL OUT OF A LOT OF PEOPLE, GREG.

"DON'T THINK FOR A MOMENT THAT YOUR FELLOW CRIMEFIGHTERS WOULD TAKE YOU IN OR FORGIVE WHAT YOU'VE DONE.

"SO, IMAGINE A SCENARIO WHERE YOU REFUSE TO WORK FOR ME.

"YOUR IDENTITY AND LOCATION GOES INTO THE HANDS OF THE STOOLIE.

"BY THAT EVENING, HE'S ARRANGED A MEET.

"AND TRUST ME, OF ALL THE PEOPLE YOU DON'T WANT TO REALIZE THAT YOU'RE BASICALLY A SERIAL KILLER?

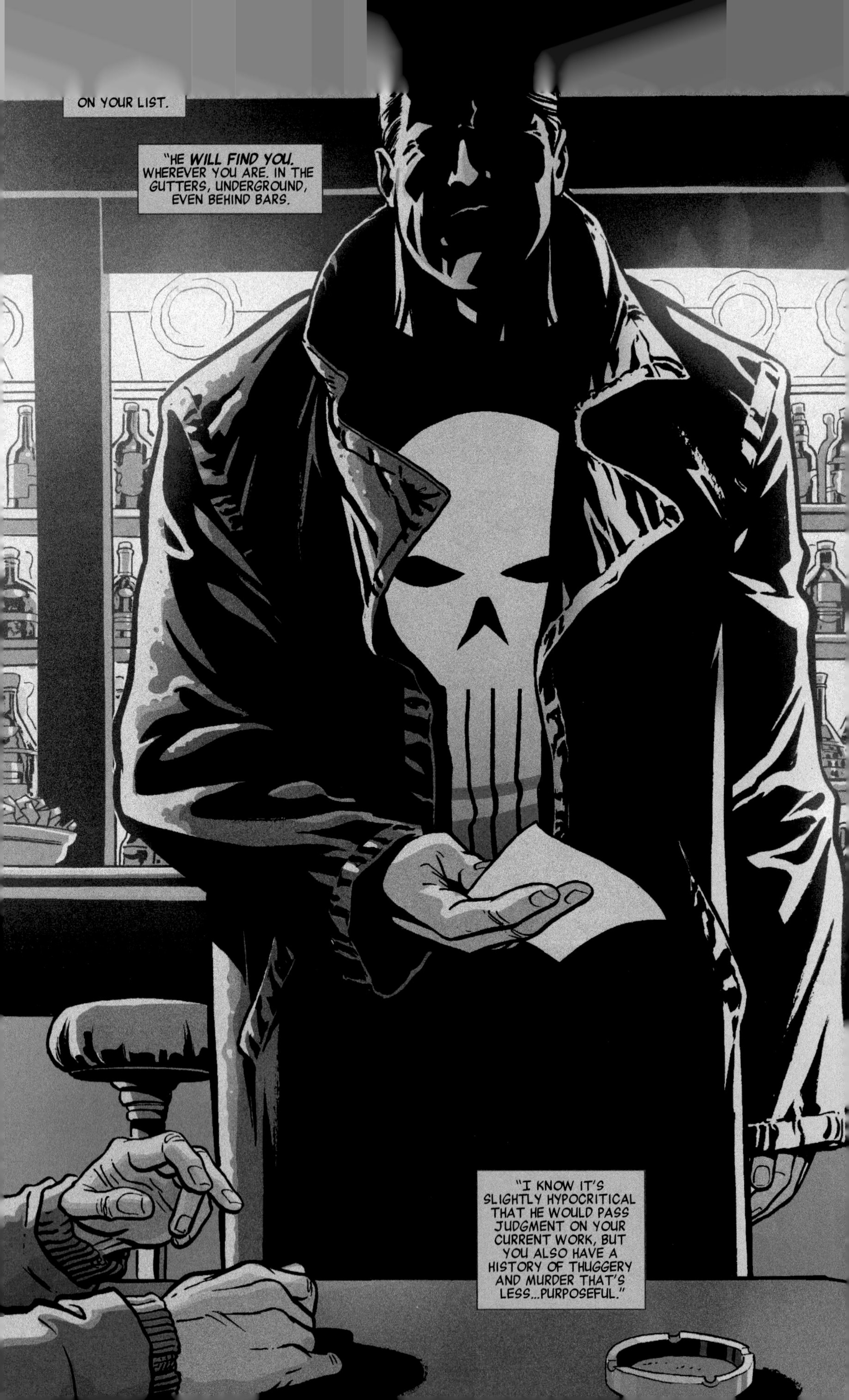
ON YOUR LIST.
"HE **WILL FIND YOU.** WHEREVER YOU ARE. IN THE GUTTERS, UNDERGROUND, EVEN BEHIND BARS.
"I KNOW IT'S SLIGHTLY HYPOCRITICAL THAT HE WOULD PASS JUDGMENT ON YOUR CURRENT WORK, BUT YOU ALSO HAVE A HISTORY OF THUGGERY AND MURDER THAT'S LESS...PURPOSEFUL."

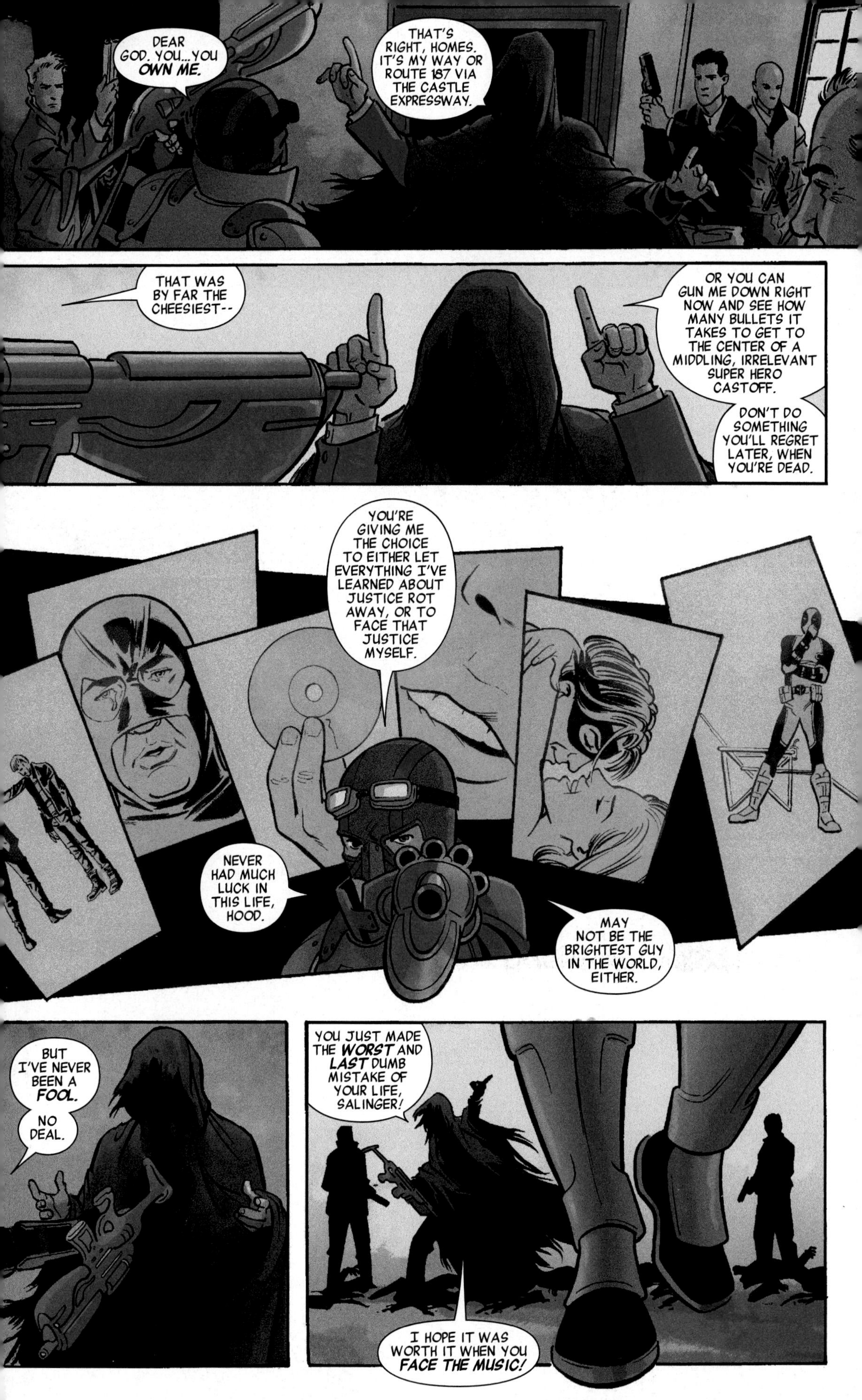
DEAR GOD. YOU...YOU OWN ME.
THAT'S RIGHT, HOMES. IT'S MY WAY OR ROUTE 187 VIA THE CASTLE EXPRESSWAY.
THAT WAS BY FAR THE CHEESIEST--
OR YOU CAN GUN ME DOWN RIGHT NOW AND SEE HOW MANY BULLETS IT TAKES TO GET TO THE CENTER OF A MIDDLING, IRRELEVANT SUPER HERO CASTOFF.
DON'T DO SOMETHING YOU'LL REGRET LATER, WHEN YOU'RE DEAD.
YOU'RE GIVING ME THE CHOICE TO EITHER LET EVERYTHING I'VE LEARNED ABOUT JUSTICE ROT AWAY, OR TO FACE THAT JUSTICE MYSELF.
NEVER HAD MUCH LUCK IN THIS LIFE, HOOD.
MAY NOT BE THE BRIGHTEST GUY IN THE WORLD, EITHER.
BUT I'VE NEVER BEEN A FOOL.
NO DEAL.
YOU JUST MADE THE WORST AND LAST DUMB MISTAKE OF YOUR LIFE, SALINGER!
I HOPE IT WAS WORTH IT WHEN YOU FACE THE MUSIC!

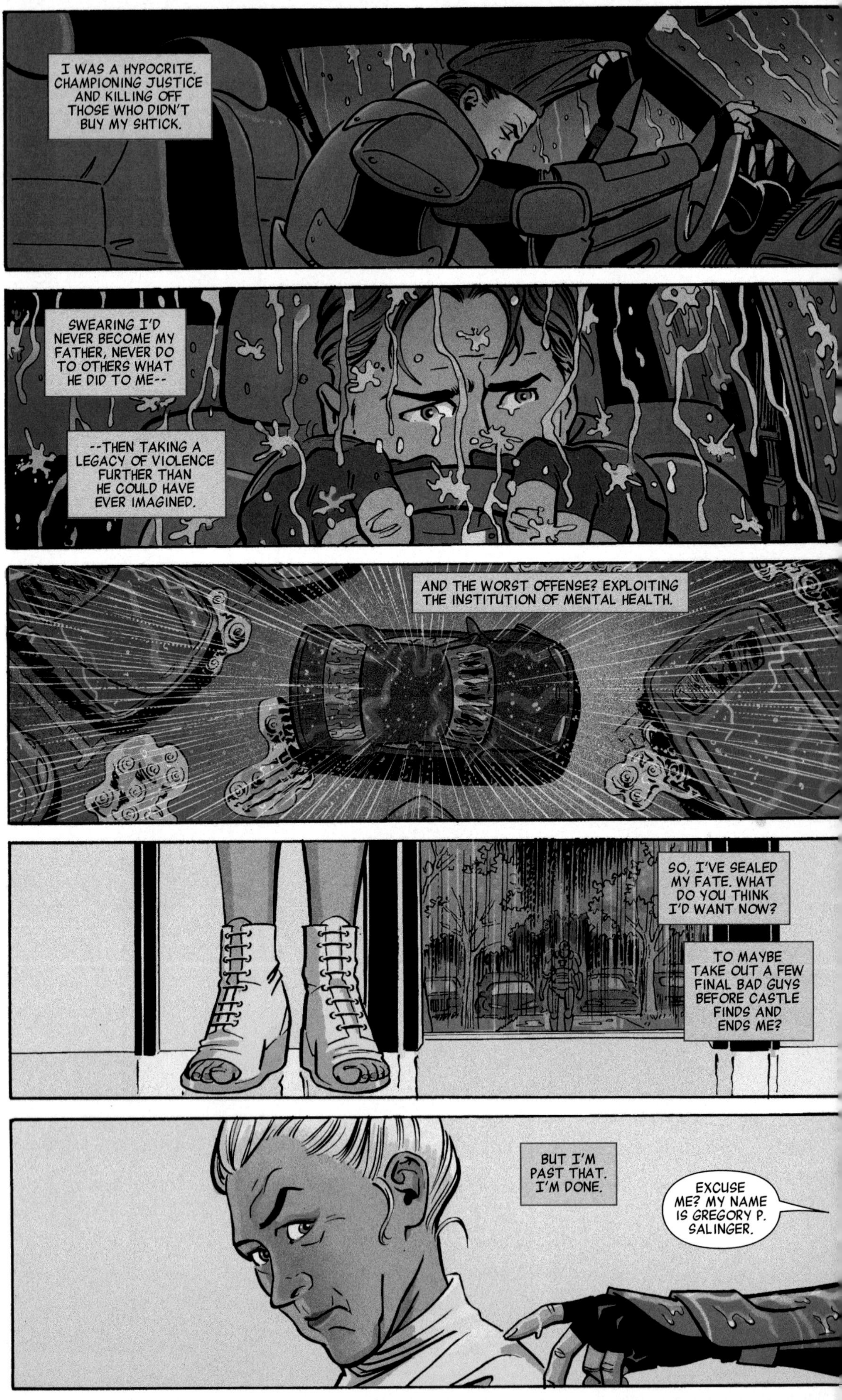

I WAS A HYPOCRITE. CHAMPIONING JUSTICE AND KILLING OFF THOSE WHO DIDN'T BUY MY SHTICK.
SWEARING I'D NEVER BECOME MY FATHER, NEVER DO TO OTHERS WHAT HE DID TO ME--
--THEN TAKING A LEGACY OF VIOLENCE FURTHER THAN HE COULD HAVE EVER IMAGINED.
AND THE WORST OFFENSE? EXPLOITING THE INSTITUTION OF MENTAL HEALTH.
SO, I'VE SEALED MY FATE. WHAT DO YOU THINK I'D WANT NOW?
TO MAYBE TAKE OUT A FEW FINAL BAD GUYS BEFORE CASTLE FINDS AND ENDS ME?
BUT I'M PAST THAT. I'M DONE.
EXCUSE ME? MY NAME IS GREGORY P. SALINGER.

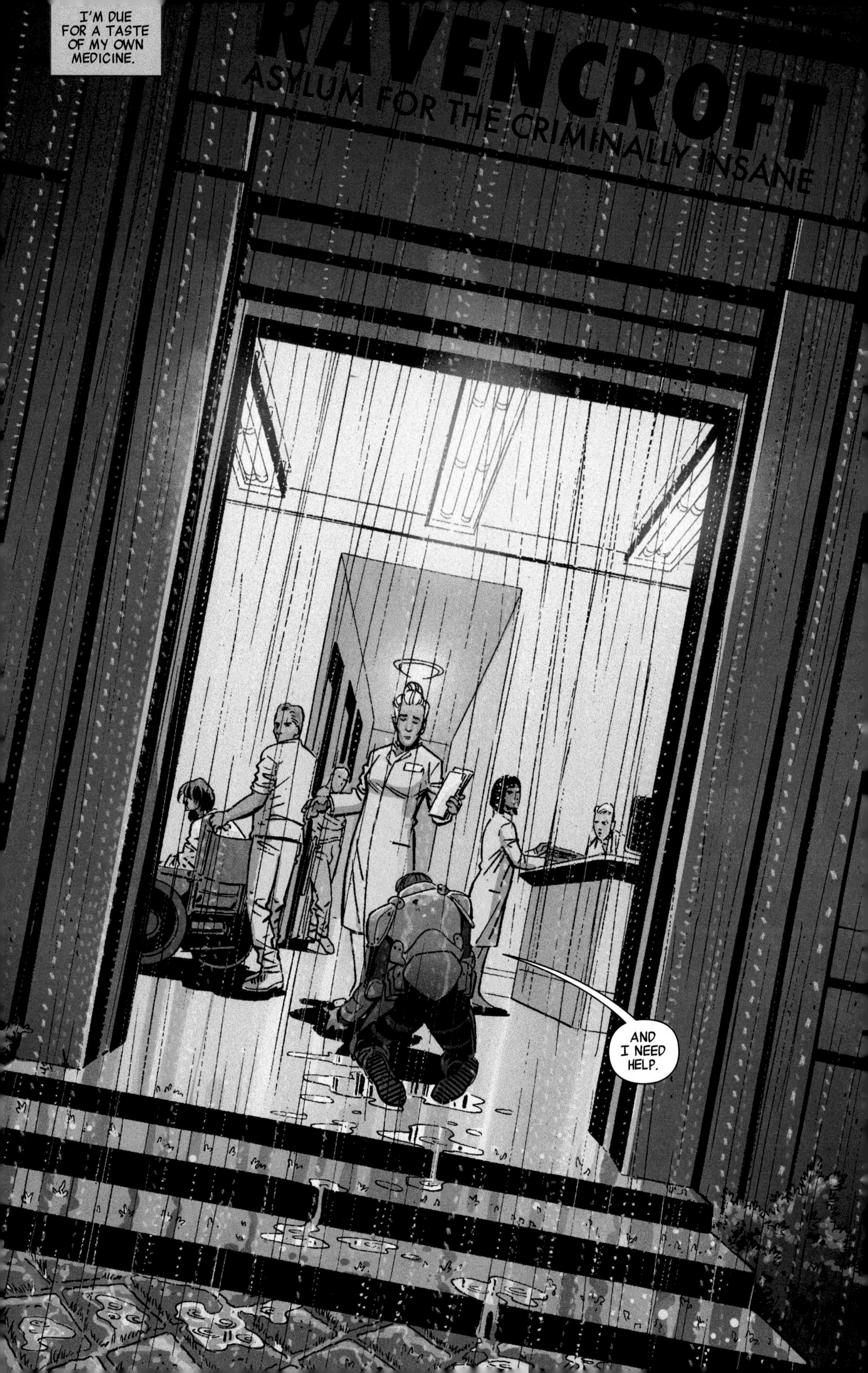
I'M DUE FOR A TASTE OF MY OWN MEDICINE.
RAVENCROFT
ASYLUM FOR THE CRIMINALLY INSANE
AND I NEED HELP.

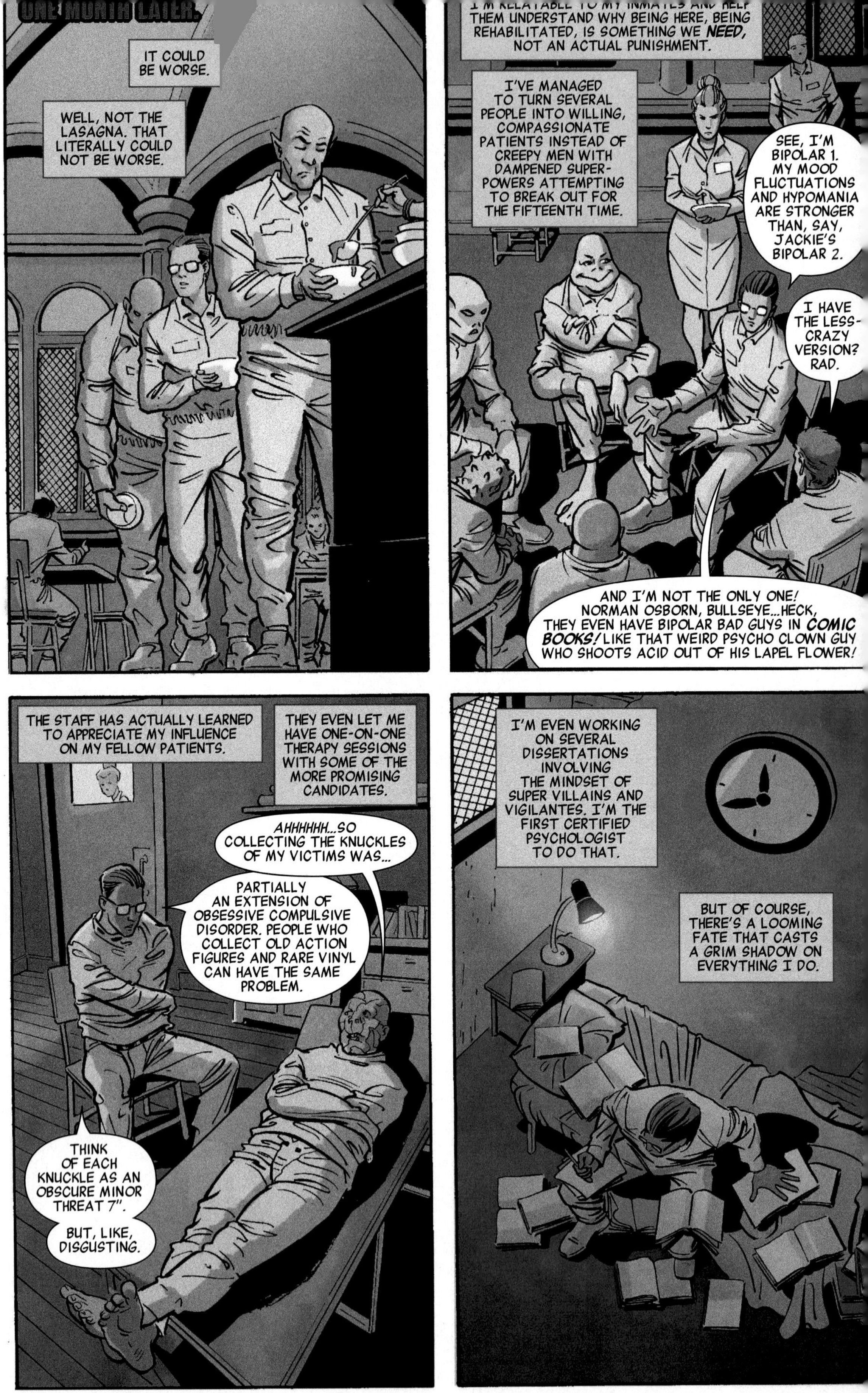
ONE MONTH LATER.
IT COULD BE WORSE.
WELL, NOT THE LASAGNA. THAT LITERALLY COULD NOT BE WORSE.
THEM UNDERSTAND WHY BEING HERE, BEING REHABILITATED, IS SOMETHING WE *NEED*, NOT AN ACTUAL PUNISHMENT.
I'VE MANAGED TO TURN SEVERAL PEOPLE INTO WILLING, COMPASSIONATE PATIENTS INSTEAD OF CREEPY MEN WITH DAMPENED SUPER-POWERS ATTEMPTING TO BREAK OUT FOR THE FIFTEENTH TIME.
SEE, I'M BIPOLAR 1. MY MOOD FLUCTUATIONS AND HYPOMANIA ARE STRONGER THAN, SAY, JACKIE'S BIPOLAR 2.
I HAVE THE LESS-CRAZY VERSION? RAD.
AND I'M NOT THE ONLY ONE! NORMAN OSBORN, BULLSEYE...HECK, THEY EVEN HAVE BIPOLAR BAD GUYS IN *COMIC BOOKS!* LIKE THAT WEIRD PSYCHO CLOWN GUY WHO SHOOTS ACID OUT OF HIS LAPEL FLOWER!
THE STAFF HAS ACTUALLY LEARNED TO APPRECIATE MY INFLUENCE ON MY FELLOW PATIENTS.
THEY EVEN LET ME HAVE ONE-ON-ONE THERAPY SESSIONS WITH SOME OF THE MORE PROMISING CANDIDATES.
AHHHHHH...SO COLLECTING THE KNUCKLES OF MY VICTIMS WAS...
PARTIALLY AN EXTENSION OF OBSESSIVE COMPULSIVE DISORDER. PEOPLE WHO COLLECT OLD ACTION FIGURES AND RARE VINYL CAN HAVE THE SAME PROBLEM.
THINK OF EACH KNUCKLE AS AN OBSCURE MINOR THREAT 7".
BUT, LIKE, DISGUSTING.
I'M EVEN WORKING ON SEVERAL DISSERTATIONS INVOLVING THE MINDSET OF SUPER VILLAINS AND VIGILANTES. I'M THE FIRST CERTIFIED PSYCHOLOGIST TO DO THAT.
BUT OF COURSE, THERE'S A LOOMING FATE THAT CASTS A GRIM SHADOW ON EVERYTHING I DO.

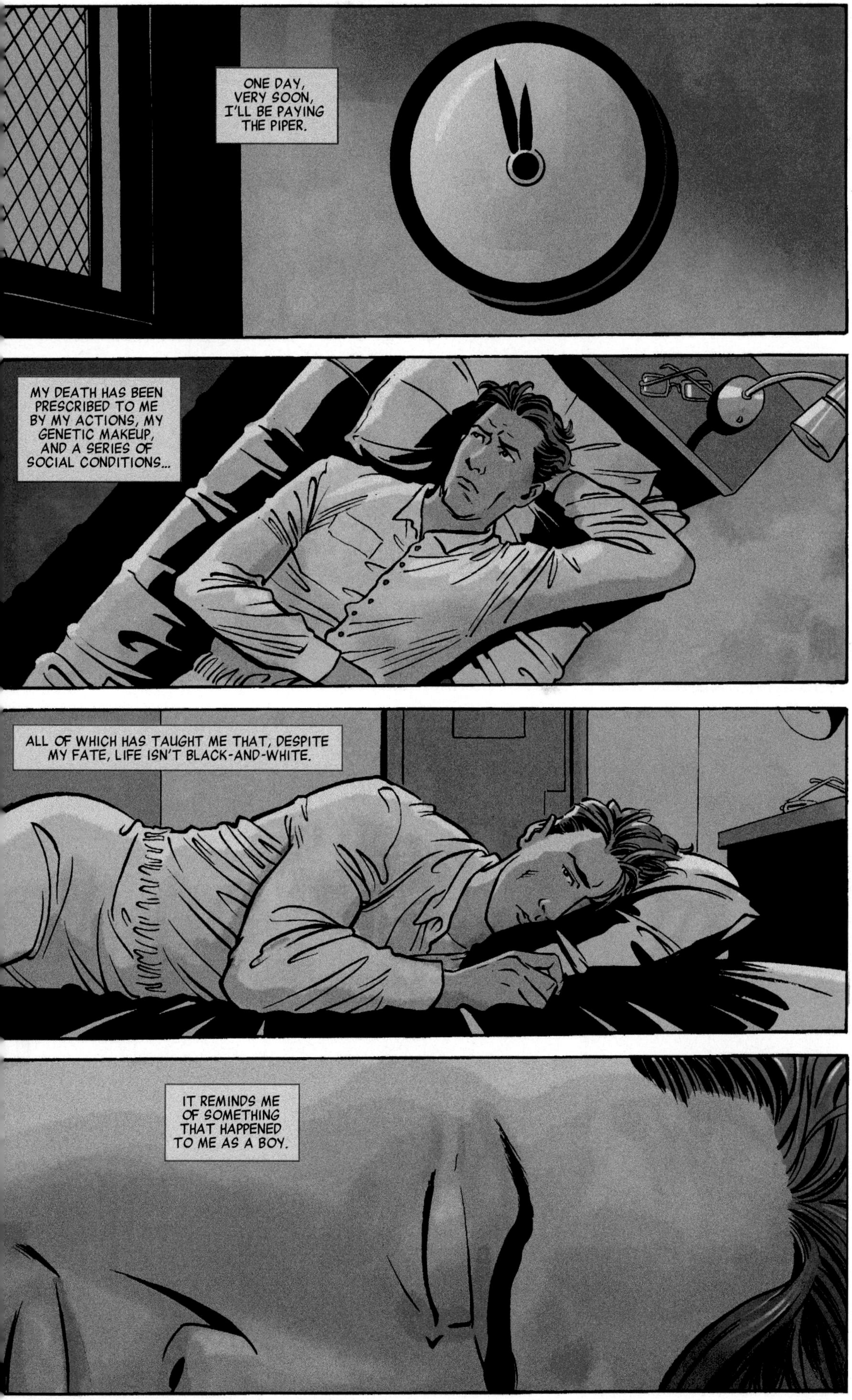
ONE DAY, VERY SOON, I'LL BE PAYING THE PIPER.
MY DEATH HAS BEEN PRESCRIBED TO ME BY MY ACTIONS, MY GENETIC MAKEUP, AND A SERIES OF SOCIAL CONDITIONS...
ALL OF WHICH HAS TAUGHT ME THAT, DESPITE MY FATE, LIFE ISN'T BLACK-AND-WHITE.
IT REMINDS ME OF SOMETHING THAT HAPPENED TO ME AS A BOY.

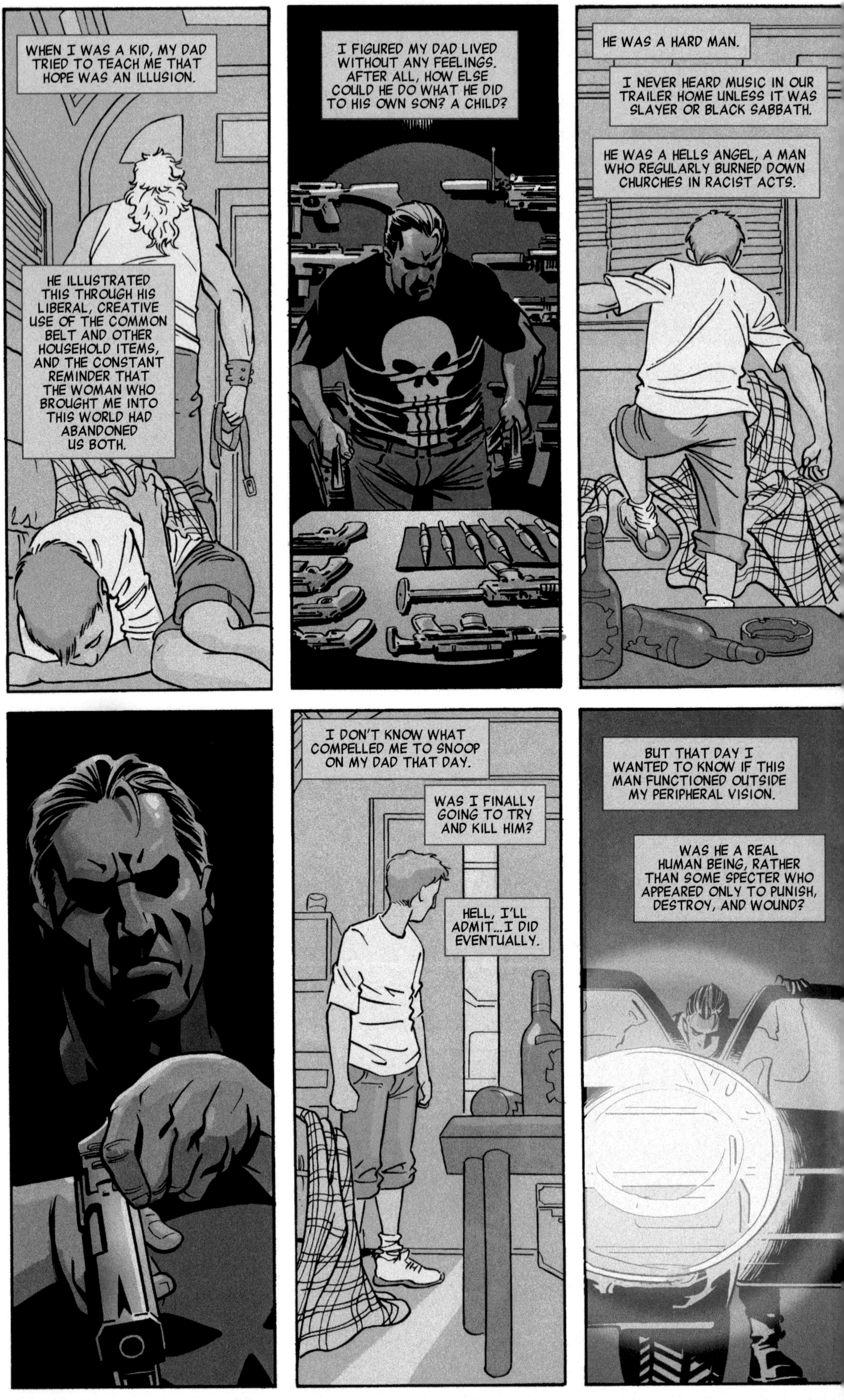
WHEN I WAS A KID, MY DAD TRIED TO TEACH ME THAT HOPE WAS AN ILLUSION.
HE ILLUSTRATED THIS THROUGH HIS LIBERAL, CREATIVE USE OF THE COMMON BELT AND OTHER HOUSEHOLD ITEMS, AND THE CONSTANT REMINDER THAT THE WOMAN WHO BROUGHT ME INTO THIS WORLD HAD ABANDONED US BOTH.
I FIGURED MY DAD LIVED WITHOUT ANY FEELINGS. AFTER ALL, HOW ELSE COULD HE DO WHAT HE DID TO HIS OWN SON? A CHILD?
HE WAS A HARD MAN.
I NEVER HEARD MUSIC IN OUR TRAILER HOME UNLESS IT WAS SLAYER OR BLACK SABBATH.
HE WAS A HELLS ANGEL, A MAN WHO REGULARLY BURNED DOWN CHURCHES IN RACIST ACTS.
I DON'T KNOW WHAT COMPELLED ME TO SNOOP ON MY DAD THAT DAY.
WAS I FINALLY GOING TO TRY AND KILL HIM?
HELL, I'LL ADMIT...I DID EVENTUALLY.
BUT THAT DAY I WANTED TO KNOW IF THIS MAN FUNCTIONED OUTSIDE MY PERIPHERAL VISION.
WAS HE A REAL HUMAN BEING, RATHER THAN SOME SPECTER WHO APPEARED ONLY TO PUNISH, DESTROY, AND WOUND?

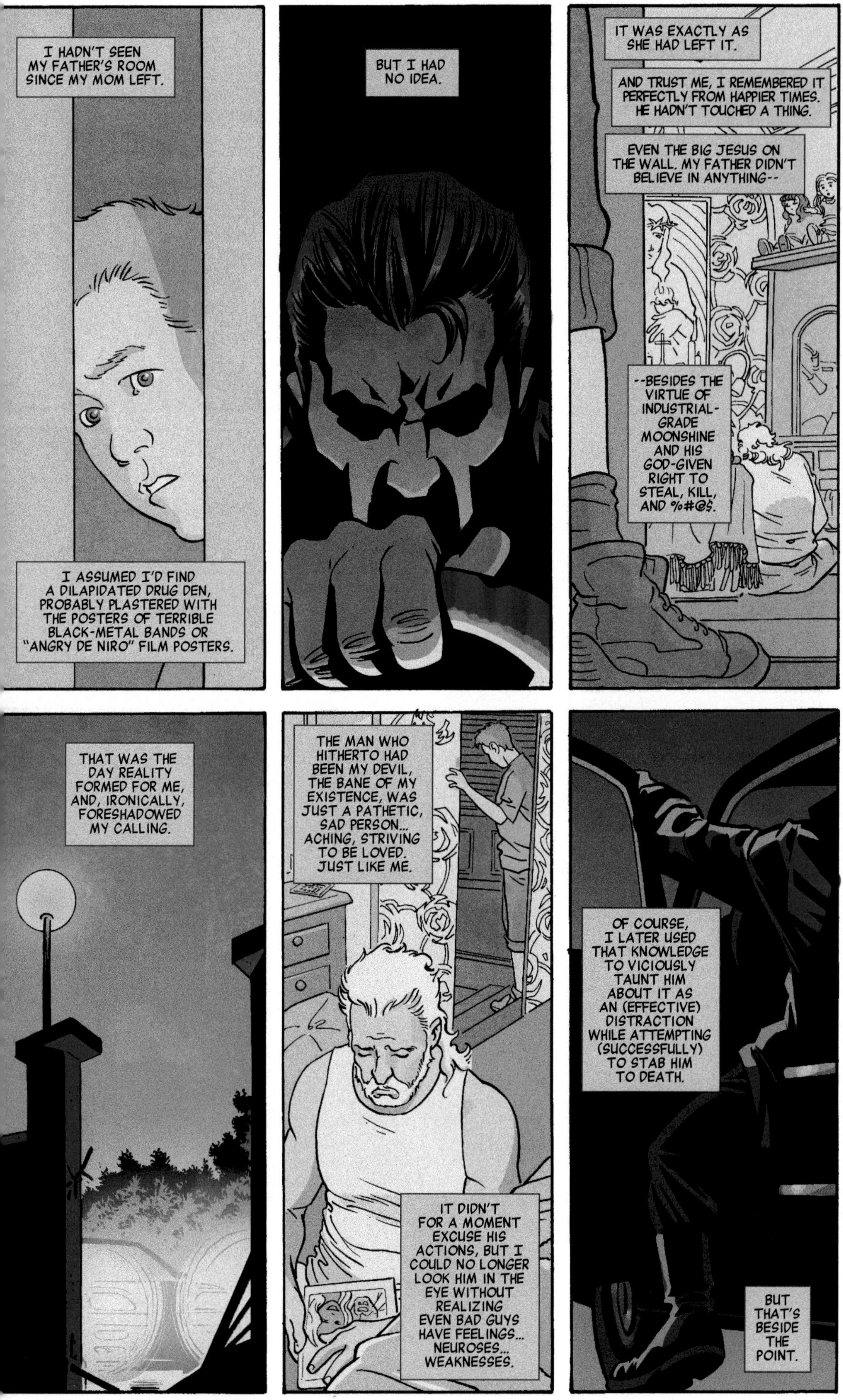

I HADN'T SEEN MY FATHER'S ROOM SINCE MY MOM LEFT.
I ASSUMED I'D FIND A DILAPIDATED DRUG DEN, PROBABLY PLASTERED WITH THE POSTERS OF TERRIBLE BLACK-METAL BANDS OR "ANGRY DE NIRO" FILM POSTERS.
BUT I HAD NO IDEA.
IT WAS EXACTLY AS SHE HAD LEFT IT.
AND TRUST ME, I REMEMBERED IT PERFECTLY FROM HAPPIER TIMES. HE HADN'T TOUCHED A THING.
EVEN THE BIG JESUS ON THE WALL. MY FATHER DIDN'T BELIEVE IN ANYTHING--
--BESIDES THE VIRTUE OF INDUSTRIAL-GRADE MOONSHINE AND HIS GOD-GIVEN RIGHT TO STEAL, KILL, AND %#@$.
THAT WAS THE DAY REALITY FORMED FOR ME, AND, IRONICALLY, FORESHADOWED MY CALLING.
THE MAN WHO HITHERTO HAD BEEN MY DEVIL, THE BANE OF MY EXISTENCE, WAS JUST A PATHETIC, SAD PERSON... ACHING, STRIVING TO BE LOVED. JUST LIKE ME.
IT DIDN'T FOR A MOMENT EXCUSE HIS ACTIONS, BUT I COULD NO LONGER LOOK HIM IN THE EYE WITHOUT REALIZING EVEN BAD GUYS HAVE FEELINGS... NEUROSES... WEAKNESSES.
OF COURSE, I LATER USED THAT KNOWLEDGE TO VICIOUSLY TAUNT HIM ABOUT IT AS AN (EFFECTIVE) DISTRACTION WHILE ATTEMPTING (SUCCESSFULLY) TO STAB HIM TO DEATH.
BUT THAT'S BESIDE THE POINT.

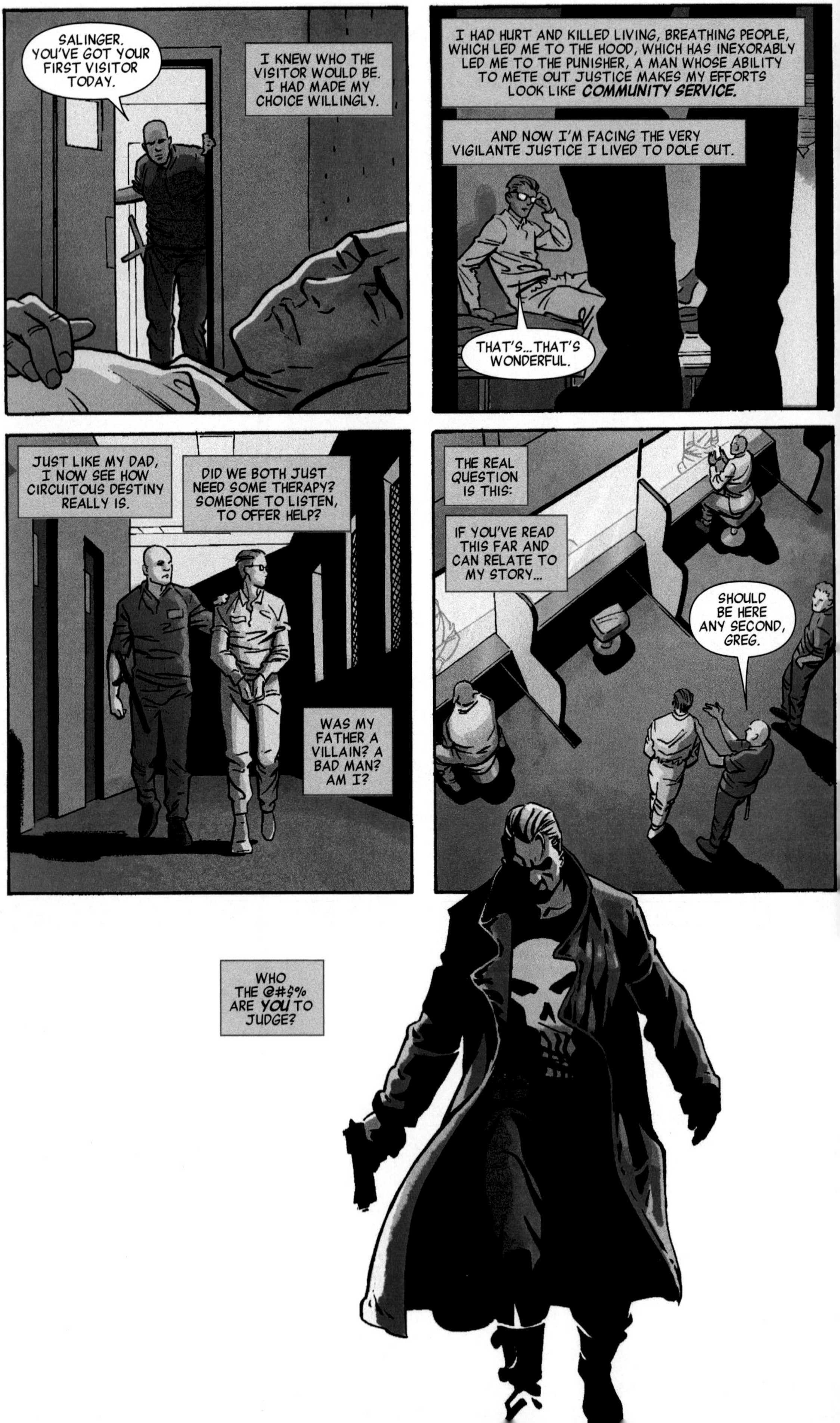
SALINGER. YOU'VE GOT YOUR FIRST VISITOR TODAY.
I KNEW WHO THE VISITOR WOULD BE. I HAD MADE MY CHOICE WILLINGLY.
I HAD HURT AND KILLED LIVING, BREATHING PEOPLE, WHICH LED ME TO THE HOOD, WHICH HAS INEXORABLY LED ME TO THE PUNISHER, A MAN WHOSE ABILITY TO METE OUT JUSTICE MAKES MY EFFORTS LOOK LIKE COMMUNITY SERVICE.
AND NOW I'M FACING THE VERY VIGILANTE JUSTICE I LIVED TO DOLE OUT.
THAT'S...THAT'S WONDERFUL.
JUST LIKE MY DAD, I NOW SEE HOW CIRCUITOUS DESTINY REALLY IS.
DID WE BOTH JUST NEED SOME THERAPY? SOMEONE TO LISTEN, TO OFFER HELP?
WAS MY FATHER A VILLAIN? A BAD MAN? AM I?
THE REAL QUESTION IS THIS:
IF YOU'VE READ THIS FAR AND CAN RELATE TO MY STORY...
SHOULD BE HERE ANY SECOND, GREG.
WHO THE @#$% ARE YOU TO JUDGE?

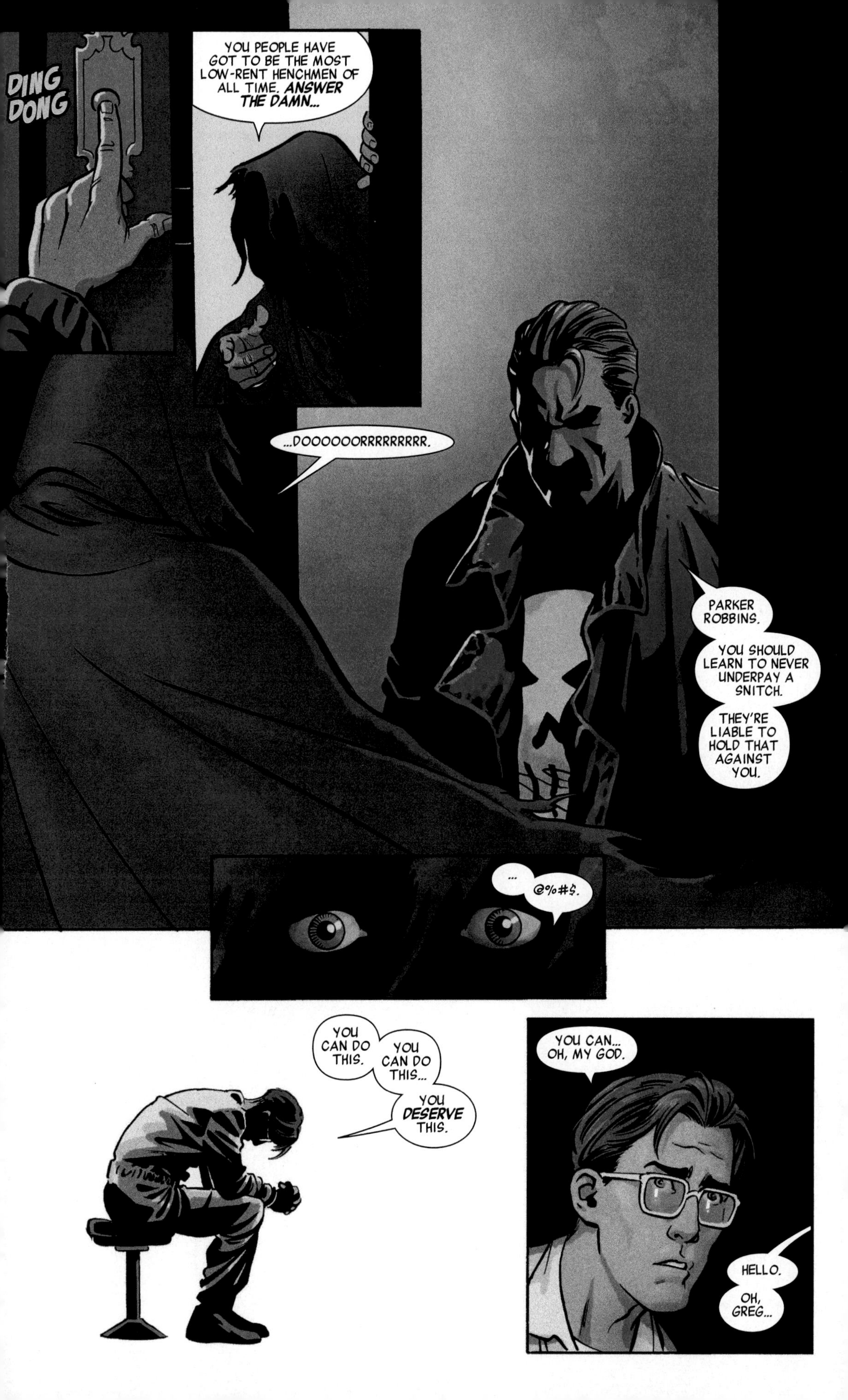
DING DONG
YOU PEOPLE HAVE GOT TO BE THE MOST LOW-RENT HENCHMEN OF ALL TIME. ANSWER THE DAMN...
...DOOOOOORRRRRRRR.
PARKER ROBBINS.
YOU SHOULD LEARN TO NEVER UNDERPAY A SNITCH.
THEY'RE LIABLE TO HOLD THAT AGAINST YOU.
...
@%#$.
YOU CAN DO THIS.
YOU CAN DO THIS...
YOU DESERVE THIS.
YOU CAN... OH, MY GOD.
HELLO.
OH, GREG...

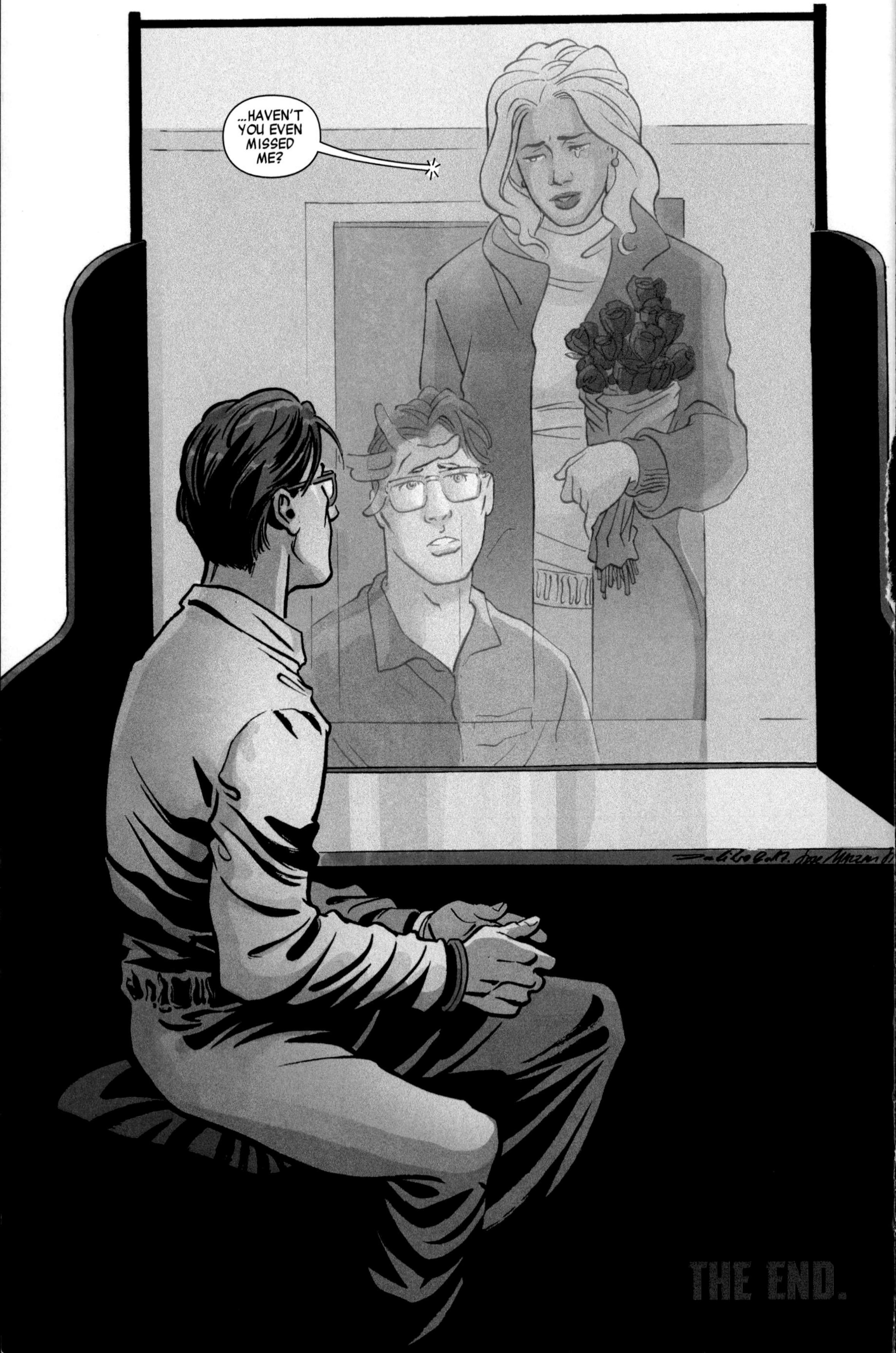
...HAVEN'T YOU EVEN MISSED ME?
THE END.

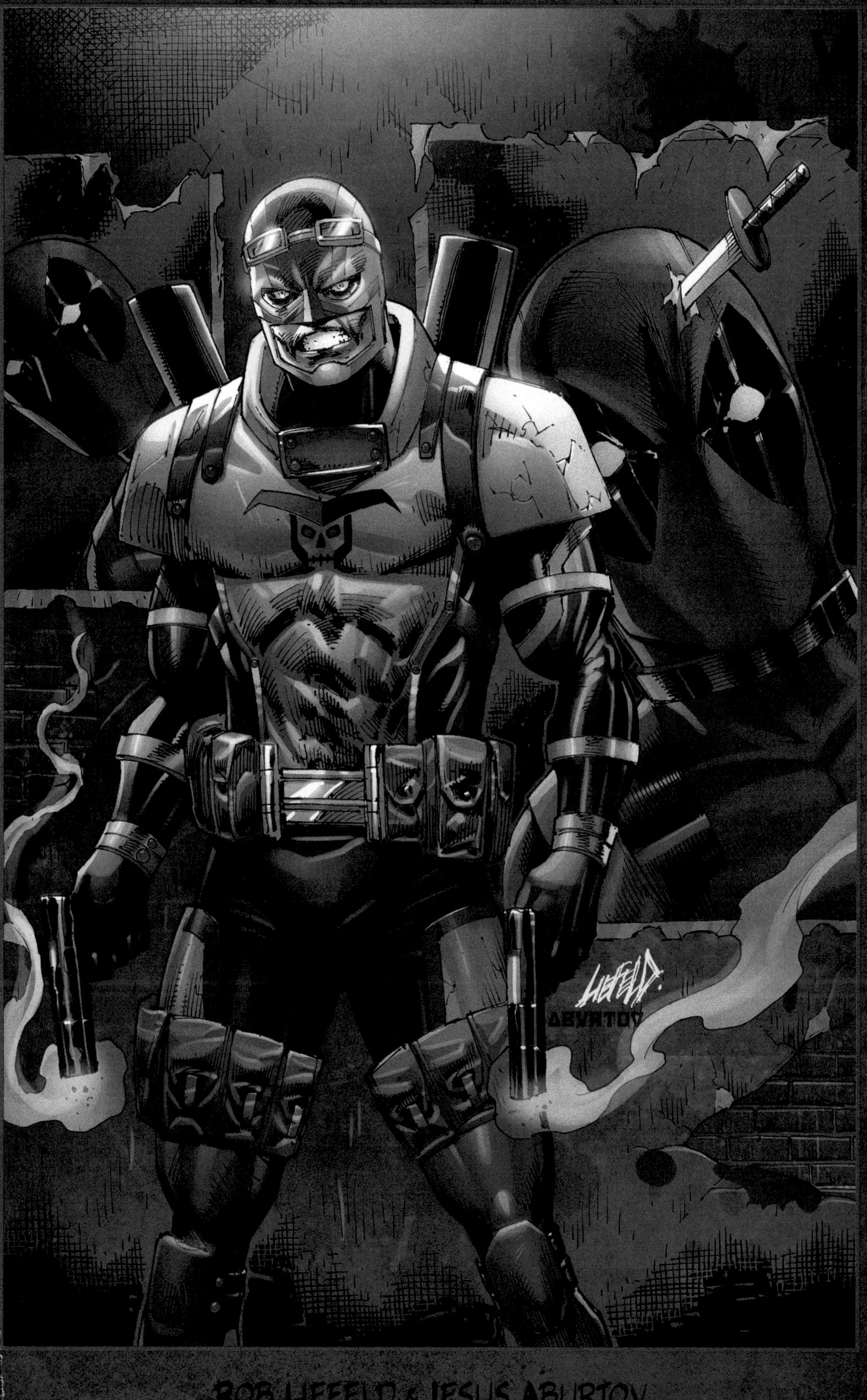

ROB LIEFELD & JESUS ABURTOV

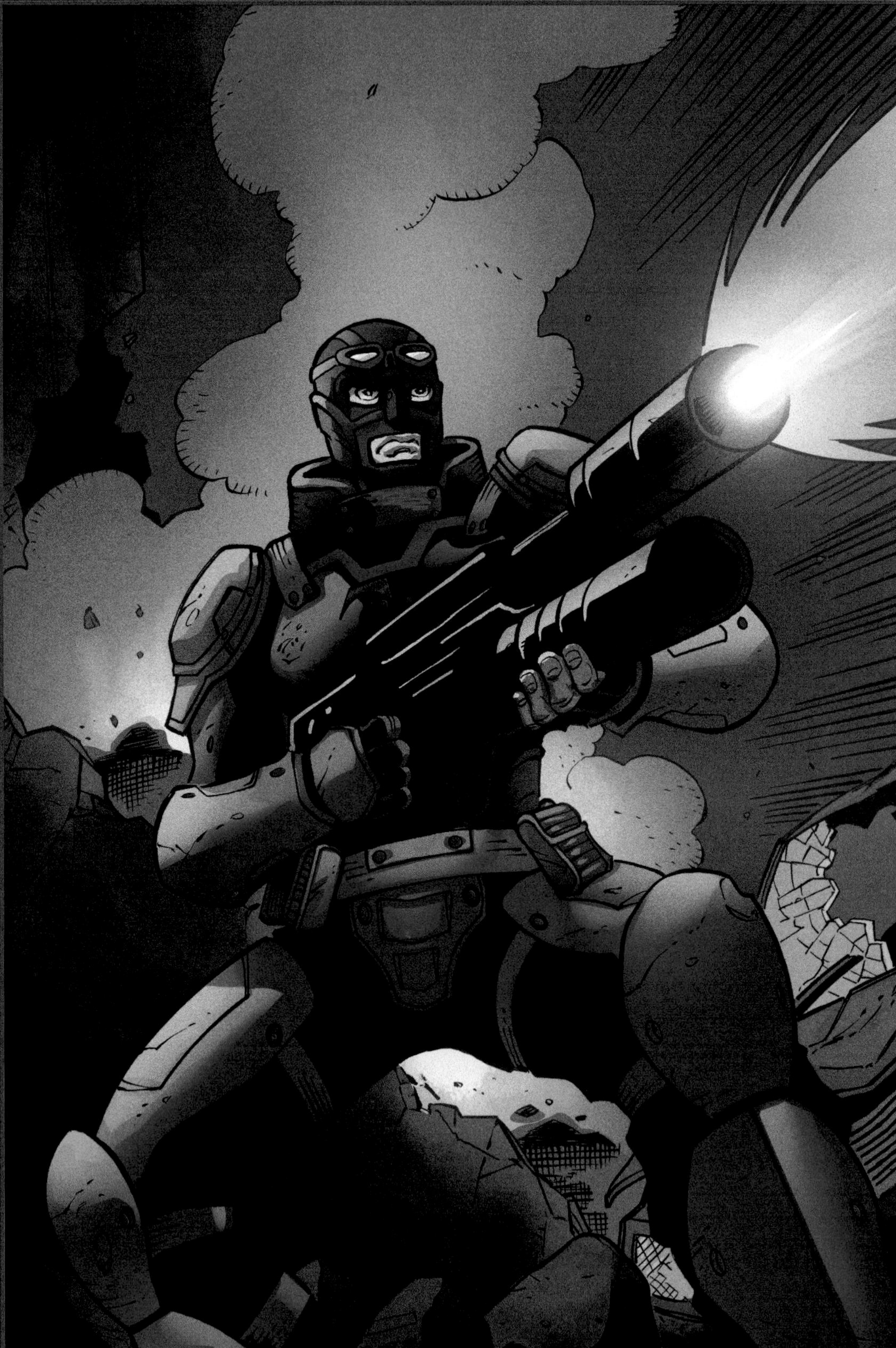

RON LIM, TOM PALMER & ANDY TROY
variant

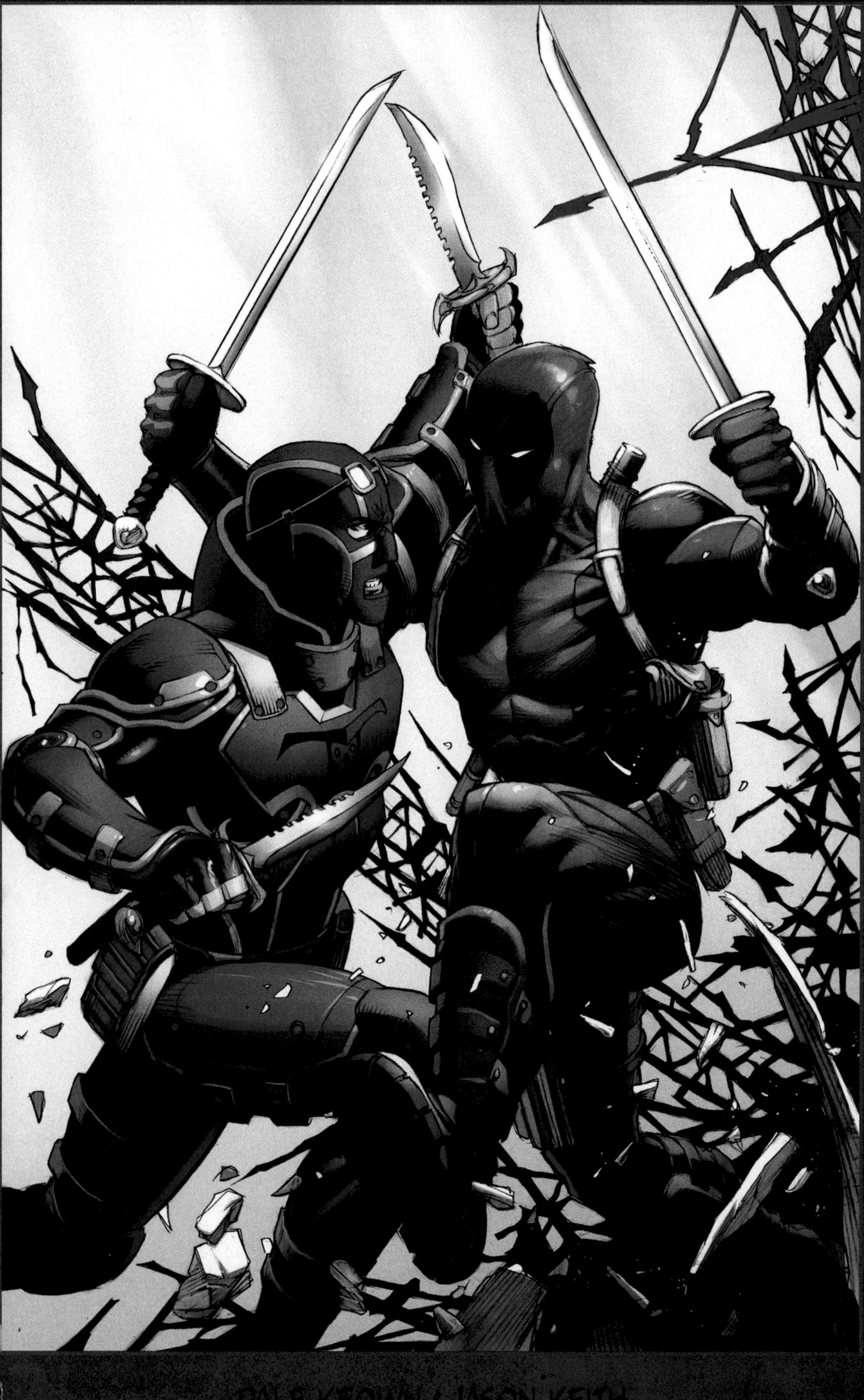

DALE KEOWN & JASON KEITH

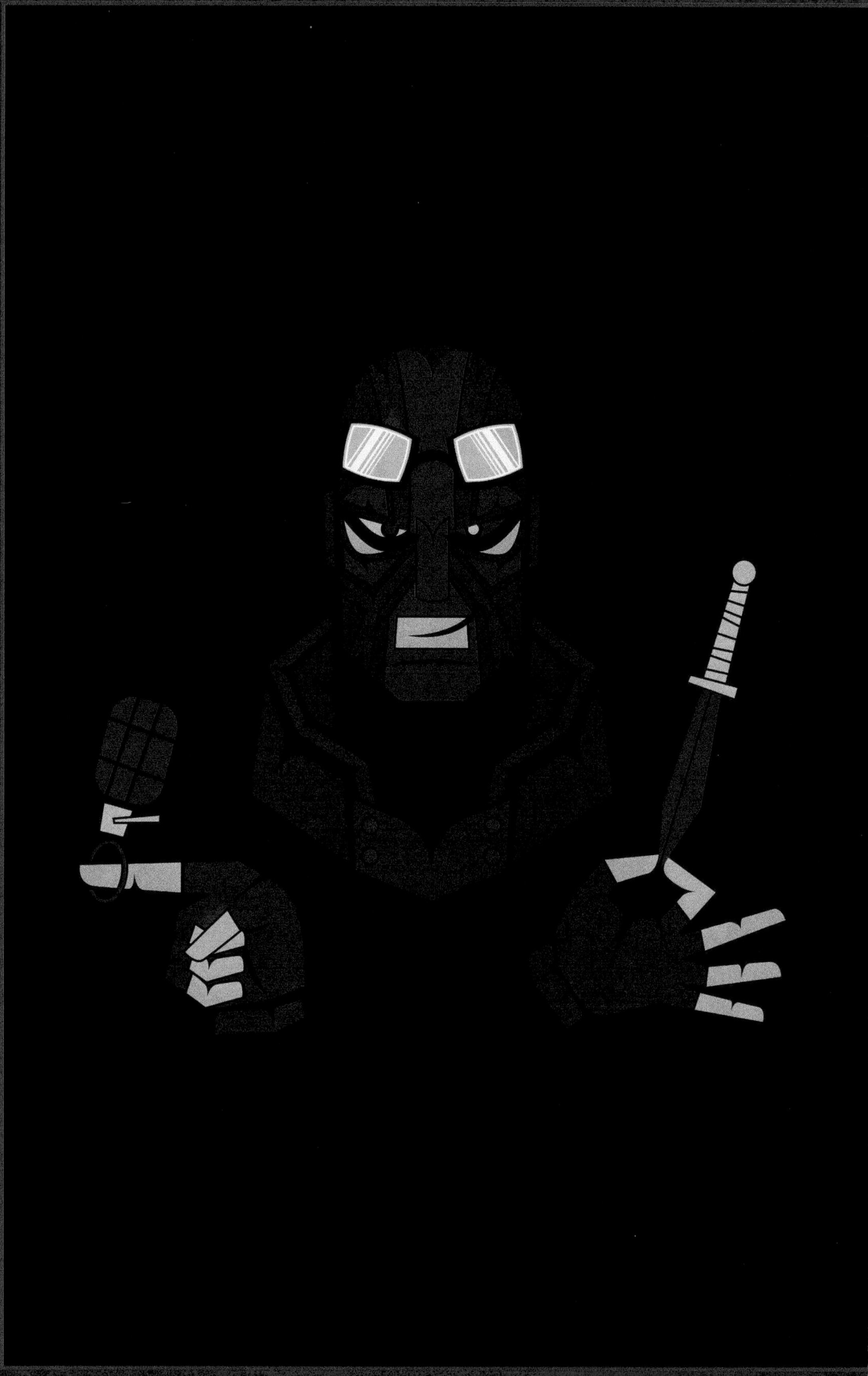

JEFFREY VEREGGE

MIKE DEODATO JR.
& FRANK MARTIN

MIKE
ANDY

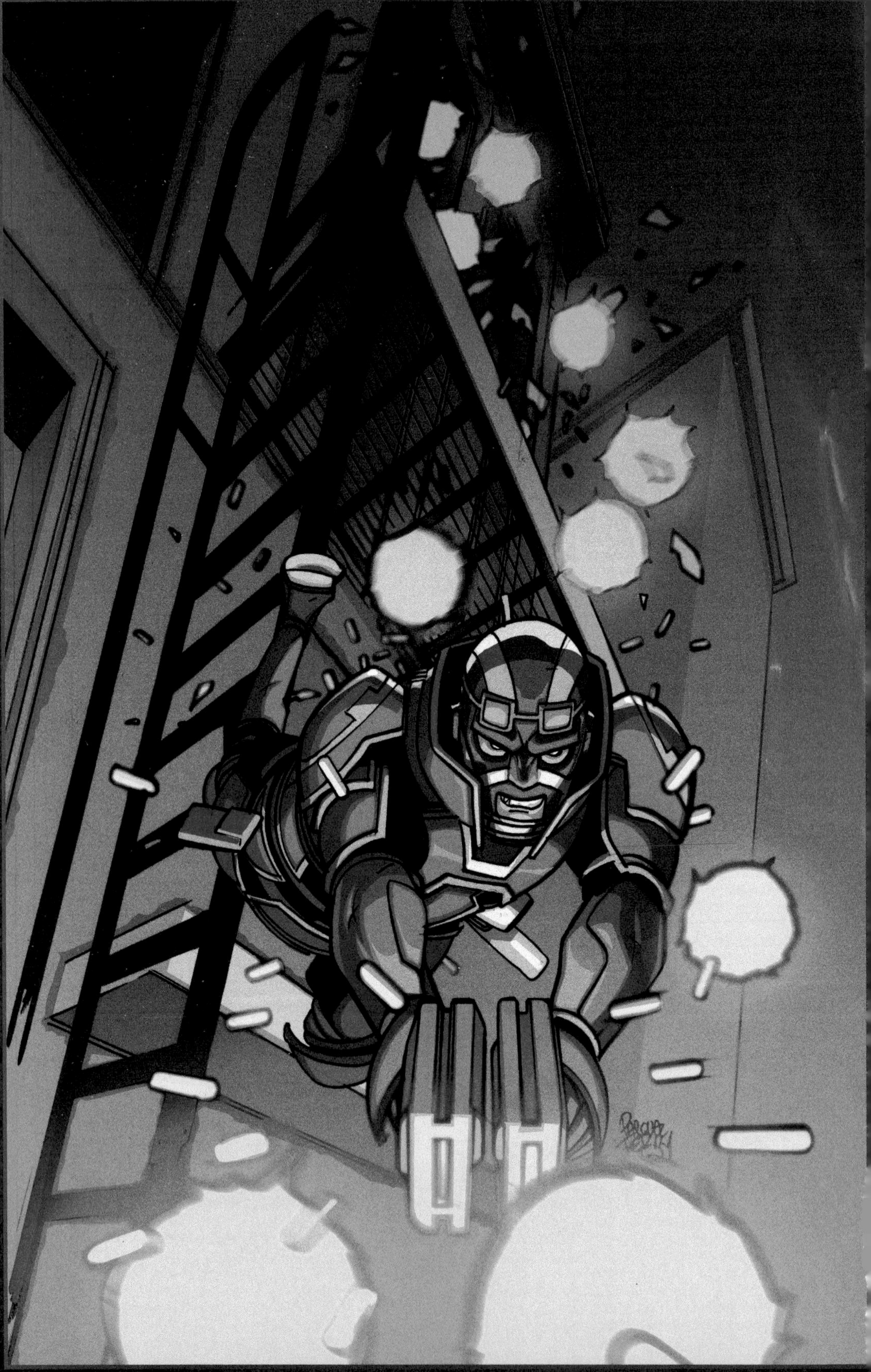

DAVE McCAIG